Adolescence and Delinquency

Adolescence and Delinquency

An Object Relations Theory Approach

Bruce R. Brodie

A JASON ARONSON BOOK

ROWMAN & LITTLEFIELD PUBLISHERS, INC.
Lanham • Boulder • New York • Toronto • Plymouth, UK

A JASON ARONSON BOOK

ROWMAN & LITTLEFIELD PUBLISHERS, INC.

Published in the United States of America
by Rowman & Littlefield Publishers, Inc.
A wholly owned subsidary of The Rowman & Littlefield Publishing Group, Inc.
4501 Forbes Boulevard, Suite 200, Lanham, Maryland 20706
www.rowmanlittlefield.com

Estover Road
Plymouth PL6 7PY
United Kingdom

British Library Cataloguing in Publication Information Available

Library of Congress Cataloging-in-Publication Data

Brodie, Bruce R.
  Adolescence and delinquency : an object relations theory approach / Bruce R. Brodie.
    p. ; cm.
  "A Jason Aronson book."
  Includes bibliographical references.
  ISBN-13: 978-0-7657-0474-0 (pbk. : alk. paper)
  ISBN-10: 0-7657-0474-9 (pbk. : alk. paper)
  ISBN-13: 978-0-7657-0473-3 (cloth : alk. paper)
  ISBN-10: 0-7657-0473-0 (cloth : alk. paper)
  1. Juvenile delinquency—Treatment. 2. Adolescent psychology. 3. Object relations
(Psychoanalysis) 4. Adolescent analysis. I. Title. [DNLM: 1. Adolescent Behavior.
2. Adolescent Psychology. 3. Juvenile Delinquency. 4. Object Attachment. 5.
Psychoanalytic Theory. WS 462 B8627a 2007]
  RJ506.J88B78 2007
  616.8900835—dc22   2006037922

Printed in the United States of America

∞™ The paper used in this publication meets the minimum requirements of
American National Standard for Information Sciences—Permanence of Paper
for Printed Library Materials, ANSI/NISO Z39.48-1992.

For Janet

~

Contents

Acknowledgments ix

Prologue xi

Introduction xv

Part I: Theoretical Issues

Chapter 1   Adolescents and Adolescence 3

Chapter 2   Adolescents and Part-Object Thinking 19

Chapter 3   Identity Formation 43

Chapter 4   Resistance and Addiction to the Bad Object 57

Chapter 5   Into Adulthood 69

Part II: Treatment Issues

Chapter 6   Respect and Intersubjectivity 79

Chapter 7   Individual Therapy 95

Chapter 8   Group Therapy 129

Chapter 9   Family Therapy 145

Part III: Afterthoughts

Chapter 10   Thoughts on Delinquency 155

Chapter 11   Object Relations Theory in Clinical Supervision   163

              References   175

              Index   181

              About the Author   185

~

Acknowledgments

This book arose out of two sources. First is my work of almost twenty years with the adolescent wards of the "Center." I am deeply grateful to all of these courageous young people who, despite backgrounds of abuse and abandonment, chose to entrust me with facets of their innermost selves. I am touched and humbled by their generosity to me. Second is the course on object relations theory that I developed and have taught for several years at the California School for Professional Psychology at Alliant University in Los Angeles. I wish to thank my students there, who sharpened my thinking by their incisive questions and who provided valuable case material to me, some of which is included in this book. I have also had the honor of supervising interns at the Saturday Center for Psychotherapy in Santa Monica, and I am deeply grateful to those who have been willing to share with me the terrors and exhilaration of becoming a therapist.

There are certain individuals who need to be singled out for particular thanks. I need to acknowledge my deceased parents, Fawn and Bernard, who insisted on intellectual rigor and honesty as well as helping to inspire my interest in psychology. My wife, Janet, has sustained me with thirty-six years of love and support that at times dumbfounds me. My two sons, Jedediah and Nathaniel (not just in their adolescent years) have taught me more than I can ever hope to have taught them.

The discerning reader is certain to recognize my considerable intellectual debt to Thomas Ogden, whose voluminous works and brilliant theories have informed and inspired me.

Colleagues, family, and friends have kindly read various stages of my manuscripts and have provided support and encouragement as well as invaluable suggestions. These include Janet Brodie, Judith Davenport, Monica Farassat, Sue Frankel, Denny Klos, Leonia Kurgan, Peggy Porter, Ken Scott, Judy Swerling, and Stone Wiske.

~

Prologue

Shannon, who will appear frequently in this volume, had two complete stays (of about nine to ten months each) at the Center. She graduated the first time after ten months and returned to live with her mother. Her stay with her mother lasted about a month, after which she gradually returned to drugs (including heroin), and finally ran away from home. She was arrested and returned to the Center.

I met with her while she was detained in juvenile hall while awaiting a bed at the Center. I was surprised at what good humor she was in. However much she claimed to love her freedom, part of her was clearly relieved to be out of the maelstrom that was sucking her down. We spoke about what had gone wrong. She had insisted on being released to the care of her mother, in what was a highly problematic relationship. Next time, we agreed, it would be different.

Shannon and I had grown close during her first stay. Suddenly she suggested, jokingly but wistfully, "Maybe I could come and live with you. I wouldn't take up much space. I don't even need to live inside. Does your wife have a garden? She could plant me in the garden. My legs could grow down into roots. My arms could reach up and soak up the sun."

Disturbed by the fusion implied in this fantasy, I, after a moment's hesitation, offered an alternative fantasy. "My fantasy," I said, "is very different. I have the fantasy of driving you up to Evergreen State College in Oregon [Shannon was a time-warped hippie, and we had talked about this college earlier as being perfect for her], giving you a good-bye kiss on the cheek, and tucking you into a dorm room."

To my enormous surprise, Shannon burst into tears. "That would be," she finally managed to say, "the happiest day of my life."

There are myriad lessons to be learned from this story, but I wish to focus here on two. The first is what a clear, Janus-faced picture it presents of adolescence: extraordinarily powerful emotional valences surging in opposite directions. Shannon herself presented the fantasy of utter passivity and dependency, in her case of almost a return to the womb. Yet she responded with even more emotion to the fantasy I provided of separation and individuation, growth and ultimate autonomy. Adolescents are children in adult bodies. They are also adults with children's minds. They are not "in between" anything. They are in two different places at the same time. It is part of what makes them so exciting to work with.

The other point to this example has to do not with adolescence, but with therapy. Orthodox psychodynamic therapists will no doubt look with some horror (perhaps justifiably) at my intervention. It violates a host of fundamental rules of therapeutic intervention, not the least of which is that when a therapist feels a sudden impulse to say something, it is usually best to quash that urge. Also, it is a fundamental rule of psychotherapy that interventions should be directed at the current affective (feeling) state of the client. Certainly, my response was at the opposite pole from the affective state of Shannon's fantasy. Finally, the intervention appeared to come more out of my own needs (my discomfort at the fusional implications of Shannon's fantasy) than out of my client's needs. But object relations therapists, and especially therapists of an intersubjective persuasion (as I discuss in chapter 6), might be more forgiving. I had, after all, been working closely with Shannon for almost a year, and we knew each other very well. There was a distinct possibility that I was "carrying" something for Shannon, that however disparate my material appeared from that which Shannon herself presented, that it was more out of a "shared" consciousness than purely out of my own. And Shannon's response seems to bear this out.

Object relations theory in general, and intersubjectivity in particular, present a radically different model of psychotherapeutic intervention than that of classical psychoanalysis. Gone is the model of the therapist as a personally and emotionally withholding "blank slate," the detached and neutral scientific observer and interpreter of the client's associations. Instead, the *person* of the therapist becomes central, not only as an alternate and interactive subjectivity, but also as a "container" or "carrier" of split-off parts of the client's own psyche.

Over the years I have come increasingly to believe that my effectiveness as a therapist is directly proportional to my ability to contain and process the split-off projections of my clients. Most of what I do is rarely as dramatic as the case just presented. Usually it is simply being able (and willing) to sit and listen to the tragic stories told by my clients, told as if they were jokes or something that happened to someone else, someone they barely knew, and allow myself to *feel* and contain the sadness that my clients will not allow themselves to experience. If I do this well enough, if I am able to walk the thin line between dismissing or blowing off their feelings on one hand (this often takes the form of an attitude of condescension), and being overwhelmed by the feelings on the other (quickly reassuring the client that his or her feelings are "normal," for example, and then "moving on to other things), clients just might be able to see in me the very feelings that they had convinced themselves were unbearable. And if I can bear them, maybe they can as well.

In this current case Shannon was almost instantly able to reidentify with that half of her fusion–individuation ambivalence that I momentarily carried for her, suggesting that while her separation–individuation impulses were split off and out of consciousness, they were very far from being repressed or unavailable. Shannon, after all, had just been plucked back from a foray into separation and individuation that had degenerated into a nightmare. Fleeing one kind of death (the annihilation of her individuality through fusion with a mother who had no awareness of boundaries) she had ended up facing the kind of death that is always latent in the opposite pole (death from isolation and abandonment in a world one has been prematurely sent into, and with which one is not equipped to cope). It is not surprising then, that at the moment of our talk Shannon was quite open to her dependency needs, and not particularly interested in indulging her needs for individuation and autonomy.

In response to the nightmare she had just experienced, Shannon had "split off" and alienated herself from the positive feelings associated with individuation and separation. When I contained (carried), for a moment, the positive feelings associated with growth, and presented them back to her in a way that was not antagonistic to her dependency needs, but rather complementary to them, Shannon was able to reidentify with those split off and denied feelings. In doing so she became (momentarily) more whole, and less "self-alienated."

~

Introduction

The Kids, The Center

The "kids" I write about are primarily a group of troubled, delinquent, four-teen- to seventeen-year-olds who reside in the residential treatment center in which I work. They come largely from impoverished backgrounds; they are the products of our black and Latino ghettoes. Most are gang entrenched. I often say that "if you can name it, it has been done to them." They are the victims of neglect, abuse, abandonment, rape, and violence. It is equally true that "if you can name it, they have done it to someone else." They have com-mitted robberies, assaults, rapes, prostitution, and murder. They are angry, mistrustful, often disrespectful adolescents. They tend not to like themselves, and they do not expect to be liked by others. But they are also starving for attention and understanding and respond positively to a modicum of both. They can genuinely appreciate real caring when it is shown them, and they can blossom when it is given in abundance. They are surprisingly easy to love.

The "Center" mentioned throughout this book is a "level 14 equivalent"[1] residential therapeutic placement serving one hundred seriously delinquent teenagers, where I have worked for the past eighteen years, many of those as clinical director. The clients are adolescents ranging in age from thirteen through seventeen. They stay an average of eight to ten months, and during that time the clients receive individual, group, and family therapy as well as a range of adjunct therapies.

I have found the Center to be a healing place, a place for coming of age. It has been so as much for me as for the clients.

Psychotherapy

Let me add to the many definitions of psychotherapy with my won formulation: "Psychotherapy is the process in which one person works to understand another person, and to communicate that understanding to that other person." To this I would also add one critical element: The therapist must also care. Without caring, the experience of being understood is the experience of being under a microscope, dissected. It leaves one feeling naked, violated, and dehumanized. With caring, the experience can become profoundly satisfying.

This book is an elaboration of each of these two elements of psychotherapy: the understanding and communication of understanding on one hand, and caring on the other. Each element carries considerable complexity. The level of complexity is further elevated by the choice of disturbed and acting-out adolescents as the focus of my discussion. Simply understanding adolescents can be itself a mind-boggling task. But the task is made even more daunting by the adolescents' frequent determination *not* to be understood.

And caring for an adolescent is no easy task either. What form should the caring take? Should it mimic the caring of parents? How does one respect the adolescent's conflicting needs for autonomy and for attachment? And how does one manage to sustain and communicate genuine caring for those adolescents who choose to project onto you all the loathed and reviled antagonists from past representations, and to react to you accordingly?

Any definition as succinct as the one given above is bound to omit as much as it says. Two words are particularly glaring in their absence: help and change. Psychodynamic therapies in general differ from cognitive–behavioral and even systems approaches in their insistence that "the job of the therapist is to understand, not to help or to change." To a large extent this difference is tactical rather than strategic. All therapists are in the business of helping, and, ultimately, all help must be measured in terms of some kind of change. But the tactical difference is not inconsequential. Especially in work with adolescents, too direct a focus on helping ends up being unhelpful, and too strong an emphasis on change produces stubborn retrenchment.

The question of why (and whether) self-understanding is helpful and leads to change has been debated since Freud's earliest postulations regarding the psychoanalytic process. The tenet that such understanding constitutes the basis of change has become part of the credo common to all branches of the psychodynamic paradigm. Yet, interestingly, each school of psychodynamic thought offers a significantly different explanation for why this is so.

Classical Freudian theory sees self-understanding (insight) as a by-product of the real work of the psychoanalysis, which is the removal of the repression that has prevented understanding. The repression, along with its intended purpose of preventing the entry of unacceptable thoughts and feelings into consciousness, also has the unintended effect of blocking the normal discharge of instinctual tension through healthy channels. What Freudians see as producing change is the removal of this "blockage." Understanding, rather than being the cause of the change, is simply a welcome by-product of the process of the removal of the repression and the redirecting of libidinal energy.

The role of understanding in object relations theory is quite different. Object relations therapy works toward self-awareness or, more precisely, toward a more fully experienced sense of self. The difference in experience between the sense of self-as-subject or agent (self as "I") of the depressive position and the sense of self-as-object (self as "me") of the paranoid–schizoid position was originally developed by Melanie Klein and has been beautifully developed and articulated in the work of Thomas Ogden and is elaborated on later in this book in the context of adolescents. For now let me present a case illustrating the importance of a sense of self (or lack thereof).

A sixteen-year-old boy (Mark) was admitted to the Center with a history of impulsive, sadistic acting out, particularly against his younger siblings. He had also set some fires and had been cruel to animals. Even when he was released from the Center a year later, his mother refused to allow him back into the home because she did not feel she could trust him with her younger children.

At the Center Mark appeared slow, even dimwitted. His therapist and I speculated that he might have some kind of brain damage. His behavior improved, but he never seemed to gain any insight. In one therapy group he was asked about his future plans, and he reported thoughts of becoming a mason. His peers in the group nodded knowingly. Yes, they could see him doing that. They could see him spending his life laying brick, after brick, after brick. When he left the Center his therapist and I gave him the proverbial snowball's chance in Hell of making it.

He did make it. He did not become a mason. He became an auto mechanic, and he soon moved up to managing the auto shop he worked in. He found a girlfriend and they married. His mother reported that she would not have believed such a change was possible. Of all her children, he had become the most responsible.

Years later we invited Mark back to speak at an assembly of the Center wards. We invited him partly because we thought he would be an inspiration to the others, and partly because we were just curious. At the assembly he spoke articulately, intelligently, and with confidence. "When I first came to the Center," he said, "people would ask me how I felt about something and I couldn't answer because I didn't know. It was embarrassing. You're supposed to know how you feel. I also didn't know why I did things because I had never thought about it. That's what I learned at the Center: how to look at my feelings and how to think about why I do things."

Object Relations Theory

I am an object relations therapist not because I believe that object relations theory is "right" and that other theories are "wrong," nor even because I find the theory aesthetically satisfying. I use object relations theory in my work with adolescents because it is singularly helpful to me. It helps me understand behavior and thinking in adolescents that otherwise make no sense. When I read object relations theory (particularly the theory of the paranoid–schizoid position) I have had the classic "aha experience": "Oh, now what he said makes sense. Now what she did makes sense."

Most of us have had the experience of thinking we understand something and then realizing that we do not. I remember in my youth visiting a cousin's farm where chickens were raised. I expressed some distress at seeing my cousin pick up some chickens by the feet and carry several, squawking, with feathers flying, in each hand. My cousin responded off-handedly, "Don't worry. It doesn't hurt them." I remember wondering how he could be so sure, never having been inside a chicken's skin and obviously being deaf to the language of their cries. I later realized that I had completely misunderstood my cousin. Our thought processes were different, and we therefore spoke in different languages. We were confused because the languages had overlapping vocabularies. I had heard "hurt" as "cause pain." He had meant "hurt" as "cause damage."

This same kind of confusion happened when I first started working with delinquent adolescents. I was interviewing a fifteen-year-old boy, and he asked me if I had read in the newspapers about a particularly heinous gang shooting in which an entire family had been executed in their home in cold blood. In a particularly cruel irony, this horrible crime turned out to be a case of mistaken identity: The gang had intended to attack the people in the neighboring house. I told him that I had read about it, and he said, "That was my gang that did that." I asked him how he had felt when he learned about it, and he said, "I felt bad." Upon seeing the relief in my face he immediately recognized that I had misunderstood him. "No, you don't understand. I felt *baaad!*" Again, same word, different language, different mentality. I had understood "bad" as "remorseful." He had meant "bad" as in "bad-assed," which he admired.

Object relations theory focuses much more on the differences in thinking than on the differences in languages. I easily overcame the above confusion over the word *bad*. What was enormously more difficult was understanding the difference in mentalities. How could an event so horrendous (and, as it turns out, so stupid) have produced a feeling of aggrandizement in this child rather than shame?

My first impulse is to describe object relations theory of the "paranoid–schizoid position" (to be discussed in detail in chapter 2) as a "Rosetta Stone" for the understanding of the adolescent mentality. But this may itself still be too focused on language. The Rosetta Stone provided fragments of the same story told in three different written languages, two known, the other (hieroglyphics) unknown. The known languages were then used to decipher the unknown one because they told the same story. But the difference between the paranoid–schizoid (part-object) position and the depressive (whole-object) position is far more complex. This difference is not the same story being told in two different languages. It is the same incident experienced as two entirely different stories. *Rashomon* is a more fitting metaphor than the Rosetta Stone. The Kurosawa film *Rashomon* presents the same event as seen through the eyes of several different participants or observers. All the observers speak the same language, but for each of them it was essentially a different event. Object relations theory of the paranoid–schizoid position and the depressive position essentially describes two fundamentally different ways of seeing (attributing meaning to) the same world.

Intersubjectivity

Only one chapter of this book deals specifically with the concept of intersubjectivity, but the concept permeates the book in more subtle ways. I believe that the concept of intersubjectivity speaks most directly to the question of "caring" that I introduced at the beginning of this section. The terms *caring* and *intersubjectivity* are not synonymous, and I submit that of the two, intersubjectivity is the more profound. Intersubjectivity refers to the interaction between the subjectivities of the therapist and the client, and to the effect each has on the other. When a client finally decides to fully and freely open his or her heart to you and invite you in, you cannot decline the offer. And when you do build the courage to accept the offer and to "walk around in there," you cannot do so with the attitude of a disinterested observer or with "therapeutic neutrality." One can enter another's heart only with an air of profound humility and gratitude, as one would enter a medieval cathedral or an ancient redwood grove. And when one emerges from that experience, one cannot be unchanged by it.

Intersubjectivity is most commonly associated with the work of Robert Stolorow (Stolorow, Brandshaft, and Atwood 1987; Stolorow, Atwood, and Brandshaft 1994), and hence with self-psychology. But object relations theorists, Thomas Ogden (1994) in particular, have shown how intersubjectivity can also be seen as arising out of the inherent tenets of object relations theory. In fact, intersubjectivity is nothing new under the sun, and is not exclusive to any particular theory. The term was originally one in philosophy rather than psychology and has only recently been borrowed by psychologists and incorporated into our theories. Perhaps the most simple and poetic expression of the essence of intersubjectivity was D. W. Winnicott's (1971) when he said that psychotherapy was something that happens in "the overlap between the play space of the therapist and the play space of the client" (p. 54).

This Book

Chapter 1 deals with a historical survey of the idea of adolescence and some of the major historical controversies relating to adolescence. This chapter enumerates the so-called tasks of adolescence and tries to place adolescent issues in the perspective of the broader developmental issues of life.

Chapter 2 introduces two key object relations concepts that are central to my study of adolescent psychology and psychotherapy: the paranoid–schizoid position and the depressive position. These represent the two key developmental concepts introduced by Melanie Klein and developed and enhanced by later object relations theorists. The chapter focuses on the paranoid–schizoid position in particular, which proves to be particularly useful in understanding adolescents in general, and delinquent adolescents in particular.

Chapter 3 continues with a discussion of the paranoid–schizoid position by applying it to a case study. Here we see how the defenses of the paranoid–schizoid position (splitting, projection, identification, projective identification, and denial) can be used to generate a stable, if pathological, character structure out of what would otherwise be an endless fluid and chaotic progression of situationally defined identity shifts.

Chapter 4 reexamines the concept of resistance in light of the object relations theories on identification with the bad object. Resistance was one of Freud's most brilliant and important discoveries, one that he explained in terms of anxiety produced as repressed material threatens to emerge into consciousness. But the tenacity of resistance perplexed even Freud, and object relations theory offers a different view of it, seeing it not merely as resulting from anxiety, but also from a kind of determined addiction to the bad object. This chapter presents several reasons for such an addiction.

Chapter 5 gets us out of the paranoid–schizoid position and into the depressive position, or, more accurately, it shows how this can or should happen, both through the normal developmental process and with the assistance of psychotherapy.

In chapter 6 we visit most specifically the concept of intersubjectivity and look at its application to a particularly difficult client population, delinquent adolescents. In this chapter I argue that in spite of the difficulty of its application, intersubjectivity is absolutely essential for a successful engagement of this population.

Chapter 7 represents a somewhat audacious attempt to apply the developmental theory of British object relations theorist D. W. Winnicott to a rationale for why individual psychotherapy works. The successful therapist, I argue here, must parallel in some way the task of the "good enough mother" in facilitating her own "destruction" as an internalized object and allowing the emergence instead of the client's "true self," one capable of forming true interpersonal relationships.

Chapter 8 discusses group therapy in terms of object relations theory. Group therapy is frequently described as the "therapy of choice" for adolescents, and a number of examples of why this is so are presented here. Of course an object relations understanding of group therapy cannot be complete without considerable reference to the crucial contributions of Wilfred Bion, essentially the creator of group therapy, and the chapter presents a series of adolescent group situations as illustrations of his "basic assumptions groups."

Chapter 9 offers a brief foray into family therapy, both in terms of object relations theory and in terms of the particularly difficult position of the adolescent in the family. The adolescent essentially has one foot in the family and the other out, and it is essential that both feet rest on firm ground while the adolescent, the family, and the therapist facilitate that delicate shift in balance from one foot to the other that will enable an eventual move into adulthood and autonomy.

Chapter 10 represents a brief epilogue offering some thoughts on the contribution of object relations theory (in particular the contributions of D. W.

Winnicott) and the problem of delinquency. Two ideas are presented: the relationship between the delinquent mentality and the object relations theory concept of the paranoid–schizoid position, and Winnicott's notion of "delinquency as a sign of hope."

Finally, chapter 11 addresses some contributions of object relations theory to the practice of clinical supervision. Here we examine the ancient but ongoing debate over the nature and location of appropriate boundaries in the supervisor–supervisee relationship and the impact of the increasing shift to intersubjectivity on that debate.

There are times in the course of this book when the reader may ask if this is a book about object relations theory, illustrated by case examples of adolescents, or a book about working therapeutically with adolescents, using object relations theory to inform the treatment. It is both. I hope that the reader takes from this book a sense of respect: respect for the complexity of the adolescent mind, respect for the tortuous nature of the psychological conflicts and dilemmas that adolescents go through, and respect for the adolescents themselves, as humans, however lost, however misguided, however much "menaces to society" they may have become.

Note

1. The highest and most intense level of residential care below psychiatric hospitalization.

PART I

THEORETICAL ISSUES

CHAPTER ONE

~

Adolescents and Adolescence

Little girls are cute and small only to adults. To one another they are not
cute. They are life-sized.

—Margaret Atwood, *Cat's Eye*, 1988

If adults, as Atwood suggests, reduce little girls to creatures that are small and
cute, what they do to adolescents is even worse. Adolescents are not even al-
lotted their own period of time. They are in a "transitional" period. They are
"between" childhood and adulthood. Their first experiences with passionate
sexual love are dismissed as "crushes." Their pain, their suffering, their angst,
is met by "Don't worry. You'll grow out of it." The word *today* can be defined
as the period of time between "yesterday" and "tomorrow." But we don't
think of today as a transitional period. Today is where we live. Adolescence
is where adolescents live.

Perhaps it is because they are near homonyms that adolescents seem to get
confused with adolescence. Family therapist H. Charles Fishman (1988), for
example, argues that because adolescence is a social construct, "it follows
that our treatment of the problems associated with adolescence must also
take into consideration the social context. In other words, what is needed
here is a contextual therapy." Since "[the] family is the social environment
out of which the adolescent emerged," it follows that "[the] most powerful social therapeutic intervention for working with adolescents is family therapy"
(pp. 4–5). Adolescence is almost certainly a social construct. Adolescents,
on the other hand, are not social constructs. They are people.

As a social construct adolescence is relatively new. Indeed, the "discovery" of adolescence did not happen until relatively late in history, and it is generally credited to a single man. G. Stanley Hall (1904) published a monumental, two-volume opus on adolescence around the turn of the twentieth century. Hall's historical importance cannot be overstated. Historians John and Virginia Demos (1969) have shown that "an examination of various written materials from the period 1800–1875 uncovers (1) almost no usage of the word [adolescence] and (2) only a limited degree of concern with the stage (and its characteristic behaviors)," while the published works of Hall and his students in 1904 "evoked a broad popular response" (p. 632).

In terms of current thinking on adolescence, Hall's importance is primarily historical. Hall believed in a "recapitulation" model of human development: that the development of the individual is somehow a recapitulation of the historical development of mankind. Hall saw adolescence, therefore, as paralleling civilization's emergence out of the barbaric dark ages of childhood. Hall also had an unfortunate (by modern standards) predilection toward eugenics, and championed the selecting out of "superior" adolescents for special education in citizenship and leadership. Adolescence was "the only point of departure for the super anthropoid that man is to become" (1904).

One of Hall's ideas about adolescence did, however, have lasting impact on the way we conceptualize the period. Hall believed that adolescence constituted a time of inevitable emotional "turmoil," and his assertion has sparked a seemingly endless debate within the field of developmental psychology. Psychodynamic theorists have, by and large, sided with Hall on this, arguing (in the extreme form) that if an individual goes through adolescence without turmoil, something is terribly wrong. I remember sitting through a lecture on adolescence at which the lecturer shook his head in apparent pity for the parents of those children who had gone through an apparently "smooth" adolescence. "Just wait . . ." was his message, making the metaphor between the seriousness of measles contracted by an adult versus that of the same disease contracted by a child.

Other psychologists have challenged this assertion. Research psychologists Offer, Sabshin, and Marcus (1965) for example, studied a group of eighty-four suburban high school boys in an attempt to define the parameters of "normal" adolescence. The summary of their findings includes the following:

1. Almost complete absence of gross psychopathology, physical defects, and physical illness.

2. Ability to experience affects flexibility and to bring their conflicts affectively to successful resolutions.
3. Evidence of specific struggles with aggressive and sexual impulses.
4. Relatively good object relationships with adults. Father is reliable and mother is understanding. Emotionally they feel closer to mother.
5. Feeling a part of a larger cultural environment and being aware of its norms and values.

With the exception of finding number 3, the evidence for a conflict-free adolescence seems fairly strong.

Psychiatrist J. Masterson (1967) attacks the inevitable turmoil position from a different tack. In a follow-up study of seventy-two adolescents admitted to outpatient clinics, Masterson found that the large majority of them "did not grow out of it." He concludes gloomily,

> Adolescence was but a way station in a long history of psychiatric illness that began in childhood and followed its own inexorable course—a course only temporarily colored by the developmental stage of adolescence. The decisive influence was psychiatric illness, not "adolescent turmoil" (p. 1343).

With a debate that has now passed its centennial mark, one might do well to step back and consider what, exactly, is being debated. Two things immediately come to mind: responsibility and response. If the *cause* of adolescent turmoil is something inevitable, some normal developmental process involving raging hormones or the like, then we of the older generation, parents, teachers, administrators, are pleasantly relieved of responsibility. If it is inevitable, then it certainly is not our fault. But while the motivation to exonerate ourselves for the pain and suffering of those we love is certainly understandable, we may err in letting ourselves off the hook too easily.

> One of our sons fell into an angry depression during his adolescence, focused in particular on high school. He hated high school with a relentless passion. My wife and I watched in despair as his grades dropped, and he began to lie to us increasingly about unfinished homework. Fortunately, he was able to graduate, with grades that were acceptable, though well below his potential.
>
> He enrolled in a countercultural college out of state. He told us later that he had dreaded going there because he had expected to hate it as much as he had hated high school. He didn't. He loved it and he excelled.
>
> The high school he had attended was a large, local public high school with a good reputation. It had good teachers who cared about our son and shared our concern for him. It was an excellent school for many kids, but it was the

wrong fit for our son. There he had become the only child I had ever heard of to be suspended from school for a day for having gone barefoot on campus. Later, at his college, barefoot was the norm.

The anguished, inarticulate cries we had heard from him in high school were the cries of the proverbial square peg being wrenched into a round hole.

The other issues emerging from the "inevitability debate" is that of response. If adolescent turmoil is inevitable, then the logical response is simply to wait it out. In spite of Masterson's findings, the "this too shall pass" approach to adolescent turmoil is not without its merits. Sending a teenager into individual psychotherapy may needlessly pathologize the teenager and the problem he or she is dealing with. Family therapy tends to mitigate this somewhat (and this is a distinct advantage of that approach), but even with family therapy it is clear to all parties involved who the "identified patient" is. In retrospect, I am glad that we sought neither individual nor family therapy for our son. On the other hand, finding an alternative high school for him might have been kind and beneficial.

To place the debate over the inevitability of adolescent emotional turmoil in its proper perspective, I believe that it is helpful to review the words of one of the major contributors to this debate. Anna Freud (1958, 1969) is regarded as one of the major proponents of the inevitability-of-turmoil side of the debate. Yet her words on the subject, rather than being argumentative or polemic, appear to me as a model of temperance, compassion, and wisdom. Freud does not rule out psychotherapy for adolescents whose issues are sufficiently problematic. To the contrary, she specifically espouses psychotherapy for adolescents whose problems appear (in Masterson's terms) to result more from mental illness than from adolescent turmoil. She argues for empathy and benevolent patience for those who, with limited emotional and cognitive resources, are facing a host of significant challenges. Anna Freud (1958) wrote,

> I take it that it is normal for an adolescent to behave for a considerable length of time in an inconsistent and unpredictable manner; to fight his impulses and to accept them; to ward them off successfully and to be overrun by them; to love his parents and to hate them; to be deeply ashamed to acknowledge his mother before others and, unexpectedly, to desire heart-to-heart talks with her; to thrive on imitation and identification with others while searching unceasingly for his own identity; to be more idealistic, artistic, generous, and unselfish than he will ever be again, but also the opposite: self-centered, egoistic, calculating. Such fluctuations between extreme opposites would be deemed highly abnormal at any other time of life. At this time they may signify no more than

that an adult structure of personality takes a long time to emerge, that the ego of the individual in question does not cease to experiment and is in no hurry to close down on possibilities (pp. 275–76).

While I believe that adolescents are an overly stereotyped group, it is nevertheless obvious that there are some monumental life events with which they must come to terms. Psychologists have historically included on the list of such events puberty and its ramifications, identity formation, and separation from the family into autonomous adulthood. It is no more stereotyping of adolescents to say that they must come to terms with these issues than it is stereotyping of the elderly to say that they must come to terms with death.

About the ramifications of puberty, much has been written (especially in the classical Freudian literature), and I have little to add. Except, that is, to add the obvious, which is that there has been a dramatic and dismaying recent change in the way teenagers deal with puberty. The ethic now seems to be (and here I admit that I deal with a skewed sample) that one deals with one's emerging sexuality by running out and having sex. Psychological issues aside, the consequences of this trend in terms of teen pregnancies are disastrous. It is comparable to a similar trend in which young teenage gangsters have replaced shooting at each other with cap guns with shooting at each other with real guns.

Identity Formation

Of identity formation I have much more to say, including bemoaning its recent fall into disfavor as a psychological concept. The concept of identity, most articulately developed by Erik Erikson (1950, 1959, 1968), began to be severely critiqued almost as soon as it was introduced. Erving Goffman, for example, argued as early as 1959 that identity could not be justified as a single, unified mental structure, achieved by the passing of a clear milestone. Identity, Goffman (1959) claimed, was a much more fluid, quixotic phenomenon that depended heavily on one's social context.

Identity, then, seems to be one of a large number of psychological concepts that has withered under too close scrutiny and too rigid a demand for clear definition. However difficult it may be to define and pinpoint identity, it remains an enormously useful concept in our attempts to understand adolescents, and in particular, our attempts to understand adolescent gangs. Teenagers with a particularly weak sense of personal or familial identity seem to be those most likely to gravitate to gang affiliation and to gratefully adopt the easy identification label that gangs provide.

A sixteen-year-old Latino gang-banger at the Center identified himself as "Frank from F-13." (Florencia Trece is a large Latino gang in the Los Angeles area.) When challenged on this, Frank would explain (with more certainty than defiance), "My name is Francisco A. But who I am is Frank from F-13."

Frank spent his youth in Mexico City. He never knew his father and was unwillingly abandoned at an early age by his mother. His mother (a tragically common story) had left him and his sister behind with some friends while she had come to "El Norte" to earn money cleaning houses. She sent most of her earnings back to her children, but little of it actually made it to them. When after a couple of years she returned to Mexico City, she was dismayed at the poor care her children were receiving. So she did what she could. She could afford to take only one of her children back to Los Angeles with her, so she took her daughter.

Frank later described his last years in Mexico City. He had asked his foster family where his mother had gone and had been told, "She has gone far away." So during his fifth and sixth years Frank would set out during the day wandering the streets looking for his mother. Since he had been told that she was "far away," he figured that the farther he walked from home, the more likely he was to find her. Each evening he would somehow find his way back home, determined that the next day he would have to walk even farther.

By the time his mother was able to take Frank to Los Angeles he was a lost and alienated soul. He had finally been reclaimed by a mother he didn't know, to reunite with a sister he barely remembered, to a land where he did not speak the language. When Frank later joined Florencia Trece, it was like being adopted by a family, and given an identity.

Adolescents only reluctantly yield such identities, however dysfunctional they may seem.

Niki, the sixteen-year-old scion of a multigenerational gangster family, swore that she was determined to leave the gang lifestyle. She had two uncles and one brother in prison for murder (both uncles murdered their wives), and she had already faced many threats against her own life. Yet Niki, who had grown up, as she put it, "in a series of motel rooms," expressed misgivings about being placed with her mother after discharge from the Center. Her mother was the only one in the family with aspirations of upward mobility, and although she was still living in a motel room, she had at least moved to a residence motel in one of the more affluent parts of Los Angeles. Niki expressed her reservations: "I don't belong in that neighborhood. I don't feel comfortable there. I belong in Watts."

Identity, not as a single unifying structure as described by Erikson, but rather as a complex set of internalized object relationships, will be revisited in much greater length in chapters 4 and 5 of this book.

Facing Adulthood

The prospect of entering adulthood looms like a Sword of Damocles over the heads of many adolescents. If I were to back off at all from my earlier polemic against stereotyping adolescents, it would be around this component of adolescent anxiety. I say this not out of an emerging desire to pathologize teens, but rather the opposite. For I attribute to teenagers what they are rarely given credit for: good reality testing. Teenagers are woefully unprepared for adulthood and they know it! Indeed it can be stated as an almost absolute rule that the less well prepared a teenager is for adulthood, the more likely he or she is to present severe pathology or delinquency. The lower the academic achievement scores are for an incoming ward at the Center, the more likely it is that he or she is gang entrenched.

This brings to mind an interesting thing about gangs. Gang members will often say that their gangs to them are "like a family," sometimes, "more like a family than my real family." Gangs offer physical support, emotional support, the promise of protection, a definable identity, status in the community, and undying loyalty. But the gang family differs from the biological family in that it is forever. Most gangs have strictly enforced codes against leaving. Most require that one be "jumped out," which is to say, be beaten within an inch of one's life and then be forever vulnerable to the impulsive wrath of the scorned gang. Many others, however, say quite clearly that the only way out of their gangs is death.

However awful this code may be to a more mature gang member who is contemplating an alternative to the dead end that gangs represent, it can be strangely comforting to the initiate. "Here is a family that I never have to grow out of, in fact, that I never even have to consider growing out of."

I sometimes find myself lapsing into a fruitless conversation (one of a number of fruitless conversations that can occur with adolescents) in which I try to explain to such a teenager the other possible models of adolescence. Adolescence (I explain) is a natural time of separation from the family and from childhood friends. I, myself (I offer), was expected not just to go to college, but to go *away* to college, to begin to experience a new world. Invariably, my lecture is met by a blank stare of incomprehension.

One girl who seemed to be an exception was Daphne (who is discussed again in chapter 8). Daphne grew up in an impoverished, gang-infested neighborhood of the city, the younger daughter of a highly dysfunctional family. Daphne had a lot going for her. She was highly intelligent, strikingly beautiful, articulate, and, with her cruel and cutting wit, she was a force to be reckoned with in her treatment unit. Daphne also stood out from her peers in having a clear sense of a future, a future different from her past.

In high school Daphne had joined the ROTC, and she had loved it. It had helped instill a kind of discipline in her of which she spoke with pride. Daphne also had a positive role model in her life: an uncle who had become an officer in the military. So Daphne graduated from the Center with a clear plan for success. She would join the armed services and she would succeed. (The military may seem to be a surprising choice for many Center kids whose rebelliousness, poor impulse control, hatred of authority, and antisocial tendencies would seem to make them particularly unfit. But the military, for them, is seen as a kind of tightly knit extended family, and thus another way of not really leaving home.)

But Daphne did not succeed, and for this I partly blame myself and the rest of her treatment team. Daphne's fierce determination to succeed had been in part a mask (reaction formation) against her underlying fear of separation and autonomy. And we had not seen this clearly enough nor addressed it thoroughly enough. I spoke with Daphne several years later when she was the impoverished mother of two young children and her gangster boyfriend was serving time in prison. I asked her what had happened with her plans for the military. "I don't know," she answered weakly. "I guess I just couldn't leave the old neighborhood."

Adolescence as the "Second Individuation" Process

An overview chapter on adolescence such as this one would not be complete without some reflection on the idea that adolescence is a kind of recapitulation of the "first" separation–individualization process. This first separation–individuation process refers to the psychological development of the child between early infancy and the ages of four or five, the period so exhaustively studied by Margaret Mahler and her colleagues in the United States and, on a more clinical level, by D. W. Winnicott in Great Britain (Winnicott's developmental theories, used as a model for an object relations therapy for adolescents, are the subject of chapter 7).

The notion that adolescence represents a kind of revisiting of this original developmental period originated with Anna Freud but was most elaborately articulated by Peter Blos (1967, 1968). According to Blos both periods are marked by (as the original name implies) a process of separation (for the infant it is separation from the mother, and for the adolescent it is separation from the family) and individuation (the formation and consolidation of personal and sexual identity). Blos points out, however, that there is a significant difference in the desired outcomes of both processes. The hallmark of a successful separation–individualization process for the toddler is, to use Winnicott's (1958a) phrase, the "capacity to be alone." In contrast, Blos points out, the mark of a "successfully" completed adolescence would be the capacity to form a healthy and mutually satisfying relationship with another human being. How this process is accomplished is the focus of the body of this book.

Depression, Anger, Boredom, and Anxiety

This quartet of affective states seems to dominate the adolescent psyche. Indeed, so jumbled together are such feelings in adolescents that it is frequently difficult to tell one feeling from another. It is clear that anger and depression are related. There is an ancient saw in psychology that "depression is anger turned against the self." Yet recent thinking also has it that, at least among adolescents, depression can be anger against others as well. The *Diagnostic and Statistical Manual, IV (DSM IV)* (2000) lists "irritable mood" as a substitute for "depressed mood" among children and adolescents among its criteria for "depressive disorder." Thus among adolescents at least, anger seems to be a part of depression whether it is directed against the self or against others. And depression, for its part (and thus anger as well?), is clearly a component of boredom. And as for helplessness, it can manifest itself as either the impotent rage of frustration or the sinking despair of hopelessness.

This kind of feeling confusion makes sense if these superficially diverse feelings can be seen as different facets of a single developmental process: the separation–individuation process. Let us start with a brief examination of boredom, which is a particularly good example of how this feeling of confusion happens.

On Boredom

Adam Phillips (1993) has written with great originality, and from an object relations perspective, on boredom. Phillips argues that boredom, rather than being merely a transient, unpleasant condition, can also form a positive, even essential part of the human potential. "In other words, the capacity to be bored can be a developmental achievement for the child" (p. 69). Phillips describes cases in which the inability to be bored becomes a particular kind of pathology, one relating to the child's inability (or refusal) to experience desire, and hence an inability to truly discover or develop a sense of self. Phillips' object relations formulation of boredom therefore appears to have far-reaching implications for the study of pathology among teenagers and is developed more fully in chapter 8. In particular, the inability to tolerate boredom may be seen as critical in the propensity toward severe drug addiction.

But boredom itself is a particularly pernicious state among many (though certainly not all) teenagers. Those who tend to dismiss this condition by saying that a child is "just" bored miss both the symbolic importance and the danger of boredom. Bored teenagers are much more likely to fall into delinquency than nonbored teens, and those who leave the Center after a "successful" program here are much more likely to fall back into their old ways if they are prone to boredom. Even with kids still in the program, I find it disconcerting to hear that they experience "doing good" as "boring" and that it is accompanied not so much by pride and a sense of accomplishment as by a wistful nostalgia for the more "fun" experience of "doing bad."

My understanding of boredom is compatible with that of Phillips, but somewhat different. Boredom (pathological boredom, that is) is, as I see it, like being on strike. When one is on strike one says, in essence, "I refuse to do my job. But I also refuse to quit my job." Boredom is similar. When one is bored one says, in essence, "I refuse to find anything interesting. But I also refuse to stop wanting to find something that will interest me." If we allow this metaphor to develop and inform us, we may note some interesting parallels. The reasons people go on strike can be broadly lumped together as "demanding better working conditions" (including, of course, better pay, better benefits, etc.). In other words, people go on strike because they want to be taken care of better. I submit that the same is true of boredom.

Boredom is a passive complaint that one is not being taken care of well enough. It is a complaint against the world that it is not entertaining enough, does not pay one enough attention, does not sufficiently stimulate. Ultimately, the complaint carries back to the mother who unconsciously is accused of abandoning the child before he or she is ready to be out in the world entertaining and stimulating himself or herself.

The fact that boredom is a thinly veiled complaint or accusation is what explains the impatient, angry reaction that it is likely to elicit in adults. When the adult/parent/mother yields to this reproach and starts making suggestions about what the child can do, the child is then getting what it wants. For the mother is then re-fusing with the bored child. But the mother's heart isn't really in it this time around, and rather than getting inside her child's psyche and making sense of it for him, the child experiences the mother's suggestions as fobbing the child off. And even if the mother were somehow able to come up with a particularly apt suggestion, it is unlikely that the child would accept it anyway. To do so would mean being on one's own again, the momentary bond reestablished with the mother through the process of suggesting being broken by the very success of the suggestion.

The significance of this type of object relations approach to boredom is that it focuses our attention not on the relationship between the bored adolescent and the potentially entertaining or stimulating things in the environment, but rather on the relationship between the bored adolescent and his or her mother, and specifically on the adolescent's sense of being abandoned, left to his or her own devices, by the mother, before he or she is really ready to be.

British object relations theorist Donald W. Winnicott (1958a) proposed that "the capacity to be alone" is the hallmark of the healthy and successful transition from infancy to childhood. Boredom among adolescents represents a fixation at, or regression back to, that emotional state in which the child experiences being alone as a terrifying abandonment. In working therapeutically with bored adolescents, we can fall into the trap of endlessly suggesting "things to do" (and endlessly having our suggestions rejected). Or we can speak more directly to the underlying issues and feelings: the terror and rage at the experience of abandonment, the despair of ever being able to survive autonomously.

On Depression

If, as *DSM IV* suggests, we include hyperirritability as a symptom of depression, then depression would appear to be only slightly short of universal among adolescents. Some psychoanalytic thinkers still assert that it should be considered universal or, at least, a necessary feature of adolescence. Briggs (2002), for example, assert that one of the necessary "tasks" of adolescence is "mourning" the passing of childhood, of the comfort, protection, and the gratification of dependency needs, that childhood represents.

While this sounds good in theory, it seems to fly in the face of what is currently observed and commonly bemoaned in modern society, which is that young preteens seem determined to rush, hell-bent, out of childhood and into adolescence. However wistful and nostalgic our adult remembrance of things past, childhood, by and large, is frequently not all that it's cracked up to be. Even among those of us fortunate enough to have our dependency needs substantially met, dependency itself is an inherently anxiety-generating state. We have to be given whatever we need, be taken wherever we need to go, be comforted in our times of distress, all by someone else. And for those who do not have good parents, childhood can be an absolute nightmare.

> Shannon, a sixteen-year-old girl at the Center (featured in the prologue and later in chapters 7 and 10) grew up with no father and a mother who severely abused drugs, fell in and out of psychosis, in and out of severe depressive withdrawals, and was verbally abusive. Shannon remembers as a child telling herself over and over again, "I have to remain responsible. I have to remain responsible. I have to remain responsible."

Exactly how this little girl conceptualized responsibility is difficult to imagine, but it must have been thought of as whatever was the opposite of her mother.

At age fifteen Shannon made an important discovery. She found that when she ran out of the house to escape her mother's wrath or abuse or psychotic process, she didn't have to come back. Shannon discovered the streets of Hollywood. She discovered panhandling (which she turned into an art form). She discovered sleeping under freeway overpasses. She discovered drugs.

When Shannon first came to the Center (following an arrest for possession of heroin), she was furiously hostile, defiant, and resistant (returning to a situation of powerlessness and dependency was not her idea of a good time). Shannon, however, bonded quickly with me. And through the course of her stay in the Center she made remarkable progress.

She came to realize that she was capable of a normal life, of normal happiness, and, most importantly, of normal, mutually satisfying interpersonal relationships. And she was able to see with remarkable clarity that drugs and mutually satisfying relationships are incompatible.

Counterbalancing this positive growth, however, was the mourning she had to do over what she was giving up. And what she was giving up was the opposite of childhood. Shannon had experienced a premature foray into an adulthood for which she was utterly unprepared. But she had also loved it. Shannon loved Hollywood and she genuinely loved drugs. However loathe I was to do so, I, as her therapist, had to come to terms with the fact that the expression I saw on her face when she talked about drugs, and when she talked about the derelicts, the speed freaks, and the low-lifes that she had come to know, was one of real joy.

The concept of "necessary" mourning for passing childhood also runs contrary to what has been observed in the "first" separation–individuation stage. Margaret Mahler (1968, 1972) carried out a systematic and rigorous observational study of early childhood psychological development, and her published results are now famous. If we extrapolate backward from theorizing on the adolescent's separation from the family to the toddler's separation from its mother's arms, we might expect to encounter some description of toddler mourning: the necessary grief process the toddler has to go through to deal with the loss of the indulged dependency needs of infancy. But we find no such thing. Mahler describes "the freely walking toddler [as] seeming to feel at the height of mood of elation. He appears to be at the peak point of his belief in his own magical omnipotence" (1972, p. 210). Greenacre (1957), somewhat more poetically, describes this period as a "love-affair with the world."

If there is a "necessary mourning" that adolescents need to go through, it seems to be more for the childhoods that they didn't have than for those they actually had. Many of the teenagers at the Center announce, some matter-of-factly, some with anger, a few with sadness, that they "never had a child-hood." The closer to literal truth this is the more difficult it is to mourn, for it may be impossible to mourn something one has never experienced. When I query these kids about what they think they missed out on, most become tongue-tied. The best that many can come up with (and this is a sad reflection of what they *did* experience rather than what they did not) is, "Well, someone to beat my ass when I was bad." It is the ones who had inconsistent parenting rather than the ones who had no parenting who really need to grieve, for they know in their guts what they should have had and yet didn't receive enough of. If they don't do this grief work (in adolescence or any other time in their lives), they are in danger of an endless and fruitless pursuit of the kind of care that is simply not given to anyone over the age of five.

> K., a young social worker who was a client of mine in my private practice, had been subjected as a child to constant verbal abuse by a stepfather, and emotional abandonment by her mother. On the day of 9/11 K. cancelled all her clients and stayed home, as did many people, horrified and transfixed by the scene on the television. When she came to see me later that week, she was enraged and indignant that her director was threatening to fire her for having abandoned her clients.
>
> She was distressed when I failed to join her in vilifying her director. Instead I explained matter-of-factly that when she joined the helping professions, she had tacitly agreed to place the needs of her clients above her own. "Who then takes care of me?" she cried out in anguish. "No one," I answered (and this time not matter-of-factly but with real compassion), "and I am so, so sorry that you didn't get that kind of care when you were young." The next several minutes in the session I sat silently but supportively by her side as she wept bitterly.

On Sadness

Sadness is a problematic feeling for many teenagers, and for delinquent teens in particular. The main problem with sadness is that there's not much you can do about it except feel it, and feeling it feels so awful. With fear one can seek the protection of others, or somehow build up defenses on your own. With anger one can punch someone in the nose or kick him in the shin and (momentarily) feel better. With sadness one seeks comfort from others, but this is a highly risky proposition. Many kids at the Center report that their families simply would not tolerate sadness. Those whose parents were themselves current or former gang members report having been beaten if they were caught crying, because only weaklings cry in that culture. The parents genuinely thought they were doing their children a service by beating the weakness (sadness) out of them.

With other parents the discouragement would be more subtle but equally effective. Seeing their child's sadness as an indictment of their own inadequate parenting, such parents react with scorn, derision, belittlement, or other invalidation.

> Marissa, a sixteen-year-old Latina, told her mother in a multifamily group about a rape she had undergone a year earlier. I am always amazed, when I see this happen, how rarely mothers give the "right" response (the one I want them to give). They rarely say, "Oh my God, my darling! I am so sorry!" Instead they start with a challenge ("Why didn't you tell me sooner?") and frequently move into blaming ("Why were you in that place? With those people?").
> Marissa's mother started out well, with a huge, tearful hug and much comfort. Then, in what appeared to be an effort to "relate" to her daughter, she started talking about the time she, herself, was raped. Even more tears followed along with tales of even more angst. This time it was Marissa who got up and walked around the table to give her mother a hug, and it was the mother who buried her face in her daughter's chest. The daughter, apparently, had gotten her allotment of comfort, and now it was time to return to the basic dynamic of their relationship: the daughter giving comfort to the mother.

But there is another problem with sadness, especially when the sadness pertains to loss. Losses are permanent. Dangers can be transitory; frustrations can be momentary. But losses can be forever. This is a problem even for the strongest and healthiest among us. We recognize, as C. S. Lewis (1989) said, that the pain of grief is the price we pay for having loved. And most of us are willing to pay that price. But many of the kids at the Center are not as convinced about the value of love. Worse yet, because so many of them have been abused, physically or sexually, helplessness is especially intolerable. And facing an irreversible loss gets them in touch with an unbearable feeling of helplessness.

So they take their sadness and transform it into anger, sometimes so instantly that they don't even feel the sadness for a moment. "Don't get sad, get even!" "Payback's a bitch." "Don't grieve for your lost 'homeboy,' get one of theirs instead." This, essentially, is the rationale of the "drive-by" shooting. It doesn't matter who you kill, any more than it matters who, in particular, killed your friend. What matters is that the balance sheet be evened. If you get revenge, you don't need to grieve.

On Anger
Anger, as I have said, is a favorite feeling for adolescents because it is experienced as being empowering.

Occasionally young neo-Nazi "skinheads" will be admitted to the center. I worked with one of these, a nice-enough young man except when he was talking about minorities. He especially hated blacks. I worked in vain to understand the meaning of this hatred. He had had some run-ins with African Americans, but nothing to explain the vehemence of his rage. It seemed, in part, to come from an identification with his father, who was also racist. But he otherwise had very little use for his father, who was an alcoholic n'er-do-well, and in and out of the boy's life, so this explanation also seemed shallow.

I was pressing him on the issue one day, and he became increasingly frustrated with me, as the question seemed to make no sense to him. "I don't know; I just hate them. I think about it all day. I *look* for reasons to hate them." This last sentence caught my attention. "So your hatred is something that needs to be fed? [I asked]. What would happen if you didn't feed it? How would it be for you if you didn't have your hatred?" He stared at me wide-eyed and began to sputter. "I wouldn't be anything! I'd be a wimp! I'd be a punk!" His voice trailed off as he contemplated the notion in mute horror.

Another aspect of anger should be mentioned here. As I discuss in more detail in chapter 2, many adolescents experience feelings not as manifestations of (expressions of) self ("This is what I feel"), but rather as "things" that happen to them, much as they experience catching a cold or the flu. With these adolescents the phrase "He made me mad" means not so much "I feel anger in response to what he did," as "He did something to me. He put this anger inside of me."

When anger is experienced as a foreign presence that invades one's being, then the logical response is to get rid of it. I have dealt with many teenagers following a verbal or physical assault. With many, their justification is "well, I had to let my anger out somehow, didn't I?" The implication is that if they did not purge themselves of this foreign invader they would somehow explode. When I respond that they might just as well have kept their anger in, they look at me with incredulity. To their minds I am telling them that they might just as well go on containing the flu forever, until it destroys them. This type of client is frequently well served by "anger management training," which (ironically) does not challenge the basic assumption that anger (feelings) is (are) something that "happen" to you. Rather, it offers the solace that "what enters you can just as easily leave you" and provides tools for dealing with the momentary discomfort.

On Anxiety

Granted once again that the population I work with is skewed heavily in the direction of delinquent coping styles, it is nevertheless still striking how few direct expressions of anxiety I see (when I do not actively pull for it). Of the admitting diagnoses of the Center wards, probably 80 to 90 percent involve either conduct disorder or some form of depression. Diagnoses of anxiety are extremely rare. This is striking because, as I have tried to point out in this chapter, anxiety pertaining both to the physical separation from the family and to the psychological transition from childhood to adulthood is a fundamental underlying background state of this period of life. The reason one so rarely directly encounters anxiety is, of course, that, as with grief and sadness, anxiety tends to get transformed into other, more acceptable feelings (especially anger).

In one particular type of case anger serves not only as a distraction from anxiety, but directly addresses the source of the anxiety: the separation from the family. Anger, especially anger directed primarily against the parents and the family, can be an adolescent's way of dealing with the terror that comes with the prospect of leaving home. For such adolescents the incessant outpouring of anger represents the burning of the boats (families) behind them lest they give in to the temptation never to leave home. "However frightened I am of leaving home [these teenagers say to themselves, at least on a preconscious level] I will make sure by my rage and hostility that remaining home is an option for neither me nor my family."

CHAPTER TWO

~

Adolescents and Part-Object Thinking

In the introduction I discussed the concept of the paranoid–schizoid position as a kind of Rosetta Stone for understanding the adolescent mentality. The concepts of the paranoid–schizoid position and the depressive position were first worked out by Melanie Klein in a series of papers between 1929 and 1935.[1] The terms themselves are somewhat unfortunate. They refer to the nature of the anxiety experienced in each position, anxiety theory being a major preoccupation of Klein. The concepts do *not* mean that in the paranoid position one suffers from delusions of persecution or from pathological withdrawal from human relationships. Nor in the more advanced depressive position is one condemned to viewing life as an endless vale of tears. I prefer, and use in this chapter, alternate terms *part-object position* and *whole-object position*.

Positions

Before delving into a discussion of the differences between these two positions (whatever one calls them), an explanation is needed about the concept of a "position." Klein herself did not distinguish carefully among terms such as position, stage, or phase. The part-object and whole-object positions clearly develop sequentially. To this extent they can be called "stages" in accordance with any developmental theory. And the achievement of the whole-object position out of the part-object position is the paramount developmental task according to object relations theory, comparable to the resolution of the Oedipus complex in Freudian theory.

19

But in classical developmental theories, one is expected to pass *through* one stage *into* the next. If one fails to do this, one has become *fixated* in the earlier stage. In object relations theory, in contrast, a complete transition to the whole-object position is considered neither possible nor even particularly desirable. Modern object relations theory sees us as living our lives in the dialectical tension between these two positions. We may spend the preponderance of our time in one position or the other, but never without awareness of the attractions and perils of the opposing position. We can move back and forth between the positions, and as we mature it is hoped that we spend an increasing proportion of our time in the whole-object position. But we never completely move into one or the other. Bion (1967) suggested that someone rigidly adherent to the whole-object position would be dull, humorless, and lifeless. My own favorite example of a healthy and emotionally rejuvenating sojourn in the part-object position is the state of being "in love."

The part-object position is, among other things, a position of magical thinking. While it is dysfunctional and unhealthy to dwell predominantly in this position, a life without magic, without some sense of awe and wonderment, without the ability to escape into and grow from one's fantasies, would be dull and lifeless indeed.

Splitting

Splitting is the sine qua non, the alpha and the omega of the part-object position (and the absence of splitting defines the whole-object position). What follows in this chapter is a listing and discussion of various characteristics of the part-object position, in contrast to comparable characteristics of the whole-object position. But the characteristics that I list and discuss separately are, in fact, not separate at all. Rather, they are all permutations, facets, logical consequences of the process of splitting.

Splitting, a term first introduced by Freud (1938) but adopted by Klein, became one of the centerpieces of her theory, and of subsequent object relations theories. Splitting seems to be based on a natural structure of the mind. We seem to be wired to process information by dichotomizing. While we are certainly capable of more complex forms of analysis, it appears to be an inherent tendency to dichotomize, to divide perceptions into opposing categories of hot and cold, tall and short, skinny and fat, good and evil.[2]

The psychological *defense* of splitting originates with the infant's inability to deal *emotionally* with the perception of good and evil (or love and hate, comfort and fear, and so on) in the same object. The infant, says Klein (1952), simply cannot enjoy a "good feed" if the warm, loving, and giving breast being sucked on is *simultaneously* perceived as being capable of being sadistic and withholding, and if the grateful and loving feelings the infant experiences toward the breast coexist simultaneously with the potential for envy and murderous rage. Even a very young infant may be aware cognitively that it is the same breast that is sometimes full and available and at other times absent, empty, or unavailable, and that it is the same breast that he or she sometimes loves and wants to suckle and at other times hates and wants to bite ("tear to bits"). But it is simply too much for the infant to deal with this ambivalence emotionally. The infant simply cannot tolerate loving something he hates or, for that matter, hating something she loves. The infant cannot be comforted by something that threatens him, nor can he wish to destroy something that gives him comfort.

The solution that Klein proposes is simple but ingenious. The infant adopts an "as if" position. The infant simply adopts the stance, "I know that the breast is one, but I will deal with it emotionally as if it were two. I will function as if there were a good breast and a bad breast that are different and unrelated to each other. The good breast I can love and worship unambivalently. It is pure nurturance and comfort and I have nothing to fear from it. The bad breast is pure evil. I can hate it without guilt or discomfort and I can seek to destroy it without concern that I might be losing something essential to me." Does the infant actually think these thoughts? No, but because splitting seems to be built on an inherent tendency to dichotomize, it appears to happen almost reflexively.

The object relations axiom that it is the emotional complexity of loving and hating the same object that pushes the infant into the split world of the paranoid–schizoid position makes sense logically but is difficult to test empirically. How can we truly know what is happening in the mind of a preverbal infant? We can, however, see the identical thing happening in the mind of the much more emotionally and intellectually sophisticated adolescent.

> Shannon was released after her second Center stay to her grandparents, whom she idolized and who, unlike her mother, appeared loving and stable. In living with these elderly people, however, she quickly saw another side to each of them. Her grandfather was kind and well meaning but did not listen well and was prone to responding to anything Shannon said with platitudes. Her grandmother had a streak of sarcasm that Shannon found piercing. In a family session about two months after she was released Shannon had turned completely against them. In the session she was hostile, rude, and unforgiving. She spoke of wanting to go back to her mother and be hugged by her but was scornful of my suggestion that she might allow herself to be hugged by her grandparents.

Suddenly, late in the session, her mood changed. Tears and sadness replaced the rudeness and hostility. "This probably sounds stupid," she said to her grand-mother, "but the other day when you bought me those cookies covered with sprinkles that I loved when I was a little girl, I was so amazed that you remembered what I loved. I wanted to give you a hug then, but I remembered how mean you could be and I was so confused. I didn't know what to do."

As with the infant described by Klein, Shannon could not handle the emotional turmoil that comes with ambivalence. She morphed seamlessly from splitting bad mother and good grandparents into good mother and bad grandparents. But in both cases she remained firmly in the paranoid–schizoid position. When she was finally able to accept that the good, nurturing grand-mother and the bad, sarcastic grandmother were one and the same person, she entered the depressive position and felt the poignant sadness that is char-acteristic of that position.

Wilfred Bion (1959) defined splitting as an "attack on linkage," and that is precisely what it is. The original Kleinian split involves a denial of the linkage between the beloved "good breast" and the hated "bad breast," though in reality they are, of course, one and the same object. But the divi-sion of a "whole object" into two "part objects" is not the only form of split-ting. Braun (1988) describes a number of different linkages that can be at-tacked in the interest of protecting the psyche from being overwhelmed by pain, anxiety, shame, or other powerful emotion. Braun lists *behavior*, *affect*, *sensation*, and *knowledge* as the four aspects of experience subject to splitting. Splitting can involve attacks on linkage within, between, or among any of these dimensions.

Max, a long-term adult client in my private practice, described two episodes of splitting, one during the birth of his first child, the other at the death of his mother. Both examples illustrate affect being split off from knowledge.

With my oldest child labor was induced so that my wife went immediately into strong contractions even before she began to dilate. After fourteen excruciat-ing hours the baby wasn't budging, so they took an x-ray and found that he had an anterior presentation. This means that the top, flat part of his skull was pushing against the cervix instead of the back, round part, and babies in my family are big and have big heads. So they gave my wife an epidural and went in with forceps. I watched as he was being pushed/pulled out and saw his head begin to emerge. Then I saw the shoulders beginning to emerge and I noticed that there was no neck in between them and the head. The head seemed to be directly connected to the shoulders. After a few more minutes the real head emerged, and I realized that what I had thought were head and shoulders were in fact a huge head with a very large topknot on top. It looked a lot like the paintings or statues you see of the Buddha. There wasn't much relief in realizing that he had a neck. My thought was, "What a horribly deformed head. No baby can have a head shaped like that and be alive. He is being born dead."

When he finally came out the nurse patted his behind and he began to cry a little. My thoughts then went to, "Oh, he's not dead. Then he must be severely brain damaged. I have a severely brain-damaged baby."

The strange thing is that as I was having all these horrible thoughts, I had no feelings whatsoever. I was pure intellect, pure observer. Then the nurse began to mould his head gently back into shape and she said, "Boy, what a funny-shaped head!" Her words triggered a dam break in me and all of my feelings rushed back. Mostly I felt like hugging her. I knew instantly that for her to make a joke about it meant that it wasn't all that serious after all.

The "linkage" between Max's thoughts and feelings was severed in the face of what would have been overwhelming angst and despair, and the split-off feelings were banished into some nether regions of his psyche. It wasn't that he didn't have feelings; rather it was that he could not allow himself to feel those feelings. When the situation changed (or, more accurately, when the meaning attributed to the situation changed) the split was no longer necessary, and the banished feelings "rushed back in."

A few years later Max's mother died.

My mother died a long, slow, wasting death. When I was called by the hospital that she had died, I went into the hospital room and my first thought was that they had already taken her away. But she was still there, covered by the sheets. Her once imposing body had shrunk down to almost nothing. I pulled back the sheet and saw her dead face. There was a small table and chair next to the bed and I collapsed into the chair, put my head down on the desk, and wept.

But as I was bawling my eyes out I was feeling nothing. It was almost like an out-of-body experience. Again, I was pure intellect, watching myself cry, feeling my wife's hands on my shoulders, thinking something stupid like, "Boy, I really am grieving aren't I," but feeling nothing.

In the first example Max's splitting ended instantaneously, as soon as he realized that there was no need to ward off overwhelming despair. The second example had no such happy ending. Max remained split off from his feelings about his mother's death for years, and the necessary grief work became a prolonged focus of the subsequent therapy. For years Max worked to recapture lost feelings about his mother. He would purposefully go to places she had loved, hoping that the tears would begin to flow, trying to feel the emotions he knew were there but could not experience.

The term *splitting* has a negative connotation that it does not necessarily deserve. This may be partly because it is such a "primitive" defense (meaning only that it arises very early in individual development), and partly because it is so closely associated with the borderline personality disorder. In any case, I am used to seeing interns and young therapists blanch and get defensive when I point out their own splitting as well as that of their clients.

But certain types of splitting are essential for a healthy psyche. Ogden (1986) presents three cases of clients whom he understands as having been "unable to use splitting effectively." These three were tortured souls who could not love for fear of destroying the loved objects by their hatred. Nor could they allow themselves to truly hate, because their hatred remained forever contaminated by their love. Ogden summarizes, "Splitting allows the infant to feed safely and to love, and to desire and hate safely, without developing overwhelming anxiety that he is being destroyed by, or destroying that which he loves" (p. 57).

Lucy (who is referenced frequently in this book) was a long-term client in her early thirties in my private practice. During the first year of therapy Lucy remained firmly entrenched in the part-object position. One internalized object relationship completely dominated her psyche: that of her unloving, verbally abusive mother, and the corresponding self-representation of the rejected, unlovable, self-hating child. Lucy's self-hatred was as pervasive and unyielding as any I had ever seen. And the presence of her internalized part object was ubiquitous: not only echoing constantly in her thoughts, but also projected onto virtually every other person in her life (including me).

Lucy was like a person whose emotional "skin" had been flayed off her psyche leaving every nerve ending raw and exposed. Every touch, however gentle, was excruciatingly painful. She became suicidal and had to be hospitalized at least half a dozen times that first year, once after her best friend told her she was "gaining a little weight."

Splitting protects the good aspects of an object by separating and distancing them from the bad aspects, and, in a way, to protect the bad aspects from contamination by the good so that they can be hated unambivalently. Bad part objects can be dealt with partly because the good part object is considered to be always nearby, and there is the hope that it may return at any moment, either spontaneously or by means of magical wooing. But with Lucy the good part object disappeared completely. I hoped to offer myself as a good object, but she insisted on projecting onto me all the critical judgments of her abusive mother.

Donald Kalsched (1996) describes how a single or cumulative trauma can become personified in the psyche of the trauma victim and achieve demonic powers to continue abusing or tormenting the victim for years to come. He claims that this abusive inner demon has a protective function as well, guarding the victim against unacceptable openness and vulnerability. These demons have much the same function, says Kalsched, as does Winnicott's (1960, 1986a) "False Self."

Lucy's internalized part-object mother achieved this demonic power and served such a function. Constantly berating her and humiliating her, it nevertheless protected her against the uncertain dangers that come with allowing oneself too much hope.

But whatever the function of this internal mother demon, Lucy's life was hell. The original function of the split, the protection of the good part object, was rendered moot, since the good part object was so far out of the picture as to be virtually nonexistent. Lucy was left with only half of the split, and that being the torturing, abusive, demonic half. Robbed of its original function, the split itself eventually collapsed.

Near the end of the first year Lucy's psyche seemed to cry "Uncle!" Unable to grow a healthy emotional skin (semipermeable stimulus barrier), Lucy instead shrouded herself in a kind of fog. All elements of good breast–bad breast, critical mother and unworthy child, disappeared into this fog. The fog even overpowered and muted the voice of the demon mother.

So thick was this fog that it affected Lucy's physical being. In my office she would look neither at me nor at anything else; instead she stared blindly into space. She got into several near accidents while driving, so she had to start taking the bus but then had to deal with frequently missing her stops. At moments in therapy she would essentially become catatonic, and at one point I referred her to a neurologist thinking she might be having petit mal seizures (she was not).

Near the end of this period (which lasted well into the second year of therapy) I impulsively asked her what it would be like for her if she were actually to allow herself to be aware. I immediately regretted my question, not because of the question itself, but because of the anger and frustration that I heard in my voice. To my surprise she was oblivious to the critical quality of my voice. Instead, she appeared to reflect for a while on my question. "Well," she said, "it would be different."

Another example of healthy, even essential, splitting is the split of the ego into "experiencing ego" and "observing ego." The experiencing ego is the bulk of the ego. It is that part of the psyche that, for example, chats with friends, drinks beer, makes jokes, and laughs. The observing ego is split off from the rest of the ego and, as its name implies, observes. It observes objectively and dispassionately, almost as though it were observing another person. It is the observational voice that interprets, "I'm having fun now."

Many modern psychotherapies emphasize the importance of enhancing the observing ego. Group therapist Louis Ormont (2006) calls observing ego enhancement one of the "five pillars" of his method. Ormont's description of the observing ego is one of a highly split-off function:

> The *observing ego* is that part of the self that has no affects, engages in no actions, and makes no decisions. It functions in conflict-free states to merely witness what it sees. It is like a camera that records without judgment. It is never weighing any thought, gesture or action on the scale of right and wrong, sane or insane, good or bad. It is a psychic entity that is intact and separate from what is taking place before it (no page number).

Dialectical behavioral therapist Marsha Linehan (1993), whose therapy is specific to the treatment of borderlines, does not try to undo the splitting that is so characteristic of that disorder but instead works to enhance the more developmentally advanced split of the observing ego (which she refers to as "mindfulness"). Observing ego enhancement is also stressed in a variety of treatment modalities developed for work with substance abusers and trauma victims.

The Part-Object Position

When one splits whole (ambivalently perceived) objects into part objects (good objects and bad objects, comforting objects and feared objects, loved objects and hated objects), one radically transforms the perceived world in which one lives. The perceived world of the part-object position is as different from the whole-object world as are the worlds on either side of Alice's looking glass. But however extreme the difference is between these two worlds, it is frequently very difficult for the outside observer to notice and therefore to appreciate. This is because of the peculiarities of the "as if" phenomenon. Remember that the splitter is saying, "I know it is one object, but I will function as though it were two." The therapist is likely to get very frustrated with the abused wife who, after weeks of threatening to leave her abusive husband, suddenly comes to a session beaming and announces that her husband brought her flowers and begged forgiveness on his knees. In vain does the therapist remind her that this is the same husband who, days earlier, beat her to a pulp (in vain because cognitively she already "knows" this). The therapist may stare in amazement and disgust as all thought of leaving the sonofabitch is tossed out the window. But from the paranoid–schizoid wife's point of view, why would she want to leave her newly returned good (part-object) husband? Indeed, her efforts must be in the opposite direction: to hold on as tenaciously as possible to the good (part-object) husband and to ward off, however possible, the return of the bad (part-object) husband. Is this a "cognitive distortion," an "error in thinking?" Yes and no. It represents someone who has intact cognitive functioning acting "as if" she did not. It is Scarlet O'Hara saying, "I won't think about that today. I'll think about that tomorrow." Does she "know" that the problem will still exist tomorrow? Yes, but she chooses to act as if she didn't know.

A World of Part Objects

It is not exactly accurate to say that part objects are "unifaceted" and that whole objects are "multifaceted." Part objects can have a number of different facets or characteristics. The rule is simply that none of the facets can be contradictory. A part object can be powerful, ugly, evil, scary, arrogant, and cunning. None of these facets is contradictory with any other. What a part object cannot be is powerful yet weak, ugly yet beautiful, scary yet desirable, and so on.

Joe (who is discussed in much greater detail in the next chapter) was a seventeen-year-old boy at the Center. When asked to describe himself, Joe would startle people with his bold, bland statement, "I'm a bad kid." To Joe, this was the beginning and the end of who he was. When people pointed out good qualities about him, he would deny, evade, or somehow distance himself from what was being said. When it was pointed out that his mother loved him dearly, he simply saw that as proof of his mother's saintliness rather than evidence of anything lovable in him. Joe lived entirely in a part-object world. If something or someone was defined as bad, that was all there was. There was no room for good in something that was bad.

Earlier in this chapter I briefly mention being "in love" as an example of a healthy regression to the part-object position. Popular love songs are full of such part-object descriptions. When one is in love, one's love object can do no wrong, can walk on water, lights up one's life, and so on. These same songs will sometimes mention the cognitive distortions that are necessary to maintain this state of bliss ("Loving eyes can never see").

Romantic love can be a wonderful state, but not under all circumstances. I strongly believe that therapists should feel comfortable in "loving" their clients. But to be "in love" with your clients courts disaster. Early in my career a successful young female attorney came in for therapy. I was immediately dazzled by the righteousness of her causes and by the passion of her crusades. Even more, I was awestruck by the fact that she had emerged a successful and principled woman out of an extraordinarily dysfunctional family and childhood, filled with abuse, abandonment, and multiple family members with severe mental illness. My client quickly dropped out of treatment, and I speculated later that she did so because she sensed my awe of her. If this is true, then she did the right thing. To the extent that I was dazzled and awestruck by her, she was a part object to me. And to that same extent, I was placing my needs (to be dazzled and awestruck by someone) over her needs (to be seen as a whole object). She was right to seek a different therapist.

A World without History

A part-object world is necessarily an ahistorical world. This comes, once again, from the nature of splitting. If I am an infant nursing at the breast and I suddenly bite down hard on the nipple, the breast is likely to be suddenly withdrawn from me, accompanied by a loud yelp from the attached mother. If I need to maintain a strict split between the good (available) breast and the bad (withdrawn, unavailable) breast, then I cannot allow myself to recognize any connection (linkage) between the two, and "cause and effect" (my biting the nipple) would be just such a connection. To maintain the split I must see the comings and goings of part objects as entirely random events. "I was happily nursing the good breast when suddenly it disappeared and the bad (tantalizingly unavailable) breast suddenly appeared in its place."

A boy at the Center puzzled and bemused people by his habit of seeming to start his stories in the middle. When asked why he had cursed out a teacher he would explain, with righteous indignation, that she had yelled at him and that he didn't like being yelled at. When asked why the teacher was yelling at him, he would supply what appeared to him to be an irrelevant detail: He had been throwing spit wads. The staff tended to interpret him as obfuscating, but I believe he was accurately reporting his experience. He simply did not make connections. When connections were pointed out to him, he could see and acknowledge them. But they were not a part of the way he normally interpreted his world.

Cognitive concepts such as cause and effect are present in the part-object mentality, but it is as though they are placed and allowed to gather dust on some back shelf of the brain. When reminded of their existence, the splitter can take them down and employ them, but always awkwardly, and with befuddlement as though never sure what they might be used for.

To say that the paranoid–schizoid position is ahistorical is not to say that people in the part-object position have no awareness of the past. Many are acutely aware of the past and often tragically trapped in it. But the past is experienced differently in the part-object position than it is in the whole-object position. In the part-object position the past is experienced as a chronology of discontinuous events. Someone in this position may be able to report with great accuracy, "First this happened, then that happened, then that happened," without seeing any connection among these events. The events were just things that happened in a particular sequence. In contrast, someone in the whole-object position experiences the past as a continuous flow, not just as chronology but as history, with events connected by a seamless fabric of cause and effect.

The lack of sensitivity to cause and effect exists not just between events, but also between events and self. I was consulting to a girls' group at the Center when the group leader brought in a special task for the group. The task was, to my mind, extraordinarily simple. The girls were asked to write down on a piece of paper three events in their lives that had contributed to shaping who they were today. I was amazed by the difficulty the girls had in simply understanding the task. These were adolescent girls of average intelligence, who kept repeating, "Wait, Ms. B. What is it we are supposed to do?" These were also girls who had suffered major traumas in their lives. They had suffered rape, molestation, abandonment, abuse, neglect—almost anything one could name—but they were unable to recognize a connection between what they had gone through and who they had become. The senior girls in the group came closer to understanding the task than the newer girls and tried to help explain it to them. But even the senior girls' comprehension of the idea of connections was rudimentary and unformed. One girl was finally able to say, "I was raped and therefore I don't like walking past dark alleys."

The absence of a sense of continuous historical flow may also help explain another phenomenon I have observed. When I first began to work at the Center, I was struck by the kids' use of the word *flashbacks*. I rarely heard an adolescent say, "I was back in my room remembering things." Rather, they say, "I was back in my room having flashbacks." At first I assumed this was simply a term drawn out of their common experience in the drug culture. But I am now convinced that the choice of words has more significance. In the whole-object position, part of the process of remembering has to do with the cellular-level awareness that an amount of continuously flowing time has elapsed since the remembered event, carrying me with it to a new place, and altering me into a changed person. I can experience a profound and powerful emotion in remembering a distant event, but that emotion is always colored by the awareness that I am no longer in the same place, nor am I the same person, as when I originally experienced the event.

If I am in the part-object position, however, time is experienced as discontinuous. My sense of chronology has not evolved into a sense of continuity. I have no experience of being carried on the flow of time into a new place. And, lacking an intuitive sense of cause and effect, I have no sense of being a different (stronger and older) person than I was when the event took place.

In the whole-object position one *remembers* past events; in the part-object position one *relives* past events (has flashbacks). Remembering involves looking back across the flow of history to a different time and a different place. Reliving is being there again, unchanged, and reexperiencing the whole thing a second (or third, or fourth . . .) time. This raises serious questions for dynamically oriented psychotherapy, for it is one thing to ask a client to remember a past trauma; it is quite another to ask the client to relive the trauma. (This is discussed at greater length in chapter 7.)

A World without Injustice

Some years ago Harold Kushner wrote the heart-and-soul-searching book, *When Bad Things Happen to Good People*, about his crisis of faith around the death of his son. This book could have been written only out of the whole-object position. In the part-object position bad things simply don't happen to good people.

Splitting divides the world into beautifully neat black-and-white packages. In this world, everything makes sense. We often fail to appreciate the capacity for logic of very small children. But in the thinking of small children (and those who perpetuate this kind of thinking in the part-object position) everything follows a simple but severe logic. If I am punished, it is because I am bad. If I am loved, then I must be lovable. If I am molested, it is because I am a sex object (later to be called a "slut" or "whore"). If I am abandoned, then I must be trash (what else besides trash is thrown away?). In the part-object position the value of a (part) object is determined by what it does; the value of the (part) self is determined by what is done to it. There can be no bad things happening to good people because if bad things happen to you, it means you are bad. Being good means that good things happen to you.

Adolescents at the Center, especially those new to the program, frequently react with extraordinary vehemence against even small punishments meted out for minor rule infractions. A simple time-out may provoke a rage reaction with behavior that escalates to the point where restraint and isolation become necessary. This behavior, bewildering from the point of view of the whole-object position, makes sense in the part-object world. Adolescents arriving at a new placement frequently come with the magical (part-object) notion that their old, bad self was left behind at the old placement and that a brand new, good self has arrived at the new placement. This notion, however, is destroyed with the first punishment given. In a world with no shades of gray, if I am given a punishment, no matter how mild, then I am being told that I am bad. And I am being told that I am entirely bad (there is no part-bad in this world). The illusion of my magical transformation becomes utterly and totally destroyed. I used to be bad. Then for a moment I convinced myself that I was good. Now I am told I am bad again. This is intolerable to me and I go ballistic.

A similar phenomenon also occurs in more senior kids at the Center. Sometimes adolescents who have been doing "well" (not getting into trouble) for weeks or months will regress instantly into old patterns following a simple disciplinary action. Their behavior returns to delinquency. Their affect shifts from ebullience to despair. And they announce that they have simply "given up." From our whole-object position we wonder why such a simple slip should have been so devastating. But in the part-object position there is no such thing as a "slip." In the part-object position, good people simply don't do bad things, whether by "slip" or for any other reason. If, after months of doing well and thinking of myself as good, I suddenly am caught doing something bad, then my new self-concept is revealed to be an illusion, a cruel hoax. I am shown to be bad after all. How can I ever hope for anything different?

The "perfect justice" of the part-object position is extraordinarily cruel in its application. When this cruelty is directed against the self, it elicits sympathy and angst in the observer. Rape victims (nearly every girl at the Center) are notorious for blaming themselves. They should have stayed home that night. They should not have been walking down that street. They should not have trusted that boy. Something horrible happened to them so somehow they must have deserved it. One girl (Lucy) described a date rape, after which she "sat in a dark room for a week just hating myself." When I asked her if she ever allowed herself to hate the man who raped her, she stared at me with incomprehension. "No, why should I hate him?" (This girl, as is so often true of delinquent girls, had also been the victim of severe sexual abuse as a small child.)

When "blaming the victim" is projected out onto external victims, it produces a chilling effect on the listener. When confronted about the deaths of innocent (non-gang-affiliated) victims of drive-by shootings, gang members will imply (in keeping with part-object logic) that there is no such thing as an innocent victim. It is the dead person's fault, gangsters imply, because the victims were "at the wrong place at the wrong time."

A World of Self-as-Object

People in the part-object world reject or ignore cause-and-effect connections because of their unacceptable linking of good and bad. Without cause and effect, however, events are experienced as essentially random, and people are essentially helpless. People in the whole-object position have a sense of self-as-subject, self-as-agent; they have a proactive, empowered self with a limited but still significant amount of control over life. There is no such perception of control in the part-object position. How can one experience control over events that *need* to be perceived as random? There is no sense of self-as-subject or self-as-agent. There *is* a sense of self, but it is entirely self-as-object. I am defined not by what I do, but by what happens to me. Staff at the Center often fault the adolescents for "refusing to accept responsibility." But how can they accept responsibility if they do not experience responsibility, and the experience of responsibility is based on the underlying experiences of power and agency. If there is a motto of the part-object position, it is "*Shit happens!*"

I actually had a girl say this to me in (what was to me) an extraordinary context. Something had upset her, and she responded in her usual way, which was to find some sharp object and make hamburger meat out of her forearm. As I walked her to the nurse's station I asked her (without much therapeutic finesse) how she could have done such a thing to herself. She answered with condescending patience, "Well, Dr. Brodie, shit happens!" I countered (again, with more emotion than therapeutic technique) that this wasn't something that just "happened," that it was something she did to herself. But I was speaking out of the whole-object position, and she was entrenched in the part-object position. This girl really did not experience any responsibility for what she had done to herself or, for that matter, any volition. This, to her, was simply a part in a cosmically determined sequence of events, at one point in which she had done what she "had to do."

Ogden (1986) described life in the part-object position as being "lived by experience" (p. 83). Adolescents at the Center tend to define themselves by what has happened to them rather than by any consistent sense of who they are. "Who am I? Well, first this happened, and then that, and then that." Staff at the Center strongly discourage "war stories." But deprived of the arena for these stories, many teens experience a sense of alienation, a loss of self. I was once staggered by the perspicacity of a senior girl who, in a therapy group, gave some advice to a more junior member that appeared to be right out of Winnicott and object relations theory. What she said (with considerable passion) was, "You've got to stop telling these war stories and get in touch with your feelings!" In the jargon of object relations theory, what I believe she was telling her friend was, "You've got to stop being lived by events (war stories) and get in touch with your self-as-subject (feelings)."

The experience of self-as-object is reflected in the language of these adolescents: their propensity to speak from a passive stance. One sixteen-year-old boy explained to a multifamily group how he had become a father: "Well, something just came up." He was obviously making a joke, but I believe that he was also speaking about his experience: "Shit happens!" Teens speak from a passive poisition even to describe their own feelings: "This anger just took over." "The tears just came up." "I got caught up in a car theft." One girl at the Center who was notorious for "not taking responsibility" finally won the staff's approval when she acknowledged, "My mouth gets me in trouble." But she is still in a passive stance and still in the part-object position. True, she no longer blamed outside people for her troubles, and this was progress. But she had merely transferred blame to her "mouth," an organ over which she experienced no more control than she had over the tides or the freeway traffic.

People in the part-object position experience their own behavior as something that "just happens" (even if that behavior includes severely cutting oneself); they experience feelings as things that happen to them. This becomes an important basis of the defense of projective identification, which I discuss at greater length in the next chapter.

The part-object position also involves a kind of concreteness of thought that sometimes appears in the language used, but is more dramatically seen as a frustrating absence of both (outwardly directed) analytic thought and (inwardly directed) introspection. In the whole-object position one experiences oneself as a subject or agent. Part of this experience of agency is the unspoken recognition of oneself as the interpreter of, the attributor of meaning to one's universe. This process is not one we are normally aware of as it happens, but, in the whole-object position, we are capable of scrutinizing it if the need arises. In the whole-object position the attribution of meaning is almost constant. If someone passes us on the street and smiles at us, we attribute any of a number of meanings to that smile. It could be a sign of courtesy (a polite smile), of warmth (an affectionate smile), of connectedness (a friendly smile), of contempt (a smirk), of seduction (a sexy smile), or of manipulation (an insincere smile). To say that we attribute meaning to the smile is not solipsistic. In the whole-object position we are constantly comparing and contrasting our attributions of meaning with those of others, and subsequently modifying them in a dialectic process of change.

To someone in the part-object position, however, things are what they are. In this position I cannot experience attribution of meaning as a personal act, any more than I can experience my own behavior or my own feelings as truly "mine." A sixteen-year-old boy at the Center explained a fight he had gotten into by saying that the other boy had "mad dogged" him (a kind of provocative staring). When asked if the staring might not have meant something else (curiosity, for example, or absentmindedness), the boy looked at us with a total lack of comprehension. Mad dogging is simply mad dogging (staring is staring) in this position. There is no place for interpretation.

Another boy, seemingly more introspective, but in fact still firmly in the part-object position, explained to his therapist why he had such a hard time allowing himself to feel close to anyone. "You don't understand," he said. "When my parents split up and I started to live alone with my mom she said to me, 'You're my kid now!'" His interpretation of those words was clearly "I own you now!" When the therapist pointed out that other interpretations were possible, such as, "You are my responsibility now," or "I set the rules now," the boy responded as though the therapist had simply not heard him. Words mean what they mean.

Still another boy, several months into the program, was confronting his therapist in one of the groups. "I know you don't like me, Ms. B. You've never liked me. You've been hostile to me and out to get me since the day I got here." The therapist, after a moment of self-reflection, respectfully demurred. "I believe that you see it that way, but I can honestly say that I am not aware of any dislike or feelings of hostility to you, and I certainly don't think I am out to get you." The boy stunned everybody in the group with his retort: "Are you calling me a liar?" Again, there is no room for questions of interpretation. My perception *is* reality, even my perception of *your* internal dynamics.

A World of Omnipotence and Magic

It may initially seem contradictory that in the preceding section I argue that the part-object position is marked by perceptions of helplessness and powerlessness, and in this section I discuss the same position in terms of omnipotence and magical powers. The apparent contradiction is resolved (I hope) by the assertion that the part-object fantasies of omnipotence and magic are *reactions to* underlying perceptions of helplessness and futility and never really replace them. An analogy can be made to a primitive tribe that exists with an acute and fundamental awareness of its inability to control the eruptions of a nearby volcano. The best the tribe can do is try to keep the volcano gods happy with an endless series of sacrifices. But however pleased the tribe may be at its success in keeping the gods at bay, no one in the tribe would ever harbor even a momentary thought that they could *control* the gods (or the eruptions). Gods are, by definition, capricious and unknowable powers unto themselves.

Earlier I argue that the infant cannot acknowledge that her biting of the breast causes it to be withdrawn (causes the good breast to be replaced by the bad breast) because an acknowledgment of cause and effect would be an acknowledgment of the oneness of the good and the bad breasts. At this point, however, I find that I need to amend that argument. What one *cannot* say in the part-object position is, "I realize that my just having bitten (aggressed against) the nipple of the beloved (undeserving of aggression) breast caused it to be withdrawn (withholding) yet still lovable." Such a statement can come only from the whole-object position since it recognizes that giving and withholding are merely two facets of the same object, connected by the effect of my action. What I *can* hope for in the part-object position is that my behavior might possibly *influence* the comings and goings of good and bad part objects. Again, this is like saying that all the power is in the hands of the gods, but that I might just hope to influence the gods in their capriciousness and whimsy.

Let me give an example that is not from the world of delinquent adolescents. Loving husband A, who dwells primarily in the whole-object position, comes home and finds his beloved wife angry and withdrawn. He is told that he has forgotten their wedding anniversary. Filled with guilt, he apologizes for having hurt her. He promises to make it up to her, but more important, he promises to do some soul searching to see how he could have done such a thing. His counterpart, loving husband B, who dwells primarily in the part-object position, comes home and finds that his loving wife is gone and has been replaced by his angry, withholding wife. He is told that he has forgotten their wedding anniversary. He is filled with shame for doing something so stupid and says, "My bad!"[3] for having forgotten. He immediately runs out to buy flowers in an attempt to send his angry wife away and woo back his loving wife. Soul searching is unnecessary because "hey, anyone can forget."

There are essentially four kinds of magical rituals in the part-object position, although some frequently overlap. These are *rituals of holding*, which attempt to lengthen the stay of a good object; *rituals of wooing*, which attempt to woo back a lost good object; *rituals of exorcism*, which attempt to drive away a bad object; and *rituals of warding*, which attempt to keep the absent bad object absent. To call these behaviors magical rituals is not to say they are not sometimes effective. Husband B's flowers and boxes of candy may have quieted his wife's wrath and soothed her hurt feeling. But at best, they give one a feeling of being able to cope with life's exigencies rather than having any real control over one's life. At worst, the recipients of these rituals become weary of being treated as part objects (even good part objects) and leave. There is a certain point in well-functioning groups at the Center when the group will stop accepting the apologies of a chronic misbehaver. The misbehaver knows that he or she has misbehaved but has no sense of power to change. The apologies are not *real* apologies because they do not come from any experience of responsibility. Rather, they are rituals of wooing, hoping to win back the favor of the lost good objects. The group, in getting fed up with and rejecting the apologies, performs an essential service, saying to the misbehaver, "We are not interested in your magic rituals. We are interested in you changing your behavior. You may not believe that you have any control over it, but we know that you do!"

The belief in the power of magic rituals can be tenacious. A seventeen-year-old girl at the Center reported that she had "given" her live-in boyfriend sex every morning that they lived together. She was stunned when he left her. Another girl was delightful and angelic, until she was the slightest bit chastised, challenged, or even questioned. At that point she would consider that her good therapists had disappeared and been replaced by their bad look-alikes. She would then snarl and argue ferociously in an attempt to drive us (the bad therapists) away and open a spot for the return of the good therapists. Her snarling arguments were not real arguments, of course (there is no point in arguing with a bad object); they were rituals of exorcism. What she was trying to do was say, "If you are a nasty bad object, I can be even nastier and drive you away." The fact that they had the opposite of their desired effect never dawned on her.

Although a belief in magic allows the part-object position dweller some hope of influencing events, in a huge area of his or her psyche he or she assumes absolute control. This area of "omnipotence" has to do with the intrapsychic defenses and processes based around splitting. These defenses include splitting, denial, projection, identification, and projective identification. They are discussed at length in the following chapter, but for now, let us look at splitting as an example of omnipotence. The extraordinary power assumed in splitting comes from the "as if" assumption mentioned at the beginning of this chapter. Splitting involves the unconscious statement, "I know that it is one object, but I will function *as if* it were two." This is omnipotent in that it involves the assertion that one can change reality to one's liking. Or, more accurately, it is the assertion that one can *function* as though reality were one way, even while *knowing* that it is another way. To some extent, then, splitting has to be seen as arising out of a powerful infantile grandiosity. It is an assertion that the reality of the world, while acknowledged, is irrelevant to one's functioning.

If one further breaks down spitting into its derivatives, one finds that dwellers in the part-object position can, willy-nilly, transfer characteristics of one object onto another (projection), claim desired characteristics of another as their own (identification), and simply choose to ignore altogether other characteristics of self or others (denial). Splitting, then (and the resulting part-object position), can be seen as a give-and-take compromise. Sacrificed is any *real* power over the universe that would come with an acknowledgment of cause and effect. Instead, a *fantasy* of omnipotence is adopted in which the world can be chopped up into manageable pieces, and the pieces rearranged at will, so that the universe becomes bearable, if not completely controllable. It is a world in which one can love freely (unambivalently) and hate freely (unambivalently), in which good is good and bad is bad and never the twain shall meet.

A World of Limited Feelings

It is a joke at the Center that the adolescents we work with (especially the boys) have only one feeling: anger. What truth there is in this comes from the fact that many teens will do whatever they can to turn all other feelings into anger. Loss becomes fantasies of revenge, humiliation becomes outbursts of rage, and fear is transformed into belligerent aggression. But some feelings simply cannot exist in the part-object position. Among these are guilt, jealousy,[4] and sadness.

In the part-object position, the concept of guilt (defined in this usage as the feeling one gets when one recognizes that one has hurt someone who does not deserve to be hurt) does not compute. In the part-object position such a feeling is an impossibility. In the perfect justice of the part-object world, people get what they deserve. In fact, what one gets *determines* what one deserves. Shame, on the other hand, can exist in the part-object position. Shame is here defined as the feeling one gets when one has violated (or, more accurately, been caught violating) some agreed-upon rule. If even shame sometimes seems in short supply at the Center, it is because the teenagers there do not all agree on these rules. Stealing and lying to authorities, for example, are acceptable in the delinquent subculture, and there is frequently a disturbing absence of shame when perpetrators are caught in the act. Stealing from one's parents, however, is a serious rule violation within this culture, and violators of that rule quickly find themselves dismissed by their peers as "scandalous." Ironically, this is not because of any concern that the parents in question might be hurt unjustly. Rather, it is because parents are deemed sacrosanct, and any sin against them is cardinal in nature. Ironically, among the adolescents at the Center, the most shameful thing to have been arrested for is the "victimless" crime of prostitution. Teens at the center will essentially brag about having been arrested for assault, burglary, and carjacking, but will go mute with shame when confronted with their prostitution.

Envy and jealousy are both complex feelings. Envy is more than just wanting something you don't have. It is wanting something you don't have and hating the person who has it instead of you. There is nothing incompatible between envy and the part-object position. If you have something I covet, then I can easily project onto you meanness, selfishness, and cold-heartedness ("You are purposefully withholding from me what I need or desire") and hate you unambivalently for not giving me what I want.

Jealousy, on the other hand, involves wanting a *relationship* one is not a part of. Since a relationship necessarily involves people, one cannot simultaneously want the relationship and hate one or both components of the relationship, not, at least, in the part-object position. Jealousy can occur only in the whole-object position because jealousy necessarily involves ambivalence. It involves wanting something one is excluded from, but not being able to hate (freely and unambivalently) the objects that are doing the excluding. In the depressive position one cannot simply turn the withholding breast into the bad breast; the withheld or withholding breast remains good.

The adolescents at the Center reduce jealousy to envy. They do this in one of two ways. Sometimes they decide that it is not the relationship they covet, but one of the two parties. The split then becomes easy and obvious. There is a good party and a bad party and the bad party is stealing the good party away from me. In this split the good party is always held pure and blameless and receives no rage or anger. All the blame, all the rage, and all the vilification get directed toward the second party.

The alternative, while still remaining within the part-object position, is still to ignore the relationship, but this time to split the more desired of the two parties. This is what the infant does when it splits the mother into the good breast and the bad breast. This time, however, attention rather than milk becomes the determinant. When you pay attention to me you are the good object, and I love you. When you give your attention to a rival, you are the bad, withholding, betraying, or malicious object, and I hate you. As with everything in the part-object position, these two part objects are seen as coming and going randomly, and without connection to one's own behavior. These types of relationship are the basis of what the kids at the Center call "drama."

The third feeling that cannot exist in the part-object position is true grief: the kind of profound sadness that comes with permanent object loss. This is why Klein labeled the whole-object position the "depressive position" in the first place. Other kinds of lesser sadness can exist in the part-object position. Many Center kids who come from intact homes will complain of a powerful homesickness when they first come in. They maintain such homesickness by a different kind of split. Rather than being seen as maliciously unavailable (as is the bad breast), the goodness of the unavailable home is maintained by having all the blame projected onto a third party (the court, the "system"), or by being accepted by the self ("it's my fault that . . ."). The absent home is still seen as good, loving, and longing for the return of the child, as long as the anger and hatred can be directed elsewhere.

Other feelings can mimic sadness, especially self-hatred. Adolescents who cut themselves (they refer to it as cutting "on" themselves), self-mutilate, and maintain chronic suicidal ideation or behavior, certainly meet some of the *DSM IV* (2000) criteria for depression. Yet many persist in these behaviors with an eerie lack of sadness. Cutters report experiencing relief, excitement, or even glee when carving themselves up. And they describe the relief they get more as relief from "emptiness" than from sadness. Similarly, teens who attempt suicide or obsess on suicidal thoughts frequently also do not report feelings of sadness. Rather, the impulses come from the association of the self as the bad object in any relationship, and, in the part-object world, bad objects *should* be destroyed.

True grief, and the sadness that expresses it, comes from the fact, or the prospect, of permanent object loss. As such, it exists only in the whole-object position. Permanent object loss simply does not happen in the part-object world. In that position part objects come and go at random. I am basking in the presence of a good object. Suddenly the good object is gone and a bad object is here in its place. There is nothing to mourn or to grieve. I may be angry, and I certainly miss the good object. But my efforts are to try magically to drive the bad object away and woo back the good object. What is there to be profoundly sad about?

When deep sadness does occur in these teens, it can be a sign of a foray into the whole-object (depressive) position, and therefore a sign of health. How long the adolescent will be able to *stay* in this new position, and bear this new feeling, is the relevant prognostic question.

A seventeen-year-old girl at the Center (Maria) had a long and extreme drug abuse history. Months into the program she would still grab and swallow any pill she could get her hands on. It didn't matter what kind; if it was a pill she would swallow it. She came from an infamous drug-dealing family. Her grandfather (who had found religion and now came in to the Center solely to preach to the girls) had been a major amphetamine manufacturer. Her mother was addicted to both drugs and men. Her mother had long ago established a pattern of getting pregnant, delivering the baby, and then leaving the newborn with a relative so that she could go out and "party" again.

I came into the Center one morning and found Maria in the front office weeping. I have rarely heard such sadness. It was as if her heart were literally breaking. She had just learned that her mother had done it again. Seventeen years after she had done it to Maria, the mother had given birth again, and again abandoned the newborn with a relative. Maria's grief and pain were for the mother who would never be a mother, for the future pain of her innocent new sister, and most of all for herself.

Half an hour later Maria was out on the playing field, laughing and having fun with her peers. The pain of the whole-object position was simply more than she could bear. Pushed by the crisis involuntarily into the whole-object position, the splitting had collapsed under the weight of the objective reality. But she could not bear the pain of this new position and, as soon as she could, she rebuilt the split and returned to the haven of the part-object position.

The inability to deal with ambivalence pushes the infant into the part-object position. The inability to tolerate the pain of permanent object loss prevents a person, later on, from leaving. The part-object position begins as, and remains, a coping mechanism. It protects the infant from overwhelming cognitive–affective complexity. It protects children, adolescents, and adults from overwhelming pain.

A World without Ruth

Ruth is a wonderful word, dating back to Middle English, pulled out of the archives and dusted off by D. W. Winnicott (1954–1955). It is an attention-grabbing word because one thinks one doesn't know what it means until one hears its negative. If one doesn't have ruth, one is ruthless. Ruthlessness is the final facet of the part-object position, the final permutation of splitting, that I will discuss here.

For those of us who dwell primarily in the whole-object position, the ruthlessness of the Center adolescents never ceases to be painful and shocking.

Among them there are many who blandly blame the innocent victims of drive-by shootings for "being in the wrong place at the wrong time." It is difficult to convey the apparent utter lack of feelings, concern, or remorse when they say this. I have seen therapists confront young gang-bangers with the fact that the "enemies" they shoot at are human beings too, with mothers, fathers, and siblings who love them. The look these young gangsters give in response to this confrontation is one of complete incomprehension and bewilderment. To them, an enemy is an enemy. An enemy is, by definition, a part object. It is someone upon whom I can project all of my own and the world's badness. It is someone I can love to hate. It is someone who allows me to love and respect myself because I can hate and disrespect him. How can an enemy be useful to me as a part object if I allow myself to recognize that he is a whole object?

It is one thing to see such ruthlessness directed at enemies and strangers. It is even more disturbing to see it turned against loved ones. It is not uncommon at the Center to arrive in the morning and find that two adolescents, who had been best friends for months, are now worst enemies. It is particularly painful to witness the cruelty (ruthlessness) with which they act out their new enmity. Dark and embarrassing secrets that before the breakdown of the friendship had been shared with no other living soul are now thrown back publicly in each other's faces, with the purpose of hurting and humiliating. From our whole-object perspective we plead with these kids, "Wait a minute! Don't you remember that yesterday this person was your dearest friend?" But from a part-object perspective this is not true. From their perspective the good object friend they had yesterday has disappeared and a bad object has taken its place. Or, with some adult logic superimposed, this was a bad object all along, tricking and deceiving me into thinking it was a good object. And what is the appropriate thing to do with a bad object? One hates it and tries to destroy it.

Dictionaries define ruth as compassion or empathy for others and remorse for one's own faults. Object relations theory sees ruth as the recognition of self and others as whole objects. If one recognizes people as whole human beings, people with good and bad qualities, with strengths and weaknesses, with altruism and selfishness, then one cannot be ruthless. With part objects, one cannot be other than ruthless. Evil part objects are to be hated and destroyed. Where is there room for compassion for something that is pure evil? For us to "love our enemies" requires more than an emotional leap, more than an act of faith. It requires a quantum shift in the way we think.

Notes

1. Klein originally wrote of the "paranoid position." She did not use the term "paranoid–schizoid position" until 1946 in response to the challenging theories of W. R. D. Fairbairn.

2. See Ogden's (1986) discussion of Klein's "phantasy" in terms of Chomsky's "deep structure."

3. The current slang, "My bad," ("Am I bad" elided into "'M I bad" or "My bad") is as emblematic of the part-object position as "shit happens." It is a wonderful phrase that pretends to accept responsibility while, in fact, totally rejecting it.

4. I am using the terms *jealousy* and *envy* here rather idiosyncratically to denote specific cognitive–emotional states. This usage does not necessarily conform to common usage.

~

CHAPTER THREE

Identity Formation

The original model for an "introject," or internalized object, is Freud's (1923) concept of the superego. In Freudian theory, the superego is the internalized voice of the punitive (part-object) father, *as heard and interpreted by a four-year-old*. The italicized part is important but frequently underappreciated. What is internalized is a two-fold distortion of the real parent. First, the superego represents the internalization of only the punitive part of the parent. The real parent is a complex mixture of love and hate, joy and anger, nurturing and threatening behaviors. Since only *half* of this complex object is internalized, the initial distortion from the original (external) object is considerable.

Second, even the angry, hating, punishing side of the external object is internalized *not as it is, but as it is seen and interpreted by a small child*. Obviously, Freud had no intention of implying that the Oedipal boy was ever *truly* threatened with castration by his father. But in the simple (part-object position) logic of the four-year-old boy, the putting together of his newly phallic competitiveness with the father with his observation of the penisless state of girls and women, and arriving at castration anxiety, makes perfect sense.

This is true of *all* introjected part objects. They are a reflection at least as much of the child's internal dynamics as they are of the real attributes of any external object.

A young woman client of mine, adamantly nonviolent in her philosophy of mothering, did not tolerate any form of corporal punishment and never touched her young daughter in anger or discipline. It was with considerable distress, therefore, that she reported observing her three-year-old girl spanking her doll's exposed behind during play, saying, "bad dolly, bad dolly!"

This was clearly not *learned* behavior. It arose out of the child's complex need (at least for the moment) to maintain a split between good object and bad object, good self and bad self.

Melanie Klein took the concept of the internalized part object, as presented in Freud's concept of the superego, and made it one of the centerpieces of her theory. Klein's model of the psyche consists not just of the ego and one internalized part object (the superego), but rather of the ego and a *collection* of internalized part objects. The original internalized part objects are the good breast and the bad breast. To these are quickly added a host of others: the sexual mother, the punishing father, the sexual father, the abusive mother, and so on.

Klein's psyche, then, consists of an id, an ego, and not just a superego, but a collection of internalized part objects to which the ego must respond. The potential of this model for intrapsychic chaos is obvious. Contemporary critics (Freudians) complained that Klein populated her model psyche with a collection of "demons," disembodied voices, immutable and forever alien to the ego. The demon critique was answered largely by the combined contributions of subsequent object relations theorists, especially Fairbairn[1] and Bion.[2]

Fairbairn postulated that for every introjected part (split) object, there is a "corresponding split in the ego." Thus the introjection of a part object necessarily generates a corresponding part-self representation, one that exists only in relationship to, in response to, the introjected part object. What we internalize, then, is not a part object, but rather a part-object *relationship*. We internalize, for example, not simply a rejecting, abandoning (part-object) mother, but instead the relationship (dialogue) between the abandoning (part) mother and the corresponding part self, in this case the worthless-piece-of-trash (part) self. What we internalize is not a voice, but a relationship.

In keeping with part-object position logic, the correspondence between the internalized part object and the corresponding part self is always perfect. If I have internalized an abandoning part-object parent, then the corresponding part self *has* to be worthless trash. In the part-object position everything is perfectly logical. If something is thrown away, it is, by definition, trash. If it had value then it would be held on to. If I have internalized a loving part object, then the corresponding self-representation is loving and lovable. If I have a punishing internalized part object, then the corresponding self-representation is bad and deserving of punishment. If I have internalized a sexual or seductive parent part object, then my corresponding self-representation will be sexy and sluttish. American object relations theorist Otto Kernberg (1976, 1980) calls these dyadic internalized part-object relationships "object relations units" or "ORUs."

The contemporary conceptualization of the psyche as an aggregate of internalized dialogues or relationships is certainly less chaotic than was Klein's idea of a single ego, bombarded by the disembodied voices of a pack of internalized part objects. But the potential for chaos remains. Do all ORUs speak at the same time? If one predominates, how, and under what conditions, are the others heard? Is there a hierarchy, and if so, how is it determined?

It does appear that certain ORUs seem to take up more "space" in the psyche than others. A client I worked with for years (Lucy) seemed so locked in the unloving and critical part-object mother versus unworthy, self-hating part-self-representation ORU that I frequently despaired of making a dent in her system. When I said something meant to be caring and encouraging, she heard my words as though she were a child listening to a scolding parent. When I commented that it made me sad that she was unable to find pleasure in anything, she would hear, "Well it's pretty *sad* [contemptible] that you can't even find pleasure in things."

Object relations observers, from Klein on, have noticed that negative objects tend to be internalized first and have greater dominance than positive objects. These observers theorize that this is because the internalization of an object is a form of attaining control over that object, and negative objects, being more threatening than positive objects, more urgently need to be controlled. However, the establishment of a clear dominance hierarchy of ORUs still leaves the question of when, and under what circumstances, subdominant ORUs come into play. Why is not everyone in the part-object world the way Lucy appeared to be: possessed by a single ORU?

One of the most obvious answers is that certain ORUs seem to come to the fore when triggered by environmental events. When a staff member yells at one of the Center kids, one can almost see the relevant ORUs leap into play. Projected onto the staff is the internalized part object of the abusive or punishing parent, and reacting to that figure is the "bad" child. The particular form of the adolescent's reaction varies from child to child. The more passive and depressed among them will hang their heads in shame and self-loathing, devastated that their essential badness (there is no partial badness in the part-object position) has been revealed to the world. Those prone to acting out, (the majority at the Center) will rage against the offending object, hoping to drive it away and make room for the return of a good part object. Girls at the Center frequently misinterpret expressions of caring from male staff and clinicians, projecting onto them the internalized sexual parent and responding with their own flirtatious or seductive sexualized part-self representation. One such girl, who had been the victim of multiple rapes and molestations, protected her relationships with me and her male therapist from this reaction by mentally neutering the two of us. Explaining to new girls in the group what it was like to work with us in therapy, she said (embarrassed that she might be offending us), "It's like talking to a gay friend."

But however much sense it makes on an intuitive level, the explanation that ORUs are simply triggered by the environment is seriously flawed. This is because an ORU is much more than just a programmed pattern of reaction to an environmental stimulus; it is a way of *interpreting*, of *attributing meaning* to that event. We cannot say, for example, that a particular ORU is simply triggered by a particular environmental threat, because it is the ORU that interprets that environmental situation as being threatening. My client Lucy, as I have said earlier, interpreted all my words as being critical, even when I said them to support her.

This is a crucial point that I wish to illustrate with a brief discussion of smiling. Smiling is a wonderful thing. I try to remind myself to smile as much as possible, as it tends to offset the austerity of my lean, six-foot-four-inch, bearded presence. But I also need to remind myself that the interpretation of my smile, the meaning attributed to it, is entirely in the psyche of the observer. And that interpretation will be determined in part by the ORU of the moment. If the person I am smiling at is under the sway of a loving part object and a lovable self-representation, then my smile will be seen as caring and supportive. If that person's ORU is a persecutory part object in relationship with a frightened, defended self, then my smile will be interpreted as manipulative and sly. If the ORU is a seductive part object and a sexualized self, then my smile will be experienced as a sexual come-on. If the ORU is a critical part object and an unworthy self, then my smile will not be seen as a smile at all; it will be a smirk.

Certainly a few environmental stimuli (a sudden loud noise, for example, or the perception of a steep precipice) produce instinctual or reflexive reactions. But the vast majority of external events are open to our interpretation. And it is ORUs that, in the part-object position, determine what interpretation we give, what meaning we attribute to, those events.[3] Whatever intuitive sense it makes to see an ORU as a reaction to an environmental event, this simply cannot be: The ORU has to *precede* the event; it has to be there first so that it can play a role in *interpreting* that event.

The formation of a stable character structure (that is to say, of a consistent way of attributing meaning to the universe) is the result of a complex intrapsychic process. It is a process involving the "omnipotent" manipulation of internalized part objects and self-representations, as mentioned briefly in the last chapter. The tools of this omnipotent manipulation are the defense mechanisms of the part-object position: primarily, splitting, denial, projection, identification, and projective identification. How all these come together may be illustrated by the case of Joe.

Joe

Joe (mentioned briefly in chapter 2), a sixteen-year-old Latino at the Center, came to my attention as a prime example of a dweller in the part-object position in three ways. First, Joe actually identified himself as a part object. When asked, Joe would identify himself as "a bad kid": the beginning and end of how he saw himself. The equanimity with which Joe would thus define himself was matched only by the tenacity with which he defended this self-image. When we would point out to Joe good things that he had done, nice things people had said about him, or good qualities in his character, Joe would grudgingly acknowledge what we said, but then instantly dismiss them as irrelevant to who he was. "Ya [he would say], that's true, but that's not really me. I'm a bad kid."

Joe worked pretty hard to justify his self-concept. One of the least likable of his qualities was that he was a bully. The targets of Joe's bullying were males, both adolescent and adult, whom Joe identified as "weak." With "weak" adult males Joe would get into endless and vindictive battles, heaping upon them his scorn and contempt. The fact that, within the institutional structure of the Center, these so-called weak men actually had a great deal of power over him was irrelevant to Joe. The moral victories he scored by his public displays of contempt and disrespect were worth any concrete punishment he might receive in consequence. Toward other adolescents deemed weak, Joe was also especially cruel. Not only did he bully those unfortunates himself, but he also tried to organize his cottage mates (vigilante lynch mob style) into collective abuse. Confronted with his bullying, Joe would acknowledge it, but with an expression of bemusement, as though never quite sure why the staff was pointing it out. He would say, in effect, "Of course I'm a bully. I told you I was a bad kid!"

During the time I worked with Joe, I also consulted at a girls' cottage. Once, sitting in a circle with the girls of this unit waiting through the last few minutes before the formal start of group, I overheard two of them talking about Joe. To my astonishment, they described him using words like "sweet," "nice," and "sweetheart." A sure sign that you are dealing with someone whose primary defense is splitting comes when you have the sensation that you are dealing with two completely separate people. I checked with the girls, and yes, they were talking about the same Joe I knew.

Given how glowingly they were speaking of him, I asked the girls if either of them was "going" with Joe. I was surprised a second time by their tittering laughter in response to my question, which they appeared to consider too absurd to take seriously. When I queried them further on their reaction they got befuddled and one of them finally answered, "Well, look at him!" So I did, at least in my mind's eye. Joe was a tall, heavy-set Latino adolescent, somewhat thuggish looking, with sagging pants and his head shaved in the current gangster style. By no stretch of the imagination could he be called a "pretty boy," but Joe had a kind of masculine virility to his looks and I had seen less attractive boys successfully paired with girls as pretty as these. So I confronted the girls with the results of my mental look-over, and they acknowledged that he wasn't so bad looking after all. Forced into a deeper level of introspection, one of the girls finally said, "Well, going with Joe would be like going with your own brother." This was my third piece of evidence of splitting: a ruggedly masculine boy, perceived by these two girls as somehow asexual.

The Psyche of "A Bad Kid"

What follows is an analysis of the way Joe's character structure in general, and these three oddities in particular, could have emerged out of the interplay of the characteristic part-object defenses. First, however, I wish to emphasize a point made by Ogden (1986). Ogden says that splitting is never simply the mental division of one object into two. Rather, it is also, invariably, the first step of a process of separating these two split-off part objects, trying to create as much distance between the two as possible. Without that distance, the good part object is always in danger from the bad part object, at risk of being destroyed by it.

Second, I need to point out that the hypothesized defensive actions presented as taking place in Joe's psyche *sequentially* cannot really have happened sequentially. Defenses that serve the function of separating (creating distance between) a good part object and its endangering bad part object frequently have the effect of creating new areas of vulnerability elsewhere in the psyche. The anxiety caused by these new areas of danger is so great that it must be dealt with instantly. And these new solutions also lead to new dangers, new anxieties, and a need for new instantaneous solutions. Thus the complex pattern of splits, projections, and such that I presented sequentially for sake of clarity actually had to happen almost simultaneously. Joe's complex character had to be born whole and intact, Athena-like, in the forehead of Joe.

The first of Joe's many splits was the division of his parents into good mother and bad stepfather. The division of "parents" into "mother" and "father" is not splitting; it is a biological reality. With Joe, however, his mother could do no wrong and his stepfather could do no good. His love for his mother bordered on adoration, and his hatred for his stepfather allowed for no recognition of anything positive. As Ogden predicted, this split was not enough to assure the safety of the good part object from the bad, and Joe used the defense of denial to achieve the illusion of distance between them. Cognitively, of course, Joe "knew" that his parents were married. But this knowledge remained purely cognitive, and Joe acted as though it were essentially irrelevant. Emotionally, Joe functioned as though his parents had no relationship whatsoever. One of the crimes that brought Joe to the Center in the first place was stealing his stepfather's credit card and amassing several thousand dollars' worth of purchase debt. When staff pointed out to Joe that his parents were legally married and that therefore the credit card debt was legally as much his mother's as his stepfather's, Joe reacted with an agitated denial. "No," he would insist, "I stole from my stepfather, not from my mother."

The split, as with the denial, was an internal, intrapsychic process within Joe's psyche. His "real" (external) mother was, indeed, a kind, loving woman. But she was human, and far from the saint Joe experienced her as being. Joe's real stepfather was a policeman. He was rigid, authoritarian, and more than a little weary of putting up with Joe's abuse. But to those of us who saw him in group sessions week after week, he seemed genuinely to care for Joe and to have Joe's best interest at heart. Joe took his split, internal part objects and projected them onto the external persons of his parents. He related to the real persons of his mother and stepfather as though he were relating to angel and devil, respectively.

At a certain point, Joe's "projection" became "projective identification." His mother basked in Joe's adoration and identified with his loving view of her, becoming even more nurturing and loving. She also was put in the position of defending him from the anger of her husband, and thus became especially protective of Joe. The stepfather, rigid and uncompromising to begin with, grew less and less tolerant of Joe's delinquent acting out and of Joe's relentless hatred, and ended up partially identified with the hating monster that Joe had created.

As Fairbairn (1952) pointed out, for every split internalized object representation there is a corresponding split in the ego (self-representation). The part-self representation that corresponded to the loving, protective part-object mother was the lovable, precious self. The part-self representation that corresponded to the bad, abusive part-object stepfather representation was the bad, deserving-of-punishment self. (The word "bad" means something very different when applied to Joe's father representation than it does when applied to Joe's self-representation. With the father it is bad as in "hated but respected," and with the self it is bad as in "beneath contempt.")

The correspondence between the part-object representation and the part-self representation does not always have to have the "mirror image" quality of the traits listed above. Joe saw his mother as "weak"[4] in that she was vulnerable to attack from the bad part-object stepfather. The corresponding self-representation is also weak. The internalized representation of his hated stepfather is acknowledged to be strong, and Joe's self-representation is correspondingly weak. Here again, the word *weak* has different meanings in each self-representation. Joe's part-self is weak in the mother–son ORU in that he is unable to protect the loved object. He is weak in the father–son ORU in that he is vulnerable to attack from the hated object. Still, Joe sees himself as weak either way he looks.

Joe's rudimentary ego can be diagrammed as follows:

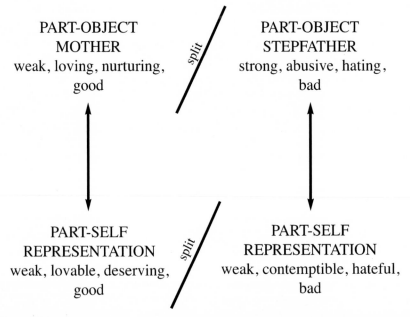

PART-OBJECT MOTHER
weak, loving, nurturing, good

split

PART-OBJECT STEPFATHER
strong, abusive, hating, bad

PART-SELF REPRESENTATION
weak, lovable, deserving, good

split

PART-SELF REPRESENTATION
weak, contemptible, hateful, bad

Figure 3.1

The protection of the valued attributes of love and nurturance by the *splitting* of the parents, the *projection (projective identification)* of those qualities onto the part-object mother and of the opposite qualities onto the part-object stepfather, and the further distance between the two by *denial*, did not accomplish Joe's task of creating a stable[5] system (ego). There remained several points of instability. One of these was the vulnerability of the part-self representation to attack by the bad part-object stepfather. In both ORUs the self-representation was weak and therefore at risk of annihilation by the bad part-object representation.

Joe solved this problem in an age-old way, as Adorno, Frenkel-Brunswick, Levinson, and Sanford (1950) described in their post-World War II study of the psychology of the concentration camp prisoners, through "identification with the aggressor." Joe identified with his hated, bad part-object stepfather. Through this identification his weakness was replaced by strength and his badness remained but was transformed from bad (contemptible) into bad (worthy of respect). Rather than simply denying his own original sense of weakness, Joe took the additional step of projecting it onto "others," thus further distancing it from himself.

What Joe did next (simultaneously) is particularly interesting. He seems to have made a second split in the newly created internal category of "weak others" into "weak male others" and "weak female others." Onto weak male others he projected the kind of weakness he experienced as part of his original stepfather–self ORU: that of vile, contemptible, worthy-of-abuse weakness. Onto weak female others he projected the kind of defenseless, in-need-of-protection weakness that he experienced in his mother–self ORU.

Again, in both cases Joe's *projection* quickly turned into *projective identification*. Joe's bullying of "weak" males had the effect of making them carry (identify with) the horrible feelings of self-loathing and vulnerability that Joe was trying to rid himself of. And Joe's care and protection of the girls he projected his more lovable weakness onto tapped into these chronically abused teenaged girls' senses of vulnerability and longing for familial protection.

It should be noted that not all of Joe's attempts at projective identification were likely successful. As noted earlier, projective identification differs from simple projection in that it requires a recipient who (in response to the manipulative behavior of the projector) "identifies" with the projection. One of Joe's targets was a male teacher whom Joe perceived as effeminate, and therefore weak. It appears that this man never really identified with Joe's projections. He viewed Joe's antics, his attempts to bully him, with mild annoyance and amused tolerance. Joe never succeeded in making the teacher feel truly bad about himself. Joe's efforts with his peers were clearly much more successful. The boys he bullied hated the position they found themselves in, and hated themselves for being in that position. And the girls that Joe protected loved being in that position, and felt special and precious under his aegis.

The fact of this second projective identification, the projection of a "good" kind of weakness onto girls, and his subsequent nurturing of them, indicated to me that along with his identification with his part-object father, Joe must also have identified in some way with his part-object mother. Joe's capacity for nurturance and protection cannot have come simply from the split in his own ego (self-representation) corresponding to any split in an internalized part object. A quick review of figure 3.1 shows no "nurturing self" in Joe's preformed ego. The quality of self that corresponded to the nurturing mother was "deserving of nurturance" rather than nurturing. The nurturing qualities in Joe must, therefore, have come from a direct identification with those qualities in the part-object mother.

This identification with the mother would have taken place for very different reasons than did his identification with the stepfather. The identification with the stepfather was purely for survival reasons: to gain the stepfather's strength. An identification with the mother can only have been to further distance the good mother from the dangers of annihilation by the bad stepfather. The other means of distancing that Joe used toward this end was *denial*, and denial is a relatively weak defense, frequently collapsing under an onslaught of harsh reality. The internalization of a valued characteristic in the mother further distances, and thus protects, that characteristic from assault by the father.

But, as I have said, one solution leads to another problem. This new problem is obvious, for along with identifying with the good part-object mother, Joe was already identified (or was simultaneously identifying) with the bad part-object stepfather. Thus internalizing the valued nurturing characteristic of the part-object mother protects it from onslaught from the bad part-object stepfather, but *simultaneously* places it in danger from the bad part-self representation.

Joe's solution to this seems to have been, once again, to split. Only this time the split was a simple split without projection or projective identification. Joe took this nurturing quality and split it off into "me-but-not-me." This was Joe's response to everyone who pointed out the nice things he had done. This was Joe saying "Ya, I did all those things. But that's not who I really am. I am a bad kid."

Joe's more fully developed ego can be portrayed in figure 3.2.

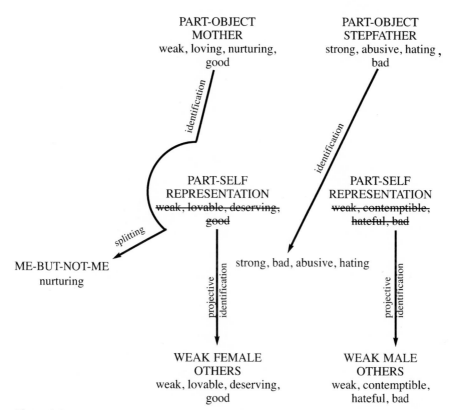

Figure 3.2

Joe's sense of identity, his psyche, as portrayed in figure 3.2, provides some potential explanation for some of the oddities that first distinguished him. Joe's self-representation is reduced to "a bad kid," regardless of the particular ORU involved. This is the result of a combination of identification (primarily with the aggressive stepfather), projective identification of all his weakness onto split male and female "others," and the splitting off of the little positive he was able to gain through identification with the mother onto a netherworld of "me-but-not-me." Not only is Joe left with nothing but a sense of badness, but he will even fight to maintain this self-concept. To acknowledge any goodness in himself is to make that goodness vulnerable to his now overwhelming sense of badness. It is much better to keep all goodness outside of his own self-representation (although still inside his psychic world of internalized ORUs). Goodness can be better protected when it is split off from the self and projected onto weak girls who can be nurtured and protected, and his part-object mother who can be adored.

My experience of hearing the girls talk about Joe but not really believing that it was Joe they were describing parallels Joe's experience of himself. This is pure splitting. Joe's nurturing capacity is not projected onto anyone else. It is acknowledged as a parallel "me-but-not-me" that exists side by side with the "real me." "I am one, but I will function as though I were two."

I believe that my final observation, that this virile and aggressive young man was experienced by his two young female friends as asexual ("like dating your own brother"), can be explained by the fact that all of Joe's nurturance (his preferred way of relating to "weak" young girls) was derived through identification with the mother. The two girls therefore experienced his nurturance as mothering, as a particularly female kind of relatedness, and thus as asexual. Nowhere in Joe's psyche is there any identification with a male kind of nurturance.

In the process of identity consolidation, Joe never left the part-object position. To the contrary, the "success" of his splitting efforts make the eventual emergence into a whole-object position all the less likely. For Joe's consolidated ORUs inform (and circumscribe) his world. Joe's ORU's act as a template through which the world is interpreted and meaning is attributed. For Joe the world is divided into strong, aggressive men who are to be respected, weak men who are to be persecuted, and weak women who are to be nurtured and protected. Other combinations simply do not make sense to him. Interestingly, Joe's therapist at the Center was a strong woman. Cognitively, Joe could recognize this. But this woman had no place in Joe's cosmology. Affectively, he did not know what to do with her and as a result, he dismissed her. He did essentially the same thing with me. He could not dismiss (or attack) me as weak, yet he did not perceive me as aggressive. I, "did not compute" for Joe. He treated me as though I just did not exist.

Notes

1. W. Ronald D. Fairbairn, 1889–1964, Scottish psychoanalyst who, working largely independently but out of the Kleinian tradition, first coined the term *object relations theory*.

2. Wilfred R. Bion, 1897–1981, British psychoanalyst as noteworthy for his pioneering contributions to the theory of groups and group therapy as for his more theoretical contributions to object relations theory.

3. The process by which meaning is attributed in the whole-object position is discussed in chapter 5.

4. Weakness is a quality that Joe would certainly define as "bad," but bad in the sense of being undesirable rather than being evil, malicious, or threatening. Thus weakness is not incompatible with the "good" qualities (love, nurturance, warmth, tenderness) of the part-object mother.

5. "Stable" in the sense of creating an ordered, predictable world in which risk is compartmentalized and minimized sufficiently that the child can go through life with a bearable amount of anxiety.

〜

CHAPTER FOUR

Resistance and Addiction
to the Bad Object

It happens all the time. Kids come into the Center and "blossom." The hard veneer of the gang-banger gradually melts away to reveal the soft, radiant face of a child. Angry defiance yields to clingy affection seeking. Behavior problems seem simply not to be an issue anymore. In "good-bye groups" I frequently have the experience of looking back, remembering the child who entered the program months earlier, and being shocked at the transformation that has occurred. Then, within a few weeks after release, I get word that the child has been rearrested, or is on drugs again, or has run away from home or from a new placement.

If one looks, the signs of these imminent failures are often present before the child is released. These kids love being loved. They bask in it, they revel in it, they seem to thrive on it, but they seem strangely unable to internalize it. No matter how much they feel loved, they never feel lovable.

One particularly introspective and articulate girl (Krystal) asked to speak with me shortly before she was due to be released to the custody of her godparents. She acknowledged that she had made a lot of progress in the program. She no longer had feelings of wanting to die. She had come to terms with her abusive (and now deceased) mother, and she recognized and accepted the love heaped upon her by her godparents. But she was troubled that she was still unable to identify anything within or about herself that she could feel was lovable. "Well," I countered, "your godparents certainly have no trouble finding you lovable." "No, you don't understand," she said. "That's just who they are. They take in stray dogs and cats all the time. They must have at least a dozen dogs and probably twenty cats." The intense and palpable love directed at her by her godparents did not increase her sense of self-worth to anything greater than that of a stray mongrel dog.

This inability (at times it appears to be a stubborn refusal) on the part of the client to take in a good object can be the most maddeningly frustrating part of being a therapist.

Lucy, the young woman I worked with for many years, was the most determinedly self-hating person I had ever met. Lucy started treatment with me at the Center at age eighteen. She had been doing prostitution for years and was addicted to heroin. After a disastrous hiatus from therapy following her release, she located me in my private practice and began three-times-a-week therapy. Over the years I developed the strong but odd sensation that I was simultaneously completely essential to Lucy and completely irrelevant to her. She inevitably went into a steep decline when I went on vacations. I would return to find her so depressed as to be almost unable to speak to me. Sometimes I found that she had been hospitalized for suicidal thoughts. Yet at the same time I had the fantasy that each time she left my office, I ceased to exist for her. No matter how animated and cheerful she was in a session (there were many such sessions, and she could be quite funny), I could almost see her deflate as she walked across the room at the end of a session. By the time her hand turned the doorknob, I was watching someone utterly and unspeakably alone in the world.

My frustration in working with Lucy waxed and waned, but it was probably out of my frustration that one time, many months into the therapy, I asked her what her goals were in therapy. I don't know what I had expected her to say, but I was shocked to find just how different our goals were for our work together. Her goal was simply to survive, to get through life, to get through each day. When I told her that my goal for her was for her to like herself a little bit more, she looked at me with an expression of utter disbelief. Such a thought had never occurred to her. It was simply beyond her comprehension.

Since the beginning of psychodynamic therapy this has been a primary focus (and source of frustration) for therapists. Freud (1910a) coined the term *resistance* to describe the phenomenon, and said that the analysis of the resistance was the primary task of the analyst. Resistance, according to Freud, is a result of the need to keep repressed material repressed, and thus to avoid the unbearable feelings (such as fear, pain, or shame) that would come with a breach of the repression barrier. Psychoanalytic therapy is necessarily slow because the repression barrier can be attacked only slowly, one bit at a time.

Object relations theorists have offered a variety of different explanations for resistance. Rather than seeing it, as did Freud, in terms of the repression of the unconscious, object relations theories attempt to offer explanations for what might well be called an "addiction" to the bad object. Some explanation for this tenacious addiction is offered in this chapter, in the context of disturbed adolescents.

Addiction as Maintenance of the Ego

"That's just who I am." We hear this often at the Center, usually offered with a defensive finality, as though "and it's not open for negotiation" were an unspoken coda. Sometimes the kids will add "It just wouldn't feel like me" if the level of change proposed is too radical.

The history of British object relations theory is, to a large extent, the history of the evolution of the concept of internalized object relationships.[1] Early critics of Klein complained that her description of internalized object representations sounded like "demons" haunting and assaulting the ego from some indeterminate place. Modern object relations theory places the internalized object relations firmly within the ego (ego is used here in its broadest sense, including what Kohut [1971, 1977] differentiated out as the "self"). This includes both parts of the internalized relationship: the internalized object representation and the corresponding self-representation are both subdivisions of a split ego.

This formulation allows for a theory of internalized object relationships that is much closer to experience. When an adolescent at the Center admits "I beat myself up a lot," we can infer that the "I" that does the beating is related to an internalized critical or abusive part object, while the "myself" that receives the beating is reflective of the corresponding self-representation. But both parts are considered to be parts of the self. And a therapist who suggests, therefore, that someone might want to "give up" an internalized bad object is suggesting that the client give up his or her experience of part of who he or she is. To do so would be experienced as a sort of amputation.

The Bad Object as an Essential Part of the Ego

The internalized bad object may also be more than just another part of the ego; it may be a part considered by the client to be essential for survival.

In the early months of my work with Lucy, while she was still at the Center, she spent hours in my office, tearful, self-loathing, and pathetic. After a great deal of work, she learned to recognize and identify the voice of her internalized mother, a woman Lucy had experienced as relentlessly critical and unloving. But this insight produced no change. Although I would plead with Lucy to let her (now deceased) mother "rest in peace," Lucy was unable to "let go" of the mother she professed to hate. Then, one day, I came across Lucy in her cottage in an angry confrontation with one of the supervisory staff. She was arrogant, condescending, and sarcastic, heaping scorn and contempt on this supervisor. I barely recognized Lucy, and I didn't like this new person I saw. However pathetic she was in my office, I liked the old Lucy. There was nothing I could like about this new young woman.

Suddenly I recognized this "new" Lucy. It was a reincarnation of, and identification with, our old adversary: her internalized critical mother. And it was the only way Lucy had of being strong. Without the ability to identify, when necessary, with the bad (strong) part object, Lucy was like a declawed kitten thrown to dogs.

The same was true of Joe (chapter 3). Joe's identification with his abusive stepfather gave him the only sense of strength he possessed. However much Joe secretly disliked his self-proclaimed identity as the "bad kid," it was infinitely preferable to being the "weak, vulnerable kid."

Addiction to the Tantalizing Object

It was Fairbairn (1952) who first discussed the implications of the tantalizing (exciting) object. The concept of the tantalizing object itself was nothing new. The original bad object, Klein's bad breast, was bad not because it was dangerous, loathsome, or undesirable, but because it was tantalizing. The bad breast was not just unavailable, but sadistically, maliciously, tauntingly unavailable. The bad breast was the ultimate tease. It derived cruel pleasure from being hugely desirable, but just out of reach. Its "badness" evolved from its desirability.

Lucy's perception of her mother had been of just such a tantalizing object. What Lucy heard from her mother was, "if you could only be perfect, then I would love you." Here, then, is a second reason why Lucy was "addicted" to the internalized bad-mother object. Not only was the internalized part object the repository of all of Lucy's perceived strength, but to give up this bad part object would be to give up its promise of the return of the good-mother object.

At the Center we occasionally hear about mothers who were so severely drug addicted that they would sell their infants' diapers, their formula, spend the food and rent money, to support their habits. These women were so lost to their addictions that they were also totally and completely lost to their children. The children of such mothers have about them a kind of grim resignation. "I love my mother," one of them said, "but I *never* want to be with her again." I have often wondered whether or not these children were luckier than their peers whose mothers were in and out of their lives, a constant tantalus. Those in the former group seem able to leave these mothers behind (without internalizing them) and go on with their lives. The latter group remain seriously addicted to the tantalus of the promised mother.

> One such girl described her mother reentering her life when the girl was twelve. The mother and daughter "bonded" by prostituting together. They would then take the day's proceeds and further bond by doing drugs together. When this girl talked about her mother, her face took on a radiant glow, and she spoke in a voice of complete adoration. She could not imagine, she would say, living without her mother.

Addiction as the Maintenance of Hate

Sometimes addiction to the bad object is supported not by desire for the return of the good, loved object, but rather by a refusal to give up hatred for the bad object. The bad object is held on to so that it can be defeated by having its awfulness proved and demonstrated to the world (or, more frequently, to an internal audience).

> An eighteen-year-old gay male (Tommy) was admitted to the Center following a series of arrests for petty crimes such as vandalism and shoplifting. After his release I followed him in psychotherapy until his death from AIDS at age twenty-seven. During this time Tommy made several moves that looked like forays into health, including enrolling in design school and, later on, in a vocational nursing school. Tommy always did poorly in these programs, and always dropped out before graduating, remaining forever financially dependent on his father.
>
> Tommy's earliest memories were of being yelled at by his father for "walking like a girl instead of like a boy." The one message he seemed clearly to have heard from his father was that he would never amount to anything, and he seemed determined to prove the old man correct. It was as if Tommy was never able to give up saying, "You want to see failure? I'll show you failure. I'll be such a failure that you will have to support me for the rest of my life."

Another teen, this one a seventeen-year-old girl, was admitted to the Center already possessed of the kind of wonderfully blithe self-awareness one finds only in borderlines and adolescents. "My parents fucked me up and I will stay fucked up. No way am I gonna let them off the hook."

Another client in a long-term, adult, private practice group reported the sudden resolution of a long and difficult transference he had had toward another group member. The client (Max) spoke of being intimidated by a fellow group member, Elizabeth. Max was not alone in being intimidated by Elizabeth. Elizabeth was very bright, and especially sure of her opinions. She was also very blunt-spoken and appeared to have little interest in pulling her punches when she confronted another group member. But Max's reaction to Elizabeth was particularly strong. He essentially cowered in her presence, unspeaking, and unable to voice an opinion. He experienced himself as "having nothing to say." A few years into the group Max reported the following experience:

"I gradually began to realize that Elizabeth was not really as I saw her. I had always seen her as brilliant and castrating. I began to see first of all that she was not so brilliant. Sure, she was smart, but in many ways she wasn't any smarter than I was. I also began to see that she wasn't really castrating. She was blunt, and she could be cutting at times. But she had a good heart. In fact, when I looked back over my relationship with her, I saw that she really liked me and that she had always been much more nurturing and supportive to me than cutting.

"The thing was, although my perception of her was changing, my feelings toward her weren't. In spite of myself, I couldn't stop acting intimidated by her. I kept telling myself that I was being unfair to her. She wasn't really the castrating bitch I was treating her as. I knew she was basically a nice person who needed understanding and support as much as any of us. I knew I was using her as a transference object but it didn't matter. No matter how much I berated myself, my feelings didn't change.

"Then, one day, as I was berating myself one more time, I had the closest thing I have ever had to an auditory hallucination. I heard this voice in my head. It was the voice of an angry, stubborn four-year-old. And it said, 'No! I don't want to give her up as a transference object. I'm not ready to stop hating her!'

"The funny thing is, as soon as I heard that voice she stopped being a transference object. I stopped being intimidated by her and hating her." When the change finally happened it was instantaneous.

Addiction as Maintenance of a Dialectical Relationship

The internalized part-object representation and the corresponding self-representation exist in a dialectical relationship with each other. Each creates the other by negating the other. There can be no worthless child without an abandoning parent whose abandonment defined his or her worthlessness. Nor can there be an abandoning parent without a child to throw away. As Fairbairn pointed out, what is internalized is not an object but a relationship, and a relationship has to have at least two parts.

If, then, we are to recommend "letting go of a bad part-object," we are really implying giving up an entire object relations unit. Internalized objects, and internalized object relationships, seem to resist such annihilation. If one pole of an ORU appears threatened, then the other pole, no matter how antagonistic the relationship, will fight to maintain its existence by defending the existence of its antagonist.

> At times I naively tried to bolster my client Lucy's self-worth by pointing out good things about her. Essentially I was trying myself to annihilate her bad-mother object representation by offering myself as a good-mother stand-in, praising and supporting her where her internal object would have been critical. She would invariably counter my efforts by heaping even greater torrents of self-abuse upon herself. It was as though any inroads I had made in building the self-esteem of the worthless child self-representation had to be counterbalanced by a comparable build-up of the abusive parent representation. Lucy would not allow any such annihilation of her bad-mother internalized object. Lucy's worthless self needed the abusive mother to define her existence. Similarly, the abusive mother needed the worthless daughter to justify her existence. The two had to stay in balance. Without this overwhelmingly dominant paradigm of Lucy's psyche, who would Lucy be?
>
> Both elements of this toxic ORU had to be supported and defended. Otherwise, what little sense of identity Lucy had would be obliterated along with the "bad-object representation."

Addiction as Protection of the Good Object

Winnicott (1947) suggested that certain children may split their universes into good and bad, accept all the bad into themselves, project the good onto their families, and then protect the good from the bad by running away from home. This pattern (which sounded very farfetched to me when I first read it) is enacted routinely at the Center. The kids at the Center, being in a locked facility, cannot complete the process by running away. But I and the rest of the clinical staff frequently find ourselves the recipients of a kind of reverential adoration. We can do no wrong. We can walk on water. Our capacity to love is infinite. We are the parents they should have had. We are the ultimate good breasts.

It is tempting to step into this role and to try and "re-parent" these children whose original parenting was, in fact, so horrible: to give them the love they so richly deserve and for which they so clearly hunger. And, in some ways, this seems to make so much sense. If these adolescents feel bad, worthless, and undeserving, why not simply shower them with love in such a way that they are able to recognize and accept that they are, in fact, "lovable"? It appears to make sense on a theoretical as well as an intuitive level. I state repeatedly in this book that in the part-object position, for every internalized part-object representation there is a *perfectly corresponding* split self-representation. Thus, if I am internalized as the loving parent–therapist, there should be a corresponding lovable self-representation.

The problem is that this doesn't happen; the kids don't internalize the lovable self-representation. In theoretical terms the key word is *internalize*. In theory, there should indeed be a good self-representation for every internalized object representation. But neither I nor any of the other canonized clinical staff seem ever to be internalized. To the contrary, we are determinedly kept external. Actually, a more accurate theoretical formulation would be that whatever split-off part of the ego, whether an internalized object representation or a self-representation, that is deemed *good* is projected onto, is *externalized* onto my colleagues and me. This is done, as Winnicott pointed out, to protect the good from the overwhelming bad with which the adolescent identifies. For this reason, the good *must* be kept external. This is similar to what Joe (chapter 3) did with his convoluted projections and identifications. Joe projected any internal experience of goodness onto the repository he labeled "weak women." This goodness then could be protected from his own essential badness ("I'm a bad kid"), while simultaneously nurtured by the split-off and disavowed "me-but-not-me" Joe.

The original perfect correspondence between the internalized part-object representation and the part-self representation is thus undone by the internal mechanisms of splitting, projection, and identification. My liking of, and caring for, the adolescents at the Center does not make them feel likable or worthy. Rather, they interpret my caring as evidence of my saintliness: "Dr. Brodie has to be a saint to care for someone as horrible as I am."

This canonization, I hasten to add, has nothing to do with any real qualities in me or in my colleagues. It is, in fact, the same process that these kids use with their abandoning and abusive mothers. The good part-object mother is not to be blamed for showing up so infrequently. To the contrary, she is idealized as "supermother," because only a supermother could love such a miserable excuse for a child. Her infrequent appearances are not a sign of any failing in her, but of her child's own unworthiness.

Addiction as Defense against Unbearable Pain

Krystal (presented earlier in this chapter), who reminded me that her ability to internalize the love of her godparents was limited to equating herself with stray dogs and cats, persisted in her work with me. "I don't love myself," she said, "and I want to be able to. I've never cared about myself. How can I love myself?" "That's easy," I blurted out, and then (shocked by my own brazenness) I added the qualifier, "at least it's easy to say. It is very hard to do. You've never cared about yourself because that way you don't have to feel the pain of everything that has happened to you. You don't have to hurt for someone you don't care about. To love yourself you have to be willing to feel that pain." She looked at me blankly. "Is there anyone you do love?" I asked her. "Oh yes," she responded instantly, "my godparents. I love them a lot." "So how would you feel if something horrible happened to them?" "I would feel terrible." "That's right," I said finally. "When something horrible happens to someone you love, you feel terrible. That's what you have to be willing to feel for yourself. In order to love yourself, you have to be willing to feel all the pain for all the terrible things that have happened to you in your life. You can't 'not care' anymore." Krystal sat silently for a long time, staring at the floor, and contemplating my words as intensely as has any client I have ever worked with. Finally she asked, "Is there any other way?"

Melanie Klein, and subsequent British object relations theorists, have tended to call the whole-object position the "depressive position." As I have said earlier, this is not because dwellers in this position are forever sad and morose, but rather because the particular anxiety associated with this position has to do with object loss. Object loss in the whole-object position is a very different thing from object loss in the part-object position. In the part-object position people expect that part objects will come and go randomly. That is the fickle nature of part objects. The disappearance of a good part object and its replacement by a bad part object is a serious thing, but it is not devastating. One can simply hunker down and await the return of the good part object. Or one can engage in any of the numerous magical incantations and rituals designed to drive away the bad part object and woo back the good.

In the whole-object position object loss is permanent and irrevocable. When Maria (chapter 3) was sobbing at the news of yet another born-and-abandoned sister, her tears arose out of a multitude of pains. She was certainly crying for her abandoned sister, and for her abandoned self, as represented by her sister. But she was also crying for the loss of her fantasized mother. The defensive split of good mother–bad mother that served to protect and preserve the fantasy of a good, loving, devoted mother, temporarily lost in the universe, but sure someday to return and love and cherish her daughter, collapsed under the onslaught of overwhelming reality. For a moment, Maria saw her mother for who she was: not as an alternating pair of split part objects, but rather as an all-too-real person, hopeless in her inadequacy, lost to her addictions to drugs, men, and narcissism. For Maria, the pain of her foray into the depressive position was more than she could bear.

Neither could Lucy stand to give up the bad mother. Lucy's part-object mother was more of a tantalus, promising Lucy all the love in the world if the poor daughter could just somehow manage to be "perfect." If Lucy had been able to recognize her mother for who she probably was, an angry, hypocritical, self-centered woman who probably did love Lucy to the limited extent that she was capable of loving anyone, it would have meant that Lucy would have to grieve, once and for all, for the mother and the childhood she never had.

In Klein's original formulation, only *part objects* could be internalized. Fairbairn's clarification, that it was *part-object relationships* that were internalized, contributed much more than a cosmetic change. With his insight we see that the split in the ego (self-representations) becomes as important as the split in the internalized object. This brings me back to Krystal, and her particular pain. As long as Krystal stayed in the part-object position, she could never be happy, but neither could she be particularly sad. She was an abandoned, unwanted child and therefore (in the logic of the part-object position), worthless. But as long as she was able to not care about herself (and who could care about something defined as "worthless"?), then she would feel no particular distress about being worthless. There was, of course, the constant background, dull pain that came with defining herself as worthless, but this could be, and was, anesthetized with drugs.

In contrast, the sharp, dagger-like pain Krystal faced with the entry into the whole-object position was daunting indeed. To "love" herself, Krystal would have to stop seeing herself as a worthless, throw-away child, not only deserving of her fate but unworthy of a moment's pity. Instead, she would have to experience herself as a lovable, precious child, deserving of love, protection, and nurturance. The magnitude of the tragedy she experienced in *not* having received all those things she would have to feel in its entirety. I can only admire the clear-sightedness with which she saw the task ahead of her when she asked, "Is there another way?"

At the Center I sometimes tell the kids that they need to learn to hate: "to hate freely and to hate consistently." This is ironic advice to be giving to a group of frequently violent, self-described "thugs," who are more frequently told that they have "an anger problem" that necessitates "anger management" training. Despite their frequent outbursts of rage and violence and their histories of aggression, I believe that my advice is good. These adolescents do not hate freely, and they certainly do not hate consistently. When they start to hate the bad (abandoning, abusive, seductive, etc.) part object, they reach a point where they must turn around and invest an equal amount of hatred in their corresponding (worthless, bad, sluttish, etc.) self-representations. In the part-object world everything must be in balance. And in the part-object world, the internalized bad part-object representation and its corresponding bad part-self representation need each other in a dialectical process of mutual definition.

What I am encouraging them to hate, freely and consistently, are the injustices that have been done to them. This is certainly not to foster any sense of "victimization" in them. That would merely be another form of splitting. Rather, I hope to introduce them to a concept not present in their part-object position mentality, the concept of injustice, and with it, to a new kind of feeling, a "righteous anger" or a "righteous hatred" that comes with the perception of injustice.

The first step in Krystal's progress toward self-love would be for her to tell herself that she did not "deserve" the abuse and neglect she received. If she were able to maintain this conviction consistently, then a powerful (and one hopes consistent) rage would emerge against the (real) mother who abused and abandoned her. This rage is the necessary corollary of the beginnings of self-love. Such rage is obviously not a desired end state, but rather a necessary intermediate state. But the process cannot be rushed or shortcut. Out of self-love would come the capacity for forgiveness, and with it a reduction in the hate. But forgiveness cannot be pushed too soon. If it is, the child will regress to a *justification* of the abuse, and will consequently relapse to self-hatred. True forgiveness can come only with an acknowledgment of the nature and magnitude of the transgression one has suffered.

Recently a girl at the Center said to me, with bitter resignation, "My mom did the best she could; but it wasn't good enough." I immediately reframed it for her. "I believe that your mom did *not* do the best she could, but it *was* good enough." What I was trying to convey to her was that she still needed to feel free to hate her mother (how can one hate someone who "did the best she could"?). But at the same time, I saw the danger that this girl would hold on to her self-concept as a "cripple," as a way of not letting her mother off the hook entirely. This girl needed to hold on to her hatred of her mother longer, as long as needed, until her self-love was strong enough that some real forgiveness might take place.

Note

1. For a more complete exposition on the development of British object relations theory the reader is referred to Thomas Ogden (1986), *The Matrix of the Mind*.

CHAPTER FIVE

~

Into Adulthood

Patricia, a girl in a group I led at the Center, called attention to herself at the beginning of group by her behavior that was simultaneously withdrawn and attacking. She sat balled up on the couch, making no eye contact with anyone, obviously unhappy, occasionally zinging her peers with verbal barbs or profanity. The group pressed her to say what was wrong. In response to the group's patient caring and persistent encouragement, Patricia began to talk about the abandonments in her life. She focused primarily on the total rejection and abandonment by her stepparents, which had happened almost a year earlier (they had suddenly told her that she could no longer live with them and that they wanted no contact with her). This pain had been rekindled by a more recent loss of a "friend" (mentor) who had been something of a surrogate mother to Patricia, but who had stopped coming to visit and who was not responding to letters. Patricia was in a state of despair and hopelessness.

As group leader I tried to focus Patricia not on the outside losses, but on her behavior in the group: on her rejection and pushing away of all the caring that the group directed at her. She acknowledged this and explained that she was loath to open up and risk being hurt again. It turned out, in fact, that Patricia had not even mailed out many of the letters to which her mentor had "not responded," because of anticipatory anxiety that they would be rebuffed. The group responded with continued support, and with corroborating stories from other girls on how they, too, retreated behind a protective wall after being hurt.

By the end of the group, Patricia was sitting up, maintaining eye contact, and even allowing herself an occasional smile. She has allowed herself to reconnect with her peers and, though still far from being happy, was no longer without hope.

What happened to Patricia in this group? The simplest explanation, that the group's caring lifted her out of depression, has a certain validity. The group's caring certainly made change possible. But the change itself was a more complex process.

At the beginning of the group Patricia was entrenched in the part-object position. She had no power, no sense of agency, no self-as-I. Alone in a world of bad objects, the most she could attempt was to try to protect herself from pain, inside some magical fortress of isolation, from which she would occasionally throw out a spear, to drive away the lurking bad objects. The change Patricia made during the course of the group was to rediscover herself as agent. In acknowledging (to herself) that she was pushing people away as much as she was being pushed away, Patricia was leaving the part-object position and moving toward the whole-object position. She was able to experience a self-as-I rather than simply a self-as-me ("this is what I am doing" rather than "this is what is happening to me").

In this transition, Patricia lost the feeling of hopelessness, which may be seen as an affect peculiar to the part-object position. Hopelessness is a downward step into despair from helplessness. One can be helpless but not hopeless. Even when one has no power, one may retain a modicum of hope: Miracles sometimes happen. But the converse is not true. While one can be helpless but not hopeless, one cannot be hopeless unless one is first helpless. Power, the power to effect changes, obviates hopelessness.

Patricia began the group feeling both helpless and hopeless. Her characteristic helplessness was exacerbated by a loss of hope. Her magic tricks no longer worked. She had run out of miracles. By focusing on her choices rather than on her victimization, the group helped Patricia regain a sense of power and thus pulled her out of hopelessness. At least part of the aloneness Patricia had been feeling came from her own choices, and over that part she had power. She recognized that she could either open herself up to people reaching out to her, and thus feel less alone, or continue to shut people out and remain "safe" from future hurt. If she chose to open up, she was taking a risk but could not experience herself as helpless. If she chose to wall herself off, then that would be her choice, and her experience would be one of stubbornness rather than hopelessness. But in either case, Patricia would be making a choice and was therefore not helpless.

Patricia's example illustrates the way change often happens: one small foray at a time from the part-object position into the whole-object position. Change in therapy, however, is not always gradual. Sometimes, after long periods of apparent stagnation, sudden and dramatic transformations occur. Such was the case with Max, and his transference with group comember Elizabeth presented in chapter 4.

After his "epiphany" Max's relationship with Elizabeth did change radically. Not only was he no longer cowed by her presence, but he could be warm, supportive, empathic, even gently confrontational with her. He was one of the first in the group to notice the unhappiness of her marriage and to offer her support in that. More important, however, Max's position in the whole group changed. He no longer acted as if he had nothing to say. He spoke his opinions in a calm, matter-of-fact way, as though he expected to be listened to and respected. Instead of being a wallflower, Max emerged as an active, valued group member. In his mid-forties, Max grew from an adolescent into a man.

Max's example illustrates an important difference between classic (Freudian) psychoanalytic theory and object relations theory. Max himself described his relationship with Elizabeth as one of "transference." In classic Freudian terms this would suggest that the relationship represented the transferring of residual feelings from an earlier unresolved relationship onto a current relationship. The resolution of the transference would free Max from an endless "repetition compulsion" and thus free up his psychic energy for more profitable, less neurotic, pursuits. This is, without doubt, a consummation devoutly to be desired.

But object relations theory frames the process differently. What Max was transferring (projecting) onto Elizabeth was not merely a fragment of the unburied past, it was one part of an internalized object relations unit: It was part of his psyche. In doing so, in *reexternalizing* an internalized object representation onto a real or external object, Max created the possibility for change. Elizabeth, however similar she may have appeared on the surface to the internalized object representation, was simply not as Max saw her. She was not a castrating bitch. She was not, for that matter, a part object.

The difference is far more than just theoretical. In resolving this ORU Max achieved a significant change in the structure of his ego. Max changed *who he was*. He became a different person: a man rather than a perpetual child. This is traditionally considered to be the "task" of adolescence.

In speaking about the original separation–individuation phase of infancy, Winnicott (1968) describes the infant's task as the "creative destruction" of the internal mother and the "discovery" of the external mother. A more modern formulation would emphasize that what needs to be "creatively destroyed" (worked through, resolved) is not simply the internalized part-object mother, but the entire ORU. In the case of Max, this was the internalized brilliant, castrating mother representation and the corresponding inadequate, cowering self-representation. When Max was finally able to let go of the castrating mother, the cowering self went with it. Once he did this, the real, external Elizabeth, like Winnicott's (1951) "good enough mother," was "there waiting to be discovered," and Max was able to begin relating to her as a real or external person rather than simply as the container of his projections.

Object relations theory is commonly misperceived as an interpersonal theory of psychology, although object relations theorists point out that it actually deals primarily with *internalized object representations* and is therefore more of an intrapsychic theory of psychology than an interpersonal theory. But in truth, object relations theory is both. *Object relations theory is a single theory about the dialectical relationship between the intrapsychic and the interpersonal, and the gradual, but never complete, shift from an autistic/solipsistic internal universe (the paranoid–schizoid position) to a reality/alterity–acknowledging interpersonal universe (the depressive position).*

For a variety of reasons, object relations theory historically has focused more on the intrapsychic, on the part-object position, than on the interpersonally oriented whole-object position. To be sure, it is easier to construct a model of the psyche in the part-object position. In its simplest form, the part-object psyche can be seen as a finite collection of dichotomous object relations units, each consisting of a matched internalized object representation and corresponding self-representation (loving parent–lovable self, abandoning parent–worthless self, abusive parent–bad self, and so on).

With the workings of internal defenses such as projection and identification, the picture can become much more complicated. But, as with Joe in chapter 3, a rough diagram of the part-object ego can still be offered.

The ego in the whole-object position defies simple description in diagram form. What seems to happen is that the ORUs simply collapse into themselves with the shift to the whole-object position. With the undoing of the split, the ORU loses both its structure and its energy. With the ORU thus collapsed, the internalized object representation is replaced by the real, whole, external object who, as Winnicott (1968) says, was waiting there to be discovered all along.

But it is clearly not enough to say simply that an external relationship replaces an internal one. An ORU is much more than just an internal relationship. It is a psychic structure: something by which a person in the part-object position attributes meaning and organizes and understands the universe. If the ego is understood as the primary organizing structure of experience, then something in the whole-object position needs to correspond to the ORU of the part-object position. I believe that Winnicott's (1960, 1986a) concept of the True Self[1] is the closest thing that object relations theory has to a structure that fulfills such a function.

The concepts of the True Self and the False Self are among the most commonly cited, and the most commonly misunderstood, of Winnicott's (frequently misunderstood) contributions. The most common misunderstanding is the equation of the False Self with what might be called a "fake self." Being "fake," or trying too hard to "fit in," is the source of much confrontation among peers at the Center. Nobody likes being lied to or feeling manipulated, and the feelings thus engendered contribute to severe ostracism for those deemed "two-faced" or otherwise inauthentic. But however admirable and valid is the current adolescent cry to "Keep it real!" this is not what Winnicott was talking about.

The False Self represents a deception to the self, not to the external world. It is a denial (to oneself) of one's true needs and feelings in an attempt to protect oneself from unbearable pain or the threat of annihilation in the face of the prospect of those essential needs not being met. This leads to the second misconception: that the False Self is nothing more than an alternative term for having defenses. For isn't that what defenses are: attempts to deny or hide from ones thoughts, feelings, and needs that produce unbearable anxiety? But again, this is not what Winnicott was talking about. The False Self is, more specifically, a denial of *who one is*, in particular, a denial of one's needs, and of the feelings associated with those needs.

As an example, if one performs Freud's original Oedipal repression, and buries in the unconscious any awareness of sexual desires for one's opposite-sex parent, but then goes on to sublimate those desires onto a partner with whom one enjoys a loving, uninhibited, and guilt-free sexual relationship, then one has *not* created a False Self. One's true needs for love, affection, physical comfort, sex, and companionship have been owned and acknowledged, and one is living within a True Self personality organization.

The adolescents at the Center live predominantly within False Self personality organizations, but not because they are "fake." Those who have been abandoned have learned to bury the terror of aloneness under a False Self structure that denies needing affection, denies needing comfort, denies needing love, and denies needing people. When asked if they ever feel lonely, they answer (honestly), "No!" Those who were abused have learned to deny their own fears and sometimes even to deny their own capacities to feel pain. Those who have been molested have managed to deny their experiences of having been violated, and have transformed the original terror into excitement and obsession.

An alternate form of the False Self organization is simply to deny any caring or concern about oneself. In the face of overwhelming pain and anxiety the simplest (and usually the last) line of defense is just to say, "Oh well!" and to stop caring. One sees this at the Center all the time. Kids working on their intentions to emerge out of lifestyles of severe drug addiction say, "I want to do it for my mom." When their peers feed back to them the conventional wisdom that this will not suffice, that they will have to want it for themselves, they are left in a position of helpless frustration. They simply cannot imagine doing anything for their own sakes.

If the predominant organizing structure of the part-object position, the ORU, consists of a dialectic between an internalized object representation and a corresponding self-representation, then the equivalent organizing principle of the whole-object position must be an analogous interpersonal dialectic between an external object (alterity) and the self. For this to be possible, the self must be functioning as a True Self structure. It is impossible to engage in a dialectic relationship between self and other if significant parts of the self are denied. The whole self must be acknowledged and owned if it is to confront alterity in an authentic way.

> A high-functioning, slightly postadolescent client (Emma) expressed considerable distress when I announced an upcoming four-week vacation. She angrily confronted me with the "coldness and formality" with which I had announced the vacation, and said that she felt "abandoned and rejected" by my plans. This angry attack was followed by a period of silence, which she finally broke. "What I really feel," she then added, "is cheated. I need you and you are not going to be there for me." I wondered out loud why she had had to go through all the pain and humiliation of feeling rejected and uncared for before she could get to the neediness. She responded, "I don't know. Maybe I just feel safer there." I gave her a look of dumb (in both senses) incomprehension, finally verbalizing my complete inability to understand that. The feelings of rejection seemed so much more painful to me than the straightforward neediness. She teared up at this point and began to talk about how ashamed she was of her neediness, and of how she expected me to be repulsed by and rejecting of it. At the end she looked at me meekly and asked, "So you don't mind my feeling dependent on you?" But her question had already been largely answered by my dumb look of incomprehension. I believe that it was this look, even more than my verbal reassurance, that enabled her to say, at the end, "I'll choose to believe you."

In the first part of this session Emma was functioning under a False Self structure. She allowed herself no awareness of her needs, and I had no existence for her as an external object. Her internal experience was not of neediness, but rather of rejection. My existence for her was limited to that of a screen for the projection of her internal objects. As she gradually began to allow herself awareness of her needs (True Self), she (simultaneously) allowed herself to see me as an external object. As long as I was nothing more than projected internal objects, she could do nothing more than rail at me impotently for the pain I was causing her. As she shifted to a True Self awareness of her needs, I became someone she could question and talk with, believe or disbelieve as she chose.

Adolescence is accurately viewed as a time of change. This is a large part of what makes it so rewarding for those of us who have chosen to work with that population. Yet if adolescence is a gradual shifting from a childhood, False Self–internalized object relationship psyche to an adult, True Self–interpersonal relationship mentality, it is ironic that the far greater potential for change and growth lies within the adult, whole-object, interpersonal dialectic. In contrast, the internal dialectic of the False Self–part-object position is frustratingly repetitious, mired, and unproductive.

Recent work in intersubjectivity, especially Ogden's (1994, 1997) perspective, which evolves out of object relations theory, focuses on the overarching dialectic between the positions: between the False Self and True Self structures, between the ORUs of the part-object position and the external relatedness of the whole-object position. But even among studies on intersubjectivity, most of the theoretical focus is on the earlier, more primitive side of the dialectic. In his almost poetical introduction to *Subjects of Analysis*, Ogden (1994) pays rare homage to the more adult way of relating:

> What I am describing is at the same time one of the most mysterious of human experiences and one of the most commonplace—it is the experience of doing battle with one's static self-identity through the recognition of a subjectivity (a human I-ness) that is other to oneself. The confrontation with alterity perceived will not allow us to remain who we were and we cannot rest until we have somehow come to terms with its assault on who we had been prior to being interrupted by it. (p. 3)

Yet in the chapters that follow, and indeed in the corps of his work in general, Ogden focused much more on projective identification ("mutual subjugation") than on the more mature "mutual recognition." Perhaps this was because of an intrinsic fascination with the primitive, and with the unending dialectic between the primitive and the mature.

But it is also possible that adolescence represents a singular foray into the realm of alterity. Like the toddler who enjoys a brief, wide-eyed "love-affair with life" (Greenacre 1957) before falling back into a more jaded nonchalance, so might the adolescent enjoy a unique period of openness to, and learning from, the world. Settling into the routines of the adult world may produce a swinging back in the dialectic to an increased amount of time spent in the staid, predictable world of internal object relations. And those of us who work with adolescents may do so to stay young and vital.

Note

1. The concepts of True and False Self functioning have been subjected to the usual criticisms of vagueness and imprecision that have been leveled at most psychoanalytic concepts. Recently, Mitchell (1993) presents a lengthy critique of the idea of a "True Self" and argues that a more useful concept might be that of "authenticity." But however cogent are Mitchell's criticisms, and however valuable is the concept of authenticity, True Self and authenticity refer to quite different phenomena. Indeed, this chapter argues that one can speak "authentically" from a "False Self" position. The concepts of the True and False Selves may be vague and flawed, but they remain valuable. To use Winnicott's (1954–1955) own words (vis-à-vis the theories of Melanie Klein), "What a pity to spoil a valuable concept by making it difficult to believe in" (p. 163).

PART II

TREATMENT ISSUES

CHAPTER SIX

~

Respect and Intersubjectivity

I have always described the population with which I work as one hundred *"severely delinquent, severely damaged* adolescents." Their criminal records testify to the severity of their delinquency. Many have been arrested more times than they are years old. Their crimes range from prostitution to rape to child molestation, from burglary to assault to carjacking, from drug dealing to arson. We rarely accept convicted murderers, but once there, many of our kids admit to numerous drive-by shootings, and quite a few talk about having killed wantonly.

As to their being damaged, there can be no doubt. One girl (Tanya) at the Center had been introduced to heroin by her mother at age eleven. She had also been molested by virtually every significant adult male in her life. Her sense of reality was so distorted that in one treatment session with an abusive stepfather she actually started to apologize to him for having masturbated him in a hot tub when she was five, saying in effect, that she was sorry that she had been such a "nasty little girl." A second girl reported having been put, at age five, in front of the television by her drug abusing and promiscuous parents not with *Sesame Street* but with pornographic videos to keep her entertained. We had a boy who described his mother playing cards with him in one room to distract him from the cries and screams in the next room as his drug-dealing father literally tortured a man to death. He told that story with the blandest of affect, and with the message that the incident was "just one of those things!" And there was Veronica, a pretty fifteen-year-old Latina with a winning smile. Near the end of her stay at the Center Veronica told her group something she had learned when she first came to the

Center. She had waited so long to tell them because she had to be absolutely sure of her trust in them. She had always, she said, had certain marks "between my legs" (said with a slightly embarrassed glance toward me). She had never known what these marks were, but she knew that she had had them since infancy and that they had something to do with her mother. Her mother had been verbally and physically abusive to her continually until the mother finally abandoned her and the entire family when Veronica was ten. When Veronica had first arrived at the Center she had a routine physical by the nurse and had finally had the courage to ask the nurse if she could say what the marks were. "Oh yes," said the nurse, "they are cigarette burns."

This chapter deals with a set of paradoxes.

Paradox Number One: Helping by Eschewing the Helping Role

The level of delinquency in the teenagers at the Center implies that they are in need of correction. The level of damage done to them implies that they are crying out for help. Yet the extent to which I personally have been effective with these kids is, I believe, the result of my trying to be neither corrective nor even particularly helpful. A seventeen-year-old girl who was brought to my office after experiencing an episode of seemingly psychotic confusion and disorientation pointed this out to me. She spoke for about an hour in my office, freely and lucidly, about herself and the horrors of her life. At the end of the session she expressed surprise about how open she had been with me. She also expressed doubts about her ability to be similarly open with the intern to whom she had just been assigned. When I asked her what the difference was between us, she reflected a moment and said, "You care about people. She wants to help people."

Let me emphasize that the intern in question cared about people at least as much as I do and that I want to help these girls as much as anyone. I think that the issue the patient was speaking to was not that I cared more than the intern, but rather that I was less focused on a need to help. The whole concept of "helping" implies an unequal relationship: a superior–inferior relationship in which one clearly has something to offer of which the other is in need. My approach to these adolescents is much more egalitarian: I genuinely believe that I have as much to learn from them as they have from me. Adolescents experience this approach or attitude as "respect."

Respect

For as long as I have worked with delinquent adolescents I have been fascinated by their passionate, even obsessive focus on respect. To be disrespected ("dissed") demands a challenge, a fight, even possibly a killing. And it takes very little to disrespect someone. If someone has "tagged" his or her name or his or her gang in a book or on a wall, someone else can "diss" that person by simply writing an "X" through the name. Looking at someone too long or too intensely can be taken as a challenge and therefore a "diss." There are ritualized ways of "dissing" enemy gangs. Members of Crips gangs are "dissed" by the word *crab*, and Bloods by the word *slob*. Any gang with the word *playboy* in its name is "dissed" by the words *peanut butter*. In a girl's unit once a girl at the lunch table innocently asked for the peanut butter to be passed. Another girl, new to the unit, suddenly dove across the table at her with the apparent intention of taking her head off.

Gangs take the issue of respect and disrespect extremely seriously. If your gang is disrespected and you do not rise to defend its honor, then you run the risk of being labeled a "ranker" or a "buster." Nothing is more reviled than this in gang culture. If word gets back to a gang that a member has "ranked out on them," they are likely to turn on the betrayer with considerable violence.

At first I saw the preoccupation with respect as a sign of pathology. These kids, I believed, thought so little of themselves that they had no expectation of ever being loved. Most had no hope of even being liked. So the least they could ask for, or dare demand, was respect. Furthermore, with the possession of a gun or the affiliation of a gang, they could insist on it.

I now see respect as being much more basic and fundamental an issue, not an "I'll settle for . . ." at all. I first began to emotionally understand the importance of respect in a boys' group at the Center. I had for months been trying to gain an affective understanding of the rage the kids felt when they had been "dissed" by an enemy gang member. Finally, one of the boys said to me simply, "It's like when somebody disrespects your race." For some reason, while I was not at that time able to put myself in the shoes of a Crip who had just been called a crab, I *was* able to put myself in the place of an African American who had been called a "nigger." I could feel the disrespect, the humiliation, and the rising, potentially murderous rage.

Disrespect is an attack on who one is, on one's identity, one's essence, one's very soul. Respect is therefore a crucial concern to everyone, but especially to adolescents, for identity formation and character formation are two of the crucial developmental tasks particular to adolescence (cf. A. Freud 1958; Blos 1967, 1968).

If the teenagers at the Center are capable of being aroused to murderous rage by a stare, or by a casual and innocent reference to foods such as crabs, beans, peanut butter, or tacos, how are they to react to well-meaning therapists whose entire raison d'être is to help them change from who they are into something else (something *better*, something *more acceptable*). A therapist's desire to "help" an adolescent client may well be experienced by that client as a kind of disrespect.

We should not delude ourselves into believing that we are ever truly "non-judgmental" as therapists. The theoretical foundations of most of our therapeutic work involve critical judgments. If we are followers of Ellis or Beck, we look for "errors of thinking" in our clients. If we are Freudians, we think in terms of inadequate superegos, or even inadequate egos. Kleinians patiently help guide our clients out of the "paranoid–schizoid position" and into the more advanced "depressive position." Indeed it is probably only the few remaining followers of Carl Rogers whose work evolves out of a truly nonjudgmental framework. Rogerians try, as much as possible, to vacate their own frame of reference in favor of seeing the world entirely through the eyes of their clients.

The psychological concept of "denial" epitomizes the paradox that I am addressing here. Denial clearly implies that there is a "truth" that the therapist sees clearly and that the client, for some reason, refuses to see. Indeed the therapist is positioned as the carrier of truth in virtually all forms of therapy, while the client is portrayed as ultimately ignorant, benighted, or self-deluded. Among therapies based on learning theories, the client's problems are formulated as either ignorance ("the client has never learned to . . .") or illogic (errors of thinking). In such theories the role of the therapist is to be the teacher, helping the client to learn what he or she has previously failed to learn, or the guru, pointing out to the client the wrongness of his or her thinking. In psychoanalytically based therapies the client is seen as either "fixated" (suffering from an arrested development) or neurotic (willfully—on an unconscious level—repressing truths that the client does in fact perceive). The therapist's role in each case is essentially to "re-parent" the client through the missed developmental stages or to be the oracular interpreter of unconscious material, which the client cannot or will not recognize.

The critical judgments built into our theoretical frameworks are often augmented by a kind of personal arrogance that takes the form of a patient (or impatient) condescension toward our clients. I have been as guilty as any of my colleagues of "telling" my delinquent adolescents that "drugs and gangs lead to an early grave." But, on reflection, surely this is absurd. Who am I, whose experience with drugs is limited to some minor experimentation in college in the sixties, to "tell" a girl who has lost several friends to drugs and who has herself overdosed twice on heroin that "drugs will kill." And who am I who, in my late fifties, have only been to one funeral of someone who died by nonnatural causes, to "tell" about the dangers of gangs to boys who themselves bear the scars of bullet wounds and for whom the gang funerals of their murdered friends are considered a normal part of their lives?

By no means do I wish to imply that we can talk to our clients only out of our own personal experiences. I know hard statistics about the longevity of drug users and gang members that may be useful to the Center teenagers. But as an experienced therapist, do I really expect my dry statistics to have more of an impact than the deaths of their friends and the wounds to their own bodies? Many of my colleagues cite these same dry statistics to their delinquent clients and then step outside the buildings after group to have a cigarette. So much for the power of statistics!

Paradox Number Two:
Respecting Those "Unworthy" of Respect

As important as differences in personal experiences are differences in perceptions of reality. A theoretical position is more than just a heuristic device guiding a therapist through the labyrinth of the human psyche; it represents the way a therapist thinks. When I look at the delinquent teenagers I work with, I truly see damaged children. I also see extraordinary errors in thinking, inadequate ego development, pervasive splitting, and all the other diagnostic judgments that are so commonly heaped upon this population. To deny these judgments would be to deny my own reality.

Nor do I believe that when I end up "telling" kids what they know better than I that I am merely indulging in arrogant condescension. Gang members and drug-using kids are highly adept in the use of denial. Indeed, gang culture teaches "formulas" of denial that become clichés of gang mentality. Gang members frequently deny responsibility for accidental killings, blaming the victims for being "in the wrong place at the wrong time." They point out with relish that gang members are not the only ones ever to be killed, with the clear (but ludicrous) implication that because one can die in peacetime, there is no particular danger from being in a war zone. Gang members also minimize their own moral culpability, arguing that "everyone breaks the law," implying a moral equivalence between jaywalking and drive-by shootings. They voice such arguments sometimes in the Center's multifamily group therapy sessions, and the results are angry intergenerational debates. I believe that at least some of the anger in such groups comes from the inanity of the debate into which the parents have allowed themselves to be pulled.

How do we reconcile the role disparities inherent in the psychotherapeutic relationship with my observation that I am most effective with my delinquent adolescent clients when I am most able to be respectful and nonjudgmental? Rogerians may come closest to offering a solution to this. Rather than a superior–inferior (enlightened–benighted) position split, Rogers advocated a therapeutic stance in which there was only *one* position in the room: that of the client. The Rogerian therapist is instructed to suspend, as much as possible, any personal frame of reference and to adopt the point of view of the client. While there is much to be admired in the Rogerian position, the intellectual vacuity of the stance severely limits the completeness of the therapeutic experience.

Intersubjectivity and Adolescent Psychotherapy

I believe that the recent emergence of the concept of "intersubjectivity" (Atwood and Stolorow 1984; Natterson 1991; Ogden 1994) in therapy offers the best resolution of the paradox I have been presenting. Intersubjectivity is a term with a long history in philosophy, borrowed by psychologists and adapted to psychotherapy in the early 1980s. In psychology the term has become associated primarily with Stolorow, who writes out of the self psychology tradition. Important contributions have also been made by Ogden, who speaks from an object relations perspective. Intersubjectivity so far has been discussed in the literature primarily as a metapsychological concept. I am unaware of any techniques or treatment strategies based specifically on "intersubjectivity." Indeed, Atwood and Stolorow (1984) are explicit in averring that *all* existing psychoanalytic treatment principles are as applicable under intersubjectivity as under the more traditional psychoanalytic paradigms. These include such fundamental psychoanalytic tenets as the "fundamental rule" of free association, the "rule of abstinence," as well as such technical rules of interpretation as Fenichel's "interpretation always starts at the surface," "ego analysis precedes id analysis," and "interpretation of resistance precedes interpretation of content."

Stolorow also makes it clear that there is nothing inherently "nonjudgmental" in intersubjectivity. He sees no incompatibility between the intersubjective paradigm and the self-psychology division of patients into those suffering from "pathological [self] structures" and those suffering from "insufficient or faulty structuralization" (Atwood and Stolorow 1984). Stolorow does offer one crucial change, however, in the way we view psychopathology, arguing that it should be understood as an intersubjective rather than an intrapsychic phenomenon. The concept of the "borderline," for example, is best conceptualized not as a stable, intrapsychic personality structure, but rather as the resulting dynamics of a particular intersubjective field—"a field consisting of a precarious, vulnerable self and a failing, archaic selfobject" (p. 56).

On one level Thomas Ogden appears as conservative as Stolorow in his presentation of intersubjectivity. As do Atwood and Stolorow, Ogden (1986) begins his work by tracing the roots of intersubjectivity back to the earliest origins of psychoanalysis, in his case through Freud, Klein, and Winnicott. And as with Atwood and Stolorow, Ogden avoids any mention of new "intersubjective techniques" to replace or even augment the classic psychoanalytic approach.

But it is in Ogden's words that the import of his message can be seen. Ogden (1994) talks first and foremost of therapy as a "dialectical" encounter.[1]

> Dialectic is a process in which opposing elements each create, preserve, and negate the other; each stands in a dynamic, ever-changing relationship to the other. Dialectical movement tends toward integrations that are never achieved. Each potential integration creates a new form of dialectical tension. That which is generated dialectically is continuously in motion, perpetually in the process of being created and negated, perpetually in the process of being decentered from static self-evidence. In addition, dialectical thinking involves a conception of interdependence of subject and object: "Dialectical thought . . . [is] a process in which subject and object are so joined that truth can be determined only within the subject-object totality" (Marcuse 1960, p. viii). One cannot begin to comprehend either subject or object in isolation from one another. (p. 14)

The "decenter(ing) from static self-evidence" is the experience of the analyst (therapist) as much as of the analysand (client).

> The analyst must be prepared to destroy and be destroyed by the otherness of the subjectivity of the analysand and to listen for a sound emerging from that collision of subjectivities that is familiar, but different from anything that he has previously heard. This listening must be done "without memory or desire" (Bion 1963), but at the same time the listener must be rooted in the history that has created (spoken) him if he is to be able to discern the sound of which I am speaking. The destruction of analyst by analysand and of analysand by analyst (as separate subjects) in the collision of subjectivities must not be complete or else the pair has fallen into the abyss of psychosis or autism. Instead, the analyst must listen to (through) the roar of the destruction from its edge, not ever being certain where that edge lies. (Ogden 1994, pp. 3–4)[2]

More than from any other modern psychoanalytic writer, one gets from Ogden an understanding of therapy as an encounter between two human beings. The two people may be very different from one another. One may be good and generous, the other cruel and selfish. One may be young and foolish and the other old and wise. But both are human beings, and it is through their humanness—their subjectivities—that their encounter achieves its power and effectiveness. In the passionate dialectical struggle between them, the creating and destroying, the accepting and negating, the real work of the therapy takes place.

This, then, is how I try to approach my adolescent clients: "I am certainly older than you and I believe I am wiser. I am certainly more educated than you and I believe I know more. You are incarcerated and I am free, and I believe that this is because my values and my choices are better than yours. But all of this is of secondary importance compared to our shared humanity. We both know what it is like to be afraid, to love and to be afraid to love, to hate and to hate ourselves for hating, to want and to feel unworthy of what we want, to mourn and to despise ourselves for our weakness."

The adolescents I work with frequently tell me that they are confused and "messed up." On one hand, this is indisputable and I can only agree with them. Yet I respond that they make perfect sense and that they are in fact in perfect balance. Their hatred, both toward themselves and toward others, is in proportion to the abuse they have received. Their fears and anxiety are in proportion to the chaos of their lives. The despair and hopelessness they feel is in balance with the abandonment and disappointments they have experienced. Nothing is "wrong" with them; nothing has to be "fixed." They merely carry more than their fair share of the world's pain. My desire is not to take their pain from them, for to do so would be to take away part of who they are. My desire instead is simply to be with them in their pain, and thus to allow them to feel less alone in their pain. If they feel less alone with their pain, they may feel less alone in the world. If they feel less alone in the world, they may have less pain. I believe that it is this approach that my young client sensed and appreciated as my "caring about people, not wanting to help people."

Let me explain this position a bit further because on the surface it seems absurd to say that "nothing is wrong with them, nothing has to be fixed."

A Center girl asked to consult with me regarding a particularly troubling and shameful recurring thought. This girl had essentially grown up "on the streets" and her only relationships with men had been sexually exploitative. With our help, she had just gotten in touch with her biological father, a man she had never known. This man turned out to be a relatively decent human being who took an interest in his newly discovered teenaged daughter. The girl, of course, was intrigued, excited, and terrified at the idea of having a "real father." What upset her was that she could not see him without having a fantasy of giving him oral sex. She told me this with a mixture of profound shame and a kind of defiance, as though she were challenging me to normalize such extraordinarily aberrant behavior. I told her that her thoughts were perfectly normal, normal that is, for someone with her background. She had been sexualized at a very young age and thus had never experienced a nonsexual type of love. Furthermore, she was terrified of losing this new object, and sought to hold onto him the only way she had ever held onto men: through sexual favors. This young girl was extraordinarily damaged, and her thoughts exceedingly aberrant. But her reaction was entirely predictable. It came out of her history and, more importantly, it came out of her humanity. In this sense there was nothing "wrong" with her. Any of us who had spent our lives walking in her shoes might well have had the same reaction.

The advantage of intersubjectivity is that it allows an approach to the client that is inherently respectful. It therefore meets what seems to be a fundamental need in the client (for respect) and speeds the formation of a working alliance or of what Ogden (1994) describes as the "intersubjective third." Respect, in this sense, is not the "unconditional positive regard" that Rogers proposed (along with the complete suspension of self to make such a thing possible). In the intersubjective sense, respect is a dynamic, paradoxical experience. It is loving and hating, accepting and rejecting, admiring and loathing.[3]

Two Particular Impediments to Respect

Before proceeding to a case illustrating an intersubjective approach to treatment, let me address two issues that potentially interfere with my capacity to be respectful toward my clients: my firm intellectual (and sometimes visceral) rejection of their values and my inability (or unwillingness) to completely divest myself of a sense of superiority to them.

Over the years of working with the delinquent teenagers at the Center my respect for them has grudgingly but steadily increased, as has my respect (though not my love) for the institution of street gangs. One need not be an apologist for gangs to recognize that they serve a function for their members. They provide respect, love, security (paradoxically), belonging, and identity to a population that may not have received much of these from their families of origin, and who lose what little of these foundations they had through the normal "second individuation process" of adolescence (Blos 1967). In some respect the gang "ethic" has elements that mainstream society might well emulate. An article in the *New Yorker* magazine (Gates 1998, pp. 34–44) bemoaned the demise of loyalty as an esteemed virtue. If this is true, then we might do well to study a group in which members willingly go to jail for a crime committed by another rather than turn "rat." I have heard judges and parents berate gang members with claims that "your home boys don't really care about you. They're not there for you." Yet I know that this is rarely true. I have sufficient imagination to be able to appreciate the impact of the gang phrase "I've got your back" when bullets are flying.

Yet however much respect one may have for gangs, one would have to be blind not to loathe them as well. Street gangs are the scourge of impoverished neighborhoods, bringing death, fear, drugs, and crime to areas with little enough hope to begin with. However important the short-term psychological benefits of gangs, the benefits do not extend to the innocent victims of drive-by shootings, to the children addicted to drugs sold to support the gang economies, and to the thousands that gangs mug, rob, burgle, and terrorize on a daily basis.

In working with adolescent gang members I make no secret of either my respect for the benefits gangs provide their members or of my horror of the price extracted by gangs for those benefits. Perhaps surprisingly, gang members do not experience the expression of the negative side of my ambivalence as disrespectful. Once again, they have been to too many funerals of their peers not to recognize the truth of the issues behind my feelings. Actually, I believe that in voicing my antagonism to gangs I am frequently speaking the negative side of *their* ambivalence as well, a side that had hitherto remained mute. It is, after all, their friends who have been killed. My task as a therapist is to remember to speak both sides of my ambivalence in order not to force them into a defensive position.

The issue of my sense of superiority in certain areas also turns out to have little effect on the therapeutic relationship. If I express to my adolescent clients the pride I take in my education and in the wisdom I have gained over the years, this is not experienced as disrespectful. Indeed, it is likely that most adolescents want an adult they can respect and admire even while they may need to rebel against that same person. If I believe that the world would be a better place if everyone shared my values than if everyone had gang values, this too need not be communicated as disrespect. In fact, if I were to allow myself to get caught up in such a debate with gang members, I believe that most of them would probably agree with me, of course dismissing me in the process as a hopelessly idealistic dreamer.

If neither my disapproval of the values of the Center adolescents nor my own perception of superiority in some areas is experienced as disrespect by clients, then what is the nature of this "respect" that adolescents value so fiercely and that I am proposing as an essential component of psychotherapy?

A Resolution of the Paradoxes: Mutuality in Therapy

I submit that the answer to this lies in avoiding the kind of arrogance that is virtually inherent in the role of the psychotherapist. The goal of most therapists is not merely to change their client's behavior, but to change who the client is. Changing a person's behavior is in itself a highly ambitious goal. Even with an incarcerated, criminal population whose behavior is inherently destructive (and illegal), we walk a fine line between authority and authoritarianism when we set out to modify a person's behavior. But when our ambition is much greater than that, when our goal is to change *who a person is*, then surely we flirt with extraordinary arrogance.

I believe the only way of avoiding such arrogance is to enter into the therapeutic relationship with the mind-set that *the extent to which I hope to change a person, I will also allow myself to be changed by that person.* This is the true equality in the therapeutic relationship and the basis of true respect. As Ogden (1994) points out, such an attitude in therapy does not imply that therapy is for both the client and the therapist. Psychotherapy is *for* the client, not for the therapist. But the emphasis on the word *for* implies that therapy is a process engaged in *for* the benefit of the client rather than being something done *to* a client. The willingness of the therapist to be changed by the client is, to my mind, the essence of the intersubjective approach.

Case Example: Alice

Let me give an example of an intersubjective interaction. I shall describe the interaction and, parenthetically, the cognitive–affective states and changes within the participants.[4]

The setting was a daily group therapy session in a girls' unit at the Center. The group consisted of ten adolescent girls, aged fourteen through seventeen, and me. All of the girls had committed multiple and serious crimes. A new girl (Alice) started out by arguing with some other girls for the right to "work" in this session. After a fairly heated discussion, the group chose her to work because she has never worked in group before. Having triumphed in getting the group to choose her to work, Alice's next step was to insist that she had nothing to work on. The group responded to this with exemplary patience, offering suggestion after suggestion (all of which were politely but firmly rejected) for what Alice might work on. My reaction to this was to remain quietly amused. I have seen too many new group members adopt the "I-want-to-work-but-I-have-nothing-to-work-on" position. (In contrast to the group's collective position of "supportive patience," I would describe my own internal cognitive–affective position at this point as "arrogant condescension.")

The first cognitive–affective shift during the session occurred in Alice and was a direct result of the group's patience (certainly not of my condescension). The group did not react as Alice had expected. She had expected impatience, intolerance, and hostility. Instead she received patience and encouragement. (The internal cognitive–affective shifts that happened within Alice may have been something like "This group (the world) is not as hostile or threatening as I thought. I am not as much at risk as I thought. This group (the world) is more caring and supportive than I thought. I might be more likable than I thought.")

This internal cognitive–affective shift allowed Alice to make a behavioral shift within the group, and she began to work honestly and openly on her resistance. She hated working in group, she explained, for two reasons. First, her mother had been extremely prying and intrusive. Second, when her mother had succeeded in prying information out of her, the mother would then either "throw it back in my face" in a hostile manner or "spread my business" throughout the extended family.

Alice's work produced a marked change in my own cognitive–affective state for two reasons. First, I knew that Alice was working in group because she was forced to work by the demands of the program. This filled me with consternation and dread because I feared that, rather than helping her, we were re-creating the trauma of Alice's intrusive mother, dragging material out of her against her will. Second, because my own parents had been somewhat intrusive (although they were not nearly as intrusive as Alice's mother), I could identify with Alice, and this stirred my empathy. (At this point I would say that my cognitive–affective state had shifted from arrogance and condescension to anxiety, guilt, and empathy.)

Alice continued to work in this group for some time on the issues of her mother and the violation of boundaries. At a certain point I felt the need (probably to assuage my guilt and reduce my anxiety) to reassure Alice. I said to her that I had no personal desire to pry into her personal business and that I certainly had no intention of using anything she said against her but that we asked her to work in group only so that we could help her. She replied to this in an audible whisper: "I know. That's why I like you."

I believe that this represented another quantum shift in Alice's experience. Her initial work on her resistance to doing work had been made possible by her new perception that the group (world) was safer than she had originally thought. Now she acknowledged not only that the world might be safe but that it might contain some benevolent elements as well. (Her new cognitive–affective state may be interpreted as "Not everyone is intrusive or assaultive as was my mother. I am not composed exclusively of badness, which my mother was trying to ferret out and punish me for. There may be some worth or goodness in me to which people can respond with love and caring.)

Here an equally profound experiential shift took place within me. Parts of this shift were in response to each of the two sentences Alice spoke. The words "I know" utterly astonished me. Here was a girl who had grown up in a world that was hostile, disrespectful of boundaries, punitive, and betraying. And yet in response to a modicum of patience and understanding she was willing to make herself vulnerable and open. (The condescension of my original cognitive–affective state was now replaced by admiration and respect.) My response to her other sentence was even more profound. Here was a girl who in the midst of her pain, anxiety, and vulnerability, chose to give me a gift: "That's why I like you." I was humbled and touched by her gift. (My cognitive–affective state had by this time been transformed from arrogance to humility, respect, and gratitude.)

I believe that Alice experienced one last cognitive–affective shift. She must have been aware, on some level, that her words to me ("I like you") were a gift. This implied a 180-degree shift from her original position of "I am full of badness that people are waiting to discover so that they can punish me." Her position now implied "I have qualities of worth that I am willing to give as a gift of thanks to this person who has been kind to me."

Two questions arise here. First, to what extent were the changes I have described in this interaction the *result* of the interaction itself? The answer is that they were *entirely* the result of this interaction *and of all previous similar interactions*. Surely Alice would not have been so ready to change her perception so radically had she not already experienced similar interactions with other benevolent people in her past. The *sum total* of all such interactions produced the character change.

Second, how permanent can we expect such changes to be? The answer here is that they are no more permanent than anything else is in this world. If Alice were to experience more such interactions, her readiness to perceive herself and the world as being good would be increasingly internalized, and her resiliency to negative input would be strengthened. I cannot, at this point, speak for Alice. But I can testify that for myself, a decade of such interactions with the adolescents I work with has changed who I am. The arrogance of my position in the beginning of the session was much more characteristic of who I was ten years ago. The children I have worked with have humbled me, and this has been an enormously positive experience. I am much happier being able to recognize, appreciate, and accept gifts of the magnitude of what Alice gave me.

Drawbacks of Mutuality in Therapy

Let me add, however, that not all the changes created in us by our interactions with our clients are welcome. I have argued elsewhere (1998) for greater awareness of the uglier human emotions that get stirred up in us by our work. When a child projects onto me the role of his abusive father, and then forces me to accept that role by provoking me by constant misbehavior, so that I find myself responding to him with consistent anger and punishment, my anger at him is only part at who he is, and part at who he has made me in relation to him. For I do not like that I have become an abusive parent, and I do not like the potential for malice and sadism that he has caused me to see in myself.

When I think of the concept of projective identification, the most powerful and dramatic example that I can think of is rape. In rape, the rapist projects onto his victim all of his own feelings of vileness and self-loathing, and then, through his behavior, makes sure that she experiences those feelings as her own. The psychological effects of rape are powerful and long-lived. It takes years for some women to get over the feelings of defilement that come with rape, if they ever do. Being raped can change who a woman is.

Those who work with rapists can be sure that they will try to do the same with us. The manipulations a rapist uses in the service of projective identification will be more subtle and more psychological than the brutality of physical rape, but the goal will be the same. And to a certain extent, he will succeed. Female therapists often end up feeling sexualized in a degrading way. Male therapists will have their competency (their manhood) seriously challenged so that they, themselves, will feel diminished. We cannot encounter the dark side of humanity and remain untouched.

Psychotherapy is an intimate dance between client and therapist, both of whom must be willing to share in the intimacy and both of whom will be affected by that intimacy. Rapists transform the ultimate act of intimacy into the ultimate act of degradation. I strongly believe that we cannot help rapists, any more than we can help anyone else, without becoming intimate with them and ultimately, allowing ourselves to be vulnerable with them. But the therapeutic dance of intimacy with a rapist has to be slow, and long, and carefully choreographed.

Notes

1. It is in his defining of therapy as dialectic that Ogden avoids the proactive–reactive schema in which Natterson gets caught.

2. Ogden's concept of the intersubjective dialectic appears analogous to what Natterson refers to as "the intersubjective principle": People seem to need simultaneously to persuade others to their positions and to be influenced by the positions of others.

3. It is not easy to find the right words and metaphors to capture the paradoxical, dialectical encounter that is psychotherapy. To my mind it is ultimately a "struggle" between two people. By this I am not referring to the kind of dead-end "fight" that happens when an ill-timed or incorrect interpretation is insisted upon or with some other breakdown of the transference–countertransference relationship. I cannot conceptualize this kind of encounter without remembering the biblical story of Jacob wrestling with the angel. As a child I remember being disturbed by this story. The idea of a man physically wrestling with an angel struck me as vaguely blasphemous: skin on skin, sweat mixing with sweat, smelling each other's smells. Yet in the story it led to an epiphany. I now see it as a wonderful metaphor for doing therapy.

4. Of course I can report with accuracy only my own cognitive–affective states and shifts. I am guessing at those of my client.

CHAPTER SEVEN

~

Individual Therapy

From the perspective developed thus far, it can be seen that the term *depressive position* is a misleading one. The term *historical position* better represents what is normative in the achievement of this psychological organization.

—Thomas Ogden, *Matrix of the Mind*

How Does Therapy Work?

The essential function of splitting is to undo or destroy history. The "original" split (the splitting of the breast/mother into good breast and bad breast) is designed to deny the fact that the breast/mother that nurtures, warms, comforts, and gratifies and the breast/mother that withholds, frustrates, and tantalizes are one in the same, differing only through the intervention of time and circumstance. In splitting, the good and bad breasts have in common only that they are both breasts and thus have at least the potential for infinite gratification. But the good breast is bountiful and fulfills its potential, while the bad breast is niggardly and withholds its potential. And, after the infant projects onto the bad breast its own rage and aggression, the bad breast becomes sadistic and malicious in its withholding. The idea that the bad breast might simply be the good breast that has just been bitten is not only rejected, it is not even allowed to be considered.

Chronology can exist in the paranoid–schizoid position, but history cannot. Good breasts can come and go and be replaced by bad breasts in some

95

kind of sequence or chronology. History, however, with its continuous flow of connectedness and separateness, change and sameness, cannot exist. If the paranoid–schizoid position is created out of the destruction of history, then conversely, the re-creation of history is a way into the depressive position. This is why psychodynamic psychotherapies so adamantly focus on *understanding* the client (as opposed to helping the client, teaching the client, getting the client to see, and so on). Over the years, I have developed the habit of checking myself whenever I feel an urge to try and get a client to see things from *my* perspective. Instead, I ask myself what it is about the client's perspective that I still do not understand. Because, on some level, the client's perspective always makes sense.

I would like to return once again to the case of Lucy, my determinedly self-hating, long-term client. During the first year of therapy she was frequently in and out of the hospital with suicidal gestures. One of her admissions followed a friend's expression of concern that she "might be putting on a little weight."

Several months into therapy Lucy told of being date-raped when she was in college. Lucy had been born with some physical deformities that had only partially been corrected by multiple surgeries when she was a child. She had grown up with a highly critical adoptive mother who had constantly reminded Lucy of her imperfections. She also had been subjected to the usual cruel taunting and teasing by her peers. So when an attractive young man asked her out, she had allowed herself a momentary lift in her self-esteem. Instead of taking her out, however, this young man had shown up at her apartment and raped her. Lucy reported that after this rape she sat in her darkened room for a week hating herself. When I asked her if she had not also directed some hatred toward the man who raped her, she looked at me with utter incomprehension. "No [she said], why should I hate him?"

About a year into treatment Lucy told me about her years-long sexual abuse by her adoptive father (she had been adopted as an infant). Her adoptive mother had been a cold, critical woman from whom Lucy had gotten the message, "If you were only perfect, I could love you." During her mother's frequent verbal assaults, Lucy would look to her father, wishing that he would come to her defense. But her father was passive and spineless and would never stand up to his wife. Then, one night when Lucy was ten or eleven and his wife was out of the house, he came to her, not to rescue her, but to rape her. When I asked Lucy what she remembered about this event, she answered with one word: "Pain!" He continued to molest her every time his wife was away until Lucy left home for college at age eighteen.

This information helped me understand Lucy's self-loathing better, but it did not appear to be helpful to her. Her trips to the hospital for being suicidal diminished as she allowed herself to trust and to depend on me more. But her life continued to be a nightmare. She engaged in daily bulimic binging followed by multiple horrific purges until she was sure there was nothing left inside her. She entered a near-psychotic state at night when she could feel the presence of her (now deceased) father literally haunting her bedroom. During the day she coped only by entering a kind of trance state that produced some near accidents when she was driving and got me to send her to a neurologist to see of she had epilepsy.

There was some gradual improvement over the next two years. She went back to work (she had been put on disability a year before coming to me) but couldn't hold a job. She despaired of ever really working again, and secretly I despaired along with her. Mostly during this period I remember pleading with her. "Be nicer to yourself." "I'm fighting this battle by myself. I need an ally." These may not have been my exact words, but that was certainly my message. I tried every trick in my technical arsenal. At one point I said, "You know, Lucy, you really aren't all that nice of a person." I said this with great trepidation remembering how she had become suicidal at being told she was overweight (it was also very important to Lucy that she be considered a "good person"). "Yes [I said in response to her look of horror], you are a very nice person to everybody in the world except one person, and you are quite horrible to that one person." But Lucy was completely indifferent to this intervention. "You mean to myself? But what difference does it make if the only one I'm mean to is myself?"

Then, early in year four, Lucy suddenly, in the middle of a session, produced a recovered memory. Unlike the memory of her father's abuse, which had been merely a secret, this was a true recovered memory of something she had completely blocked from consciousness. When Lucy was between ages three and five, her adoptive brother (who was then in his early to mid-twenties) would come by in his mobile home to "take Lucy away for the weekend." What happened then was ritualistic sexual torture. During the day he would buy her small toys. At night he would undress her, insert an enema into her rectum, and insert the toys he had just bought her into her vagina.

As I listened in horror to this story of sadistic abuse, I thought back to the story she had told years earlier about the date rape. Suddenly it all made sense. Lucy had grown up perceiving herself to be a human toilet, into which men performed their bodily functions and then left. When the handsome young college man in college had asked her out, she had momentarily allowed herself to think that she might be something more than that. The rape that followed was a brutal disillusionment of her brief hope. Of course she sat hating herself! What a fool she must have thought herself to have indulged in that momentary hope, that illusion that she might be something better. And hate the man who raped her? Of course not! Why would you hate a man for using a toilet?

The interesting thing is that not only did things make more sense to me, but they began to make sense to Lucy as well. From this point on, therapy assumed a radically different tone. Lucy began to ask questions. "I wonder [she mused shortly thereafter] if my father had some idea of what my brother was doing?" (Before this Lucy had responded to all my questions as though she were a schoolgirl being chastised for not having studied for a test. "I'm afraid I don't have an answer for that," she would say in a meek voice.) Now, not only was she asking questions herself, but she was putting things together as well. She remembered, for example, being told later on that it was her brother who had suggested to his parents that they adopt young children.

Lucy was creating a history for herself. And in doing so she was moving out of the paranoid–schizoid position and into the depressive position. Ironically, in recognizing that she had been a victim, she stopped being a victim (an object, without agency). And, enlightened by this newly created history, her self-concept began to change as well. No longer was she a "horrible little girl." Instead, she was a little girl to whom horrible things had been done.

This chapter attempts to elucidate a theory of psychotherapy based on the developmental contributions of British psychoanalyst Donald W. Winnicott. Winnicott (1896–1971) was the first major psychoanalytic theorist to appreciate fully the role of the mother in the psychological development of the child. Both Freud and Klein, for very different reasons,[1] devised essentially intrapsychic theories. Winnicott was the first to move the psychoanalytic dialogue in the direction of an interpersonal theory. This is not to say that Winnicott's was not also an intrapsychic theory or, for that matter, that Freud and Klein were oblivious to environmental influences. But both Freud and Klein paid attention to environmental factors primarily when they were "traumatic." Both considered that there was a "normal" (biologically determined) developmental progression that would unfold in a predictable sequence unless confounded by decidedly abnormal environmental influences (Freud's insistence on the universality of the Oedipus complex is but one example of his focus on the biological rather than the environmental).

D. W. Winnicott and the Mother–Infant Unit

Winnicott's theory is neither intrapsychic nor interpersonal. Rather, it can be seen as a theory focusing on how the child develops out of a purely intrapsychic mode of functioning and into an interpersonal mode. In Kleinian terms, this would be how the child grows out of the paranoid–schizoid position and into the depressive position. Winnicott (1968) framed this process in terms of the child's abandonment of ("destruction of") internal objects in favor of the embracing of external objects. Winnicott stipulated that the role of the mother is crucial in this process. In trying to understand a similar shift during the process of psychotherapy, Winnicott's role of the mother thus may be used as an informing model for the role of the therapist.

Although steering the psychoanalytic dialogue down a significantly different course from those initiated by Freud and Klein, Winnicott never formally rejected the positions of his teachers. Winnicott never denied Klein's assertion that the nascent psyche of the infant is totally instinct driven. He did deemphasize instincts, especially the aggressive instinct, arguing that anger, rage, and aggression need to be understood as reactions to frustration as much as manifestations of instinctual drive. But it is the infant's instinctual awareness of danger, and of being vulnerable to danger, that remains the focal point of Winnicott's (1968) first major axiom: that the infant is immediately (instinctually) aware of utter helplessness and vulnerability, and consequently of his or her total dependency on the mother.

Winnicott (1951) hypothesized that the infant's terror at being helpless and dependent is so great that the infant goes into complete denial at any incipient awareness of separateness between itself and its mother, entering instead into an illusion (delusion) of fusion with the mother. So powerful is this illusion that Ogden (1986) suggests the term "the illusion of invisible oneness" (p. 173). The "oneness" has to be kept invisible to the infant (by denial) because an awareness of oneness implies the possibility of "twoness," and this is intolerable to the infant.

So far this aspect of Winnicott's theory falls in line with the intrapsychic tradition of both Freud and Klein. The fusion, after all, is an illusion that takes place inside the head (within the psyche) of the infant. And it happens to protect the infant from its own internal anxiety that is at least partly instinctually produced.

But Winnicott (1956b, 1971) did not stop there. He went on to make the radical assertion that at this point the infant is joined and supported in the illusion by its mother. The mother joins the infant in the denial of separation. For the mother, as well as for the infant, the birth of the infant (or, at least, the cutting of the umbilical cord) is denied. The infant believes itself to be one with the mother. The mother believes herself to be one with the infant. Winnicott (1956b) stated that in any other circumstance, such an illusion or delusion on the part of the mother would be considered psychotic. In the context of her infant, however, the mother's denial of separateness is considered not only healthy and normal, but essential to the emotional development of the child.

The infant's contribution to the "mother–infant unit" is what Winnicott (1951) called the "illusion of creating the breast."[2] That is to say, "The breast is an extension of myself, there when I need it." The mother's contribution is "the illusion of the needless infant." This is to say, "I am so in touch with (connected to, fused with) my infant that I can anticipate and meet his or her needs before he or she even experiences them as wants."

I witnessed this at a weekend retreat. A young couple came to the retreat with their infant. Suddenly, without any indications that were visible to me, the mother announced that the infant was hungry. The infant was put to breast and, sure enough, sucked with energy. The mother was convinced that she had recognized signs that the infant wanted to be fed long before the infant itself could possibly have felt anything that could reasonably been called "hunger."[3]

The mother–infant unit is a strange, two-headed creature. Its psyche is simultaneously infantile and adult. The satisfaction that the illusion of fusion provides to the mother is essential in offsetting the otherwise exhausting demands of the "primary maternal preoccupation." It also allows her to perform the essential shift in identity from simply "woman" to "mother." For the infant component, the benefits of the mother–infant unit are even more crucial. Winnicott's (1960, p. 39 fn) famous phrase "There is no such thing as an infant" has several levels of meaning. On the most basic level, the infant alone (outside of the mother–infant unit) cannot survive physically. On a psychological level, the infant in the mother–infant unit has more than just an infant's psyche. It also possesses the surrogate ego provided by the mother's adult psyche. And this is crucial.

There are certain things that an infant has a hard time learning alone. A crawling infant can crawl along, bump his head into a wall, learn that it is hard, and, by paying attention to associated sounds, learn that it is called a "wall." But, paradoxically, an infant alone has no way of learning what is going on inside himself. This is where the mother is so important. Through her part of the illusion of the mother–infant unit, she believes that she can read the infant, that she knows (she feels) what the infant is feeling. And through her adult ego contribution to the mother–infant psyche, she so informs the infant.

The infant, on his or her own, knows (biologically and instinctually) about discomfort. But the initial knowledge of discomfort is completely undifferentiated. Discomfort is simply discomfort. The differentiation of feelings is made possible through the contribution of the maternal surrogate ego. It is the mother who says (at first nonverbally, through behavior), "There are different kinds of discomfort. There is a hungry discomfort; there is a dirty diaper discomfort; there is a tired discomfort. And you will learn these differences not, at first, by the words I use, but by the different solutions I provide for them."

The postulation of a parallel between the role of the mother as surrogate ego to the infant and that of the therapist to a client immediately puts us in conflict with one of the basic rules of psychotherapy that we learn as first-year graduate students. That rule is "Never suggest to your clients what they might be feeling. Always ask them what they are feeling." There are good reasons for such a rule. Overly compliant clients will sometimes agree with whatever their therapists suggest, regardless of its accuracy. It also makes sense to urge the client to introspect rather than feeding them possible solutions.

But if we recall Mark from the introduction, we are reminded that there are people who genuinely do not know what they are feeling. Such people are left bewildered by the simple question, "So how does that make you feel?" Psychologists have devised a variety of "feelings charts" for such clients. These are charts that include a score or more drawings of the human face, each with a different facial expression. Below each face is the name of the feeling that goes with the particular expression. But these charts miss the essential point, which is that if one is completely out of touch with one's feelings, a drawing connecting the name of an emotion with a particular facial expression is not going to be of much help.

Winnicott's (1971) contribution to this learning process was his assertion that this kind of learning depends not simply on instruction, but rather on the partial dissolution of boundaries between mother and infant. This is similar to what in other relationships is called "empathy." The word *empathy*, of course, has many definitions, but in general it refers to the capacity to imagine oneself in the skin of another, and to use one's own fantasized feelings to divine and commiserate with the feelings the other.

I rarely ask the teenagers I work with how they feel. If I am with a young gang-banger who is expressing rage at the death of one of his homeboys, I listen sympathetically and then say something like, "I understand and appreciate your anger. But if I were in your shoes I would also be feeling sad." The client can then do with this whatever he wants. If he has any unidentified or unacknowledged sadness, then he can begin to deal with it. If he is unable to relate to anything that feels like sadness, I may invite him to wonder why not. In either case I have suggested to the client neither what he *is* feeling nor what he *should be* feeling. Rather, I have simply offered myself as an alternative ego, to be used or not, as the client chooses.

Interpretations

The intervention I just described is basically a rudimentary interpretation. The term *interpretation* is another of those poorly defined parts of the therapeutic lexicon that includes a broad variety of verbal and nonverbal[4] therapist behaviors. For Freud (1900), an interpretation was basically an intervention designed to bring repressed material into consciousness. In object relations theory, with its focus more on splitting than on repression, interpretations are interventions that make connections. When I interpret to a teenager that he or she might feel sad after the death of a friend, I am making a connection between an event (a loss) and a feeling (sadness or grief). If the child rejects my interpretation, I might want to follow with a second one, pointing out the connection between feelings. Sadness, I might say, is a feeling that many people avoid because it is related to helplessness, a feeling which people who have been abused frequently find unbearable. Anger, on the other hand, is empowering in that it offers the "solution" of revenge ("pay-back"). For this reason many teens leap from sadness to anger before they even allow themselves to "feel" the sadness.

Interpretations are far more powerful than anything implied in simply helping people "get in touch with their feelings." Interpretations make connections, and in doing so act to undo splitting. As an example, referring back to Joe of chapter 3, consider the following hypothetical interpretation: "Joe! Of course you are a bully. I would probably be a bully myself if I were in your shoes. You felt brutalized by your father when you were a child and you couldn't stand it. So you decided that it was better to be the bully than the victim. You may not really like yourself as a bully, but it feels a hell of a lot better than feeling the way you did when you were a victim. So you decided to let somebody else feel those feelings instead of you. It makes sense!"

Nothing in this interpretation is particularly brilliant or radical, but to the extent that Joe would be able to accept it, he would be moving decidedly out of the paranoid–schizoid position and into the depressive position. There are a number of ways in which this might happen.

First, if Joe accepted the interpretation it would imply an acceptance of some sense of historicity. Joe presents himself as, "I'm a bad kid. That's just who I am," as though "A Bad Kid" had been inscribed on his birth certificate along with his name. To the extent that Joe is able to accept the interpretation, he is accepting neither that he was born a bad kid nor that it was foreordained that he should always be so. He acts the bully because of a historical chain of events. It is who he has *become*; it is not necessarily who he *is*.

Part and parcel with a sense of history is a recognition of cause and effect. Joe is not a bully because of the capricious whims of the gods. There are *reasons* why Joe behaves as he does, and the reasons make sense. And this allows for the possibility of change. If the reasons for a behavior pattern change, then the behavior can change as well. Joe is no longer the helpless, victimized child he once was. The behavior that made sense in his childhood no longer does in his present circumstances.

A second ramification of Joe's acceptance of the interpretation would be that he would see his behavior as the result of certain *choices* (either conscious or unconscious) that he has made. Quite simply, he chose to be the bully rather than the victim. The recognition of choice is the recognition of *agency* that is one of the hallmarks of the depressive position. No longer would Joe be able to shrug his shoulders and dismiss his life with "Shit happens!" The recognition and acceptance of one's choices is the acceptance of responsibility. It is also the essence of empowerment. If one had the power to choose in the past, then one has the power to choose differently in the present and in the future. The difference is in the consciousness of the choices.

Joe's acceptance of the interpretation would also imply a movement toward the acceptance of himself as a whole object. Joe's self-definition as a "bad kid" epitomizes the part-object (paranoid–schizoid) position. Joe sees himself as consisting of all badness. Goodness, and all its permutations (kindness, empathy, warmth), resides only in certain others (in Joe's case, only in females of the species). The extent to which Joe is able to reidentify with the victim in himself, while simultaneously acknowledging his bullying, moves him toward an identity as a whole object.

Any movement into the whole-object position would also imply a new capacity for "ruth." While stuck rigidly in the paranoid–schizoid (part-object) position, Joe remained entirely ruthless. The victims of his bullying received no mercy and no compassion, and Joe was convinced that they deserved neither. They deserved to be bullied simply because he defined them as weak. That is the way things are seen in the "perfectly just world" of the paranoid–schizoid position. But as Joe begins to accept himself as a whole object, he is put in the position of seeing others as whole objects as well. When the split is undone in the self-representation part of the object relations unit, it is also weakened in the internalized object-representation component of the ORU. The recognition of wholeness in others makes it much more difficult to be ruthless toward them. One cannot maintain the belief that someone "deserves" to be abused because he or she is weak (bad) if the perceived weakness is acknowledged to be part of a more complex collection of good and bad character traits.

Finally, the acceptance of the wholeness of others is a shift toward the acceptance of the "alterity" of others. In the paranoid–schizoid position one does not relate to real people. One projects onto other people and then one relates to the projection they then unwittingly carry. But in order for the projection to have its desired effect, the carrier must be seen as a part object. It does no good to project one's fears onto another person if one also recognizes elements of courage in that person, for one cannot then despise that person unambivalently for his or her cowardice. If one cannot use another as an object of projection, then one is forced to confront the "otherness" of that other. And when one confronts and accepts the otherness of another person, one has successfully shifted from an intrapsychic mode of being to an interpersonal mode. One has moved from the paranoid–schizoid position into the depressive position.

That such a simple and innocuous interpretation should have the potential for such far-reaching characterological changes may provide some relief for the frustrated and beleaguered therapist. But the discerning reader will no doubt have noticed my caveat, "to the extent to which Joe (the client) is able to accept the interpretation. . . ."

In Winnicott's model the infant is able to utilize the mother as a surrogate ego because of the partial dissolving of the boundaries between them. Without this partial boundary loss the infant is abandoned in its condition of utter helplessness, and the woman who gave birth to the infant never becomes a "mother." In psychotherapy, a similar boundary diminution needs to take place between the client and the therapist. With respect to the client, this is called "transference," and with respect to the therapist it is referred to as "countertransference."

Projective Identification and the Transference–Countertransference Matrix

In transference and countertransference there is a dissolution of boundaries that is similar to (though far lesser than) that of the mother–infant unit. In transference elements of the mother in the original mother–infant relationship are projected onto the person of the therapist, and the therapist is thereby "empowered." Freud's (1910a) "discovery" of transference and, more importantly, his recognition of its importance in the analytic process, are among his greatest contributions. Freud even went so far as to assert that those he deemed incapable of forming a transference (narcissists, for example) were incapable of benefiting from psychoanalytic psychotherapy. Without the transference the analyst is reduced to the role of the pedagogue, and his interpretations become just so many words.

The analyst, of course, never achieves the level of power as a surrogate ego that the mother had in the mother–infant unit. The adult patient's hold on "reality" is much stronger than that of the infant, and the dialectic of fusion and autonomy has a much different balance because of the adult's much more solid sense of "self." Nevertheless, the transference clearly empowers the therapy, making the therapist's words more than just opinions, and giving the therapist's interpretations something of the power of the client's own insights.

Bird (1972) among others, noted the relative paucity of Freud's writings on transference—clearly one of his most important discoveries—and of the uncharacteristic fuzziness of his discourse on the topic. There are times that Freud trumpets transference as one of his greatest discoveries, and others when he seems to forget that it exists. Bird speculates that Freud's discomfort with transference stems from its frequently murderous nature, the same quality that Winnicott (1968) was to claim as essential for successful separation–individuation. In "Beyond the Pleasure Principle" Freud (1920) spelled out a brief history of the use of transference in analysis. "At first the endeavors of the analytic physician were confined to divining the unconscious of which the patient was unaware, effecting a synthesis of its various components and communicating it at the right time. Psychoanalysis was above all an art of interpretation" (p. 18). This approach was frustrated by the discovery of another major psychoanalytic concept: resistance. "In this [second] endeavor the chief emphasis was on the resistances of the patient; the art now lay in unveiling these as soon as possible, in calling the patient's attention to them" (p. 18). After acknowledging the failure of this approach as well, Freud writes of the realization that the transference represents a "repetition" (as opposed to a recollection) of the unconscious material and that, as such, the original neurosis is replaced in analysis by the "transference-neurosis." The transference, therefore, not only potentiates interpretations, it becomes the subject of the interpretations. Freud ends this brief section on transference with the following sentence: "The physician makes it his concern to limit the scope of this transference-neurosis as much as he can, to force into memory as much as possible, and to leave as little as possible to repetition" (p. 19). This is done by interpreting the transference as soon as it is noticed. Thus, although Freud described here the evolution of the role of transference in analytic technique, in another aspect of technique he ends up exactly where he started: the importance of interpretation. Freud never seems to have wavered on this point. The job of the analyst was to interpret.

Freud's (1910b, 1912, 1913) treatment of countertransference was less ambivalent: He saw it as almost entirely negative. Freud gave countertransference a narrow definition. It was, for him, the manifestation of the unresolved (neurotic) material in the therapist stirred up by the unresolved (neurotic) material in the client that was the content of the transference. Since Freud defined countertransference as inherently neurotic, it could only be problematic. It was seen as interfering with the therapist's objectivity and rationality, and it could only get in the way of the treatment.

The current state of the psychoanalytic dialogue has moved considerably from Freud's original position. Countertransference now tends to be defined much more broadly, and tends to include all of the therapist's affective reactions to the transference rather than just the neurotic ones. Winnicott (1947) even went so far as to coin the term "objective countertransference," an idea that would have been an oxymoron under Freud's narrow definition. Objective countertransference is that emotional reaction that any normal person could be expected to have in response to a particular transference manifestation.

There has also been a corresponding shift in the value placed on countertransference. It is of course still appreciated that unconscious or unattended-to countertransference can be destructive to the therapy. However, there is general agreement among both neo-Freudians and object relations theorists that attention to countertransference can inform the therapy. There is much divergence among current theorists on just how much countertransference adds to the therapy. Even some object relations theorists such as Kernberg (1976, 1980) rank countertransference relatively low among the tools of the therapist's trade, while others, such as Ogden (1994, 1997), give it high esteem.

One of the main contributions of current object relations theory is its view of transference and countertransference as particular manifestations of projective identification. This, in turn, allows for an entirely different technical use of the concept of transference: a *working in the transference* rather than simply an interpreting of the transference.

Projective identification, as understood in modern object relations theory, is a defense unlike any in the Freudian lexicon. All the Freudian defenses (and this includes all those listed by Anna Freud [1936] and other ego psychologists) are *intrapsychic*. They exist in, and only in, the mind of the individual. If, for example, someone *projects* onto me some aspect of himself or herself that he or she finds unacceptable, such as aggression, I am likely to have no idea that I am being so used. The person may decide that I am cruel, violent, and dangerous and avoid me or cater to me based on that perception. I, on the other hand, may notice only that he or she is withdrawn and reticent, something I may attribute to shyness. Should I ever find out that I am perceived as a threat, I am likely to be shocked.

Similarly, if someone *identifies* with me, I may or may not notice that the person has interests similar to mine, that he or she dresses much as I do. But I may be completely unaware that I am being purposefully emulated.

Projective identification, on the other hand, is not simply an intrapsychic defense; it is an *interpersonal* defense. It is a psychological defense that involves two people. When I am the recipient of the projective identification of someone's aggression, that person will bother and annoy me until I *feel* angry. It will then take self-awareness and self-control on my part to resist the impulse to actually be aggressive toward that person.

Projective identification is the source of much pathology among adolescents. But, as with transference, it has the potential for healing growth. The difference between projective identification that leads to stagnation and pathology and projective identification that leads to growth and healing lies primarily in the recipient or "container" of the projective identification. When projective identification is in the form of transference, that container is the therapist.

When projective identification (transference) occurs in therapy, the therapist has the ability to "metabolize" the projected feelings. If the feelings are metabolized in a way that makes them more acceptable to the client, the client may then be able to reidentify with them and thus move toward wholeness.

This process sounds more mysterious than it is. On the face of it, the client's (unconscious) statement that "I feel something I don't want to feel so I will make you feel it for me," sounds absurd. But just as I argue in chapter 2, the paranoid–schizoid position (among adolescents) creates feelings are only loosely owned as belonging to self. Rather, feelings are experienced as something that happens to you, much like catching a cold or the flu. Thus in the paranoid–schizoid position it makes perfect sense that someone else should "catch" these feelings instead of you.

The role of the "container" of the projective identification is equally nonmystical. The term *container* is really just a shorthand term, describing primarily the (unconscious) point of view of the projector. It is in the unconscious fantasy of the projector that the recipient is "containing" the very same feelings that the projector has been struggling to avoid. In fact, however, the therapist/container does not "contain" the client's feelings at all. The recipient of projective identification feels his or her *own* feelings, not those of the projector, though feelings that were at least partially provoked (subtly or otherwise) by the behavior of the client. Since the feelings being experienced are those of the "recipient," they are qualitatively different from whatever feelings the projector needs to ward off.

Thus, neither is there anything particularly mysterious about how feelings get "metabolized" in projective identification. I can, in my unconscious fantasy, convince myself that you are "containing" some feelings for me that I am warding off. I can then manipulate you so that you end up feeling something akin to the feelings I am warding off. But the feelings you will have will differ from what I would have (or fantasize having) because you are a different person than I. If I am unfortunate enough to choose as the recipient of my projective identification someone who is less able to tolerate those particular feelings than I am, then I will be confirmed in my conviction that the feelings are unbearable. If, on the other hand, I choose a recipient who is comfortable with those feelings, then I may learn that the feelings are not as dangerous as I had feared, and I might allow myself to actually feel (reidentify with) some of them.

> One of my interns was seeing a severely disturbed, severely drug-addicted male in outpatient therapy. The client had once been a highly successful professional, but his addiction had cost him his career, his family, and his house. Indeed, the only thing between this man and the streets was the good will of a friend who allowed him to sleep on his couch.
>
> At one point the client came in and announced that he anticipated his one remaining friend turning on him and kicking him out of his last refuge. The client was literally sputtering with rage. For twenty to thirty minutes the therapist sat listening to the rage, the client's spittle literally hitting him in the face. When I asked my student what he had felt during this diatribe the answer was, "terrified."

To the question "What was being projected onto the therapist," the most immediate answer is "anger." But this answer is wrong. Anger was being hurled at the therapist, dumped on the therapist, used to clobber the therapist, but was not being projected onto the therapist in the psychological sense of projection. Remember that the first step in projection is the splitting off and denial of feelings that are unacceptable to the projector. This client was perfectly willing to feel and own his anger; indeed he gloried in it (it empowered him). The feeling the client could not bear, which he had to project onto the therapist and then assure (through his rage) that the therapist would feel, was fear. And I am pleased to say that the young therapist bore it beautifully. He sat with it stoically; he put up with the spittle flying in his face, and he allowed the fear to become his own. In doing so he transformed it (metabolized it) in a crucial way. The fear, when it had exclusively been the client's, was perceived by the client as unbearable. The therapist, however unpleasant he found the fear, found it bearable. When the fear shifted from being the client's to being the therapist's, it metabolized from being unbearable fear to being bearable fear. With the fear thus metabolized, the client was finally able to "reidentify" with his own fear. By the end of the session his rage subsided, and the client was able to talk about how terrified he was, as he faced the potential loss of his last safe haven.

In this process it was essential that the therapist contain the projected feeling for a period of time. If the therapist had not been able to do this, if he had said, "Calm down! Get a hold of yourself! Get yourself under control before we can go on," then I think the client would probably have bolted, and the session would never have been completed. As it was, the session was extremely successful. The following week the client returned and reported that he had been able to question his benefactor and learn that his fears had been unfounded: His friend had never intended to ask him to leave. More importantly, the client had taken a step toward wholeness. Rather than simply being a "rageful person," the client had moved toward a more complex emotional repertoire including both anger and fear.

Containment and Nonverbal Interpretations

If the therapist (or mother) is to do her job well, she must be willing to sit with the feelings projected onto her by the client (or infant) for some considerable time. The neophyte therapist is likely to try to get the client to "own" (or, "get in touch with") his or her feelings too soon. To do this, by way of offering a (premature) interpretation, is to say to the client essentially, "Hey, these are your feelings, not mine. You carry them, not me," which the client is likely to interpret as, "So my therapist can't bear these feelings either. They really must be objectively unbearable."

The whole idea of healthy projective identification is that the client projects onto the therapist feelings that the client truly experiences as being unbearable, and which are therefore projected onto someone who, because of an idealized parental transference, is experienced as being capable of "bearing the unbearable." In the case of projective identification, a premature interpretation has the effect of trying to give back to the client feelings that he is (perceives himself as) not yet able to bear. Such an interpretation is thus apt to have the opposite effect from the intended one of "helping the client get in touch with his feelings." Instead, it is likely to push the client into using less healthy defenses and coping mechanisms, to push the client deeper into withdrawal, depression, cutting, or substance abuse.

At this point Ogden's (1994, pp. 107–35) concept of "interpretive action" (interpretations given "by means of actions other than verbal symbolizations") becomes particularly salient. Ogden introduces the concept of interpretive action, places it in its historical (psychoanalytic) context, and presents cogent clinical illustrations. But he strangely omits much discussion of the importance of interpretive action. Yet from the perspective of the therapist's willingness to contain the projective identification for as long as the *client* experiences its necessity, interpretive actions form an essential component of the therapist's intervention repertoire. Let me illustrate with two cases.

Araceli was a sixteen-year-old Latina whom I had been seeing for about six months at the Center. Araceli's father had been in prison for most of her life, and her mother, with a history of considerable substance abuse, had been in and out of her life. Araceli had dealt with these losses as had many of the Center teens in her situation: She had substituted the protection of her family with the aegis of gang membership, and she had replaced the warmth of her mother's arms with the high produced by drugs.

In my office Araceli once described a period in her life when, after having run away from a placement, she had moved in with a "boyfriend" who provided shelter. Araceli readily admitted that she had never had any fondness for this "boyfriend," whom she described in extremely unflattering terms. She talked about this experience as though she were telling an amusing story. She laughed at how "stupid" and "vain" he was, and even joked about how boring sex had been with him.

In the midst of her joking diatribe against this boy, I suddenly found myself squelching the urge to say, "But you opened your legs for him!" Having fortunately recognized the hostility behind this before I blurted it out, I was then able to realize that my anger was a defense against deeper feelings of despair and sadness. I sat silently for a while, listening to her and allowing myself to absorb my feelings. A verbal interpretation, that her humor was a defense against her underlying rage and sadness, might have been appropriate. But before I had a chance to give such an interpretation, she abruptly turned to me and said, "You look so sad!" I nodded a silent acknowledgement. She was ready to hear my interpretation, ready to re-own her feelings, and had read the non-verbal[5] interpretation in my face before I had given it verbally.

A somewhat different scenario occurred just a few days later with another client.

By the age of fifteen Shannon, a sixteen-year-old Anglo girl, had become a chronic runaway and had used virtually every drug on the streets. For a month before her arrest she had been mainlining heroin (to my mind a crucial "point of no return" for drug users) and had already had one serious overdose. What was particularly disturbing to me was that she remembered this overdose with marked nostalgia. It was, she said, like what she knew of the Buddhist concept of "Nirvana": a serene place between life and death, a place of blissful absence of feelings.

My despair for Shannon was tempered somewhat by the extraordinary positive transference she had formed almost instantly for me, and I had some hopes that she might be able to use me to some good end. And, for as much as Shannon hated and ran from feelings, there had been moments in therapy when she had broken down, at times sobbing like a small child. Most encouragingly, I noticed that this chronically isolated loner had begun to open up in group therapy, and to form some real and meaningful relationships with peers.

In one particular session Shannon did everything possible to avoid a real feeling. She described herself as "feeling high" and indeed acted like someone high on marijuana. She flitted from subject to subject and giggled about everything. I was bored, and wondered aloud if she weren't dealing with boredom. "Yes," she agreed without conviction, and giggled about being bored. I got angry (she was wasting my time as well as her own), but as with Araceli, I quickly recognized that my anger was a defense against sadness. Shannon mentioned that her "boyfriend" at the Center was leaving soon, along with another boy whom she had gotten close to. I reminded her that these two losses compounded the earlier recent losses of her two closest girl friends. "Ya, but it doesn't really matter," she said in an unconvincing way. "There is a new girl who just came who is cool."

Shannon appeared completely determined to not hear anything I might say or, more to the point, to feel any of the sadness that was filling the room, but which was resting entirely on my heart. So I determined to sit with, and bear, the sadness myself. I did not make a cartoon of the sadness. I allowed myself to laugh at those of her jokes that were funny, and to smile in appreciation of my fondness for her. But I knew that, as it had with Araceli, sadness covered my face.

Shannon never overtly responded to it. But it was there, unobtrusively, all the time, for her to take or not take as she chose.

Winnicott (1956a) says that it is essential for the newborn that the mother's presence be felt but "not noticed." If the mother's presence is not felt, then the child experiences himself as being alone and abandoned in the world. It is axiomatic in modern object relations theory that the infant would have experienced this as impending annihilation. If, on the other hand, the mother's presence is prematurely "noticed," a similar anxiety arises. The noticing of the *otherness* or *alterity* of the mother again makes the infant unbearably aware of his or her own separateness from this external object, and therefore unbearably aware of his or her vulnerability to the loss of that object. What Winnicott (1951) calls the necessary "illusion of creating the breast" (the illusion that the breast is not separate at all, but rather an extension of the self, that can be called into use much like the infant's own hand or foot) is prematurely shattered. In response to this too-early awareness, the infant will either become addicted to the presence of the newly recognized mother object or (or also) internalize the mother-as-object and become a slave to this omnipotent internalized part object (see chapter 4).

In therapy nonverbal interpretation offers the analog of the behavior of the mother whose presence is felt but not noticed. It allows the client to work with the therapist intimately, without being distracted by the presence of the therapist as an *other*.

> An intern I supervised at a psychodynamically oriented training site worked with a woman in her mid-fifties who devoted all of her free time to nursing her slowly dying, ancient mother. The client was filled with both rage at the life-sapping demands of this task and anxiety at the prospect of a life without her mother.
>
> The intern, dutiful to the implicit constructs of the training institution, tried as much as possible to work "in the transference," in spite of the vehement objections of the client. "I don't want to have to think about my relationship with you," the client would say. "I don't want to have to worry about what something might mean to you or how it might make you feel," in an obvious reference to her fears that she was being pulled into another dependency/slavery relationship of the type she had with her mother. Torn between what she perceived to be the theoretical demands of her training site and the verbalized demands of her client, the intern persisted with what she thought was "good therapy." Six months into treatment, the client called the agency, spoke with genuine warmth about the intern, but nevertheless insisted that she be transferred to another therapist. The client experienced her therapist's insistence on verbal interpretations of the transference as insistence on being "noticed," something she was not yet ready to do.

After considerable reflection I must admit to still having some difficulty in clearly distinguishing between Ogden's concept of interpretive action and his much more elaborately developed concept of "containing" (as opposed to giving back to the client via interpreting) the projective identifications of the client, and "metabolizing" the projections such that the client can re-identify with them at will. Indeed it seems that much of my work at the Center consists of containing the sadness that the tragic lives of these children should have engendered, but that they themselves cannot bear to feel.

> Carla, a cohort of Araceli and Shannon (both presented above), was much more in touch with her own sadness than were either of her two peers. In our first session together, Carla was clearly uncomfortable. A sixteen-year-old, ghetto-raised Latina in the room with an older, white, male doctor was not her idea of an easy match. Carla decided that the best tactic was to entertain me,

and (under the apparent assumption that all older, white, male doctors are basically "dirty old men") she chose to entertain me with the story of how she lost her virginity.

Carla had been walking down the street when a boy she knew stopped her. They talked for a while, he told her that she was pretty, and he asked her if she wanted to go with him. Ghetto-raised girls of this age frequently pair up with boys both out of a need for protection, and out of a desire for social status. But it appeared that Carla agreed to this boy's proposal more because she couldn't think of a reason to say no. "Okay [said the boy], if we are going to be going together then sooner or later we are going to have sex, so we might as well do it now." So they did. "And that's how I lost my virginity," said Carla with a bright smile as though she were telling the punch line to a funny joke.

I stared at her for awhile before coming up with a few words about the utter absence of love in her first "lovemaking." But again, it was the sad expression on my face (as opposed to what she expected to see there, which was a look of prurience) that enabled her to drop her mask-smile and begin to weep gently at the tragedy of her own story.

The Therapist and the "Primary Maternal Preoccupation"

Much has been written in modern object relations theory about projective identification as the psychological or interpersonal mechanism in transference and countertransference. Most has focused (appropriately) on the client as the projector of unacceptable feelings or of rejected components of object relations units (ORUs). The nature of the countertransference in the transference–countertransference relationship has been analyzed in terms of the therapist as the recipient or "container" of the projected material.

Much less attention has been focused on the role of the therapist as projector in the relationship. Most of the writing that does address this topic has been cautionary or critical. Bion (1963) wrote poetically that the therapist must approach each session "without memory or desire." Ogden (1994), in arguing for a partial breakdown of boundaries between client and therapist in the intersubjective relationship (the "analytic third"), nevertheless cautions that the breakdown must not be complete lest the pair fall "into the abyss of autism and psychosis" (p. 4). Even Winnicott (1956b) noted that in any relationship other than the mother–infant unit, the mother's loss of boundaries would be considered a psychosis. One of the most impassioned voices on boundary issues is that of Alice Miller (1981), who, writing about the parent–child relationship rather than the therapist–client relationship, described the damage done to sensitive children by the projections of narcissistic parents.

But in spite of his caveat, Winnicott insisted that the mother's entry into the quasi-psychosis of the mother–infant unit was essential to the well-being and development of the infant. Without the mother's willingness to allow the infant to become the "primary maternal preoccupation," the infant is in danger of becoming (as one woman described it) "that thing that lives in my house" (Ogden 1986, p. 172).

Winnicott's insistence that the mother needs to enter into a relationship that Bion later described as being one of "mutual projective identification" is not entirely at odds with Miller's anguished objections. Winnicott is not oblivious to the dangers of a mother whose own intense neediness overwhelms the needs of the infant. But he insists that for a woman to become a mother she must loosen the boundaries between herself and her infant and be able to feel herself inside her infant's skin. Every time a mother interprets ("interprets" through her behavior as much as through her words) an infant's experience, she is employing some element of projective identification. When she "says" to her infant, "You have been startled and are frightened. Let me comfort you in my arms," she is using projective identification. When she says, "You are hungry; here is the breast," she is doing the same thing. When she says, "You are tired and cranky; let me rub your back until you fall asleep," she is again projecting herself into the skin of her infant in an effort to understand. This is obviously not *pure* projective identification. The mother has external data to rely on as well. But if she relies exclusively on external clues, something essential will be missing from the mother–infant bond.

I believe that almost every time a therapist makes an interpretation, he or she is using some degree of projective identification. I say "almost" because I am actually talking only about good interpretations, "good" not in the sense that they are "correct," but in that they are informed by empathy and emotional sensitivity to the client rather than by some textbook learning. "Bad" interpretations, however accurate, are purely cerebral and are likely to get a response in return only from the intellect of the client.

> Helen, a twenty-two-year-old girl, continued with me privately after graduating from the Center. She had come to the Center at seventeen, severely bulimic, self-loathing, cutting herself, terrified of life, and abusing almost any drug she could get her hands on. Helen worked harder in therapy than any client I have ever had. All sessions were filled with tears, angst, and self-discovery. I once had to interpret to her that her hard work in therapy actually had an element of resistance (continuing self-torture), but her work was also very real and very successful.

At one point in the therapy, when Helen was being courted by the man she would eventually marry, she came to a session and announced that the relationship was off. She had just spent the weekend with her mother, who had convinced her that the young man was wrong for her. Speaking of her decision, Helen was cold and without affect. "Yes, I know he loves me but, oh well! He'll get over it. He will hurt, but life is pain anyway." While recognizing that this coldness and insensitivity was much more characteristic of her mother than of Helen, I nevertheless was shocked to find myself suddenly hating a client whom I normally loved.

Rather than speaking my hatred directly, I acted on the hunch that what I was feeling toward her was a reflection of how she was feeling about herself. "You know," I said to her, "I'm guessing that you hate yourself right now." At these words her eyes filled with tears, and she said, "God, do I hate myself! I can't stand myself when I'm like this." What followed was an extremely productive session on how she tended to lose all sense of herself in the presence of her overbearing mother.

One could argue technically that I was not really "projecting" on to her, but rather simply offering back her own resurgent self-loathing that I was momentarily "containing." But such an understanding ignores the dialectical process inherent in both the healthy mother–infant unit and the successful therapist–client relationship. At the moment the feeling of hatred was mine. When I imagined that Helen might be feeling what I was feeling and offered that to her as an interpretation, I engaged in a form of projective identification.

Projective identification from therapist to client does not have to take the form of a verbal interpretation. It can just as easily be a look or an exclamation.

A seventeen-year-old boy, Tom, described his crime in a boys' group at the Center. Committing an armed robbery at a small grocery/liquor store, wearing a ski mask and carrying a gun, Tom knew the clerk he was robbing and told the group that he actually liked him: The man had been nice to Tom and his friends. When Tom pulled his gun on the clerk, the man refused to give him any money. "I know you," he said, "you aren't going to shoot me." Tom shot him anyway. Tom then reported that the man didn't die. Tom thought he walked with a limp now, but he wasn't sure.

Tom described the incident with a kind of intensity to his voice, but without affect. The group and I listened in silent horror, and I was convinced I could feel a kind of palpable chill descend over the room. Uncharacteristically, I was the one who broke the group's silence. "That's cold!" I said.

To my surprise, Tom did not react to my comment as though he had been slapped. To the contrary, he reacted with a sense of relief, as though he had been heard. "Yes," he said, "it sure was. My mother had just died and I didn't give a shit about myself, so I sure as hell wasn't going to give a shit about anyone else." Tom then went on to work with real feelings about the loss of his mother and the devastation it brought to him.

As director of training at the Center I have worked with a large number of psychology interns, most of whom have been noteworthy for their intelligence, technical sophistication, and dedication to their clients. What separates the successful from the unsuccessful therapists among them is their ability to be in touch with and use their feelings and their willingness to be "decentered" by their clients. The first of these qualities runs counter to much of what makes us become therapists. We become therapists because we want to help people, because we see ourselves as warm, empathic, and nurturing. We are uncomfortable when we find ourselves feeling disgust, contempt, impatience, lust, or other "unworthy" feelings toward our clients.

The second quality runs counter to what we are taught in our first-year psychotherapy classes. There we are taught to "stay centered," to "keep appropriate boundaries," both good pieces of advice unless they become shackles. In successful therapy, two people must move down a path together. If either one of them insists on staying "centered," no movement can take place. If the boundaries of either are too rigid, neither will be touched.

Joan, an intelligent and knowledgeable intern at the Center, had been given an especially difficult case. Her client Sam, a hostile and disrespectful eighteen-year-old, had been convicted of sexual battery. Sam had grown up in a family in which his father had abused Sam physically, and Sam's mother physically and sexually. Like many such boys, Sam had rejected his helplessness in the situation in favor of identification with the aggressor. Although he would occasionally acknowledge loathing his father, most of the time Sam argued vehemently that his father was right in everything he did and said. He dealt with his inability to successfully defend his mother against his father's aggression by adopting the conviction that the abuse "must have been what she wanted," a belief that he carried over to include all women.

The therapy sessions were marked by long diatribes about the need to be "hard," by expressions of contempt for anyone deemed "soft" or caring, and by crude sexual and assaultive remarks toward the therapist. Sam admitted to being somewhat obsessed with Joan, but insisted that his interest was purely sexual. Joan always met Sam's off-putting sexual comments with a "reminder" about appropriate therapeutic boundaries.

In supervision I frequently suggested to Joan that the hostility and crudeness of Sam's sexual advances might in part mask a true desire for intimacy that needed to be defended against because it made him so vulnerable. Joan invariably responded to my suggestions with a shudder of disgust. She admitted that she needed to see Sam as a monster, and that she was much more comfortable dealing with his hostility than with his neediness. To allow herself to feel warmth toward Sam made her feel unacceptably vulnerable. Thus she and Sam were both stuck on "center" (ironically on the same center). All I could do was to wait to see which one of them would tiptoe off center first.

Psychotherapy and the "Creative Destruction of the Mother"

Throughout the complex evolutionary process of his own theory development, Freud never shifted from his bedrock assertion that the fundamental task of therapy was the removal of the repression. This, as I have said earlier, was not so much because insight and self-awareness were inherently good things, but rather because the repression was seen as the pathogenic blockage of normal instinctual discharge. Once the blockage (repression) was removed, healthy psychosexual functioning should follow. Yet to his dismay, Freud (1920) found that removing the repression once was never enough. Rather, it turned out that the repression had to be removed over and over again. This process was what made psychoanalysis take so long. Freud (1914) called it "working through," and he was clearly never truly satisfied with his own ability to explain why working through was necessary, and why it took so long.

Once again, I believe that the contributions of D. W. Winnicott throw invaluable light on the process of working through. Winnicott (1971) claimed that the healthy development of the infant depended on its ability (along with that of its mother) to join into the mother–infant unit. He then claimed that the next step in that healthy development was the months-long or years-long emergence from that unit. Again, as is characteristic of Winnicott, the mother is given a crucial role in that process.

Winnicott (1968) calls this process the "creative destruction" of the internalized mother and the "discovery" of the external mother. This is the process by which the child separates from the mother–infant unit and achieves an autonomy, the hallmark of which is "the ability to be alone." This in turn is made possible by the internalization of the "mother-as-environment," or the ability to "feel the presence of the absent mother."

From the vantage point of the infant, the "mother" component of the mother–infant unit is not the real mother at all (though the role of the real mother is crucial). Rather, the infant deals with an internalized mother representation or, more accurately, a collection of internalized part-object mother representations. The developmental task of this period—what Mahler (1968) called the "separation–individuation" period—is the destruction (renunciation) of these internal part-object mother representations and the eventual embracing of the real, external, whole-object mother. This can be an enormously painful time for all involved. Winnicott (1968) says that it is the duty of the mother to allow her infant to do his or her destructive work (in the process of discovering external reality) but to ensure that she survives (as an external object) this destruction. "Survive," Winnicott notes, means "not retaliate" (p. 91). That is, the mother must be able to tolerate the child's murderous rage at the failings of the various internalized mothers and remain available as a real, external person to give understanding, comfort, and support.

If the task of working through is essentially the same task as that of "the creative destruction of the mother," then it becomes apparent why the task is so arduous, so frustrating, and so long in its resolution. The internalized part objects are not easily given up, the bad ones with even more difficulty than the good ones (see chapter 4). It also sheds important light on Freud's (1910a) observation that a successful therapy depends on the development and resolution not just of a positive transference, but of a negative transference as well.

If only the positive transference is developed, the internalized part-object mother representations are never destroyed. Instead, the part-object "good mother" is simply reinforced, and the corresponding "good-self representation" will blossom (temporarily) in its presence. This is what is disparagingly called a "transference cure," and it typically lasts only as long as the relationship on which it hangs.

> Tanya (mentioned in chapter 6 as the girl who had been molested by every adult male in her life and who had wanted to apologize to one of her molesters for having been such a "nasty little girl") was such a case. When Tanya first came to the Center, her peers immediately disliked and picked on her. She was depressed, self-pitying, and unable or unwilling to defend herself against her more bullying peers. But something about her appealed to the staff. She wore her feelings on her sleeve, which made her childlike, vulnerable, and approachable. Tanya blossomed under the positive regard of the staff. Her self-worth increased, and she learned to stand up for herself against the bullies. She became a leader both in the unit and in group therapy sessions. While never showing deep insight into herself, she was able to provide valuable feedback to other girls in her group.

When it came time for her to graduate to a less restrictive setting, I was amused and touched by her advice to her peers. She encouraged them to open up to their (male) therapist and to me, explaining with some awkwardness, "It's like talking to a gay friend." Her words should have forewarned me. In splitting us off from our sexuality, Tanya kept us safe for her, but preserved us as (internalized) part objects. Two days after transferring to her new placement, Tanya ran away, returning to the streets and to a life of drugs and prostitution. Another girl who ran away with her returned to the placement a few days later. When I spoke with her she said, "Tanya wasn't the same girl when she was on the streets. She wasn't sweet; she was hard and mean."

A more successful course of treatment can be seen with Emma.

Emma, a seventeen-year-old Latina at the Center, almost immediately formed a very positive transference with me, asking me, half seriously, if I could adopt her and she could be my "Mexican daughter." Many tearful sessions followed in which Emma talked about her rejecting parents and the abuse she had witnessed and experienced as a child. Always, I remained the good parent in contrast to her own bad parents.

Then, one day seven months into the therapy, I arrived twenty minutes late for one of the therapy sessions to which I had previously always been prompt. Instantly I was the bad parent. I had (in her new mindset) undoubtedly preferred to spend more time with another girl who was almost certainly white; I knew how much Emma cared for me, and I cynically and callously took advantage of this, knowing that she would forgive me; I understood the passivity in her character, which I again took advantage of. She and I were reenacting the entire rejecting-parent–worthless-child ORU, with me being cast in the role of the rejecting parent.

I neither disputed her allegations nor even offered an explanation for my lateness. Rather, I sat quietly and listened as intensely and as empathically as I could to her pain.

In doing this I was trying to follow Winnicott's model of the good-enough mother, allowing myself (the internalized bad part-object representation of myself/the mother) to be killed (as indeed it deserved to be), while I (the real, external, whole-object I) remained to care for her (through my demonstrated empathy). The bad object is by definition a part object and as such cannot possess incompatible good and bad qualities. When Emma experienced her purported bad object (me) behaving in a way antithetical to bad objects (that is, neither defensively justifying my failure nor defensively counterattacking, but instead listening with care and empathy), she was forced to renounce the split. I stopped being merely the container for her (good or bad) internalized part-object projections and took a step toward being a whole, external object. In this sense the session represented a step toward her liberation from the tyranny of the internalized object relations units. When, at the very end of the session, I finally explained that my lateness had been caused by my being called to a medical emergency, I was no longer speaking to the transference, but rather to what Greenson (1971) and others have called the "real relationship."

Winnicott's concept of the creative destruction of the internalized mother adds enormously to our understanding of negative transference. Not only does negative transference represent the working through of ancient, unresolved traumas, but it can also be seen in Winnicott's terms as the client's attempts to find liberation from the tyranny of internal object relationships and in the discovery of the external world.

The difference here between Emma and Tanya is that Tanya never stopped seeing me as the good breast. The good breast is the source of everything wonderful, and, rather than something to be killed, it is something to be protected at all cost. Tanya protected me as the good breast at the cost of staying in a phantasy[6] world, and the "progress" she made at the Center thus never left the realm of her phantasy life. Emma, on the other hand, allowed me to become the bad breast and proceeded to try and murder me. While allowing myself to be killed (as a part object) I simultaneously insisted on remaining alive (empathically involved) as a whole object. Ironically, in killing the bad breast, one simultaneously kills off the good breast because the split creates both dialectically. The bad breast, it should be remembered, is not that different from the good breast. The bad breast is bad not because it is undesirable. All breasts, good and bad, are infinitely desirable as they represent the source of all happiness in the world. The bad breast is bad in that it is seen as sadistically and maliciously withholding its bounty (as I was seen as cruelly withholding by my lateness). To the extent that Emma made progress in that one session in undoing the split, she was able to gain an integrated sense of identity as a whole, complex person rather than having to jump back and forth between grandiosity and self-loathing. She was also, to the same extent, able to make progress in relating to people as whole, real, external people rather than as mere carriers of her internalized object projections.

Psychotherapy and "Potential Space"

To me, one of the most exciting yet maddeningly elusive of Winnicott's concepts is his concept of "potential space" (Winnicott 1971). In understanding this concept I will gladly follow Ogden's lead and not even pretend to suggest what Winnicott is "really" saying. Instead, I will present my understanding of what Winnicott might mean or, more accurately, my understanding of what Winnicott might mean as influenced by Ogden's understanding of what Winnicott might mean, by "potential space."

My understanding (henceforth, this phrase will remain implicit) is that potential space is not a different concept from what I have discussed before, but rather a different metaphor, one that, as Winnicott seems to have intended, stimulates us to think of familiar ideas in new ways. Potential space starts out as the potential space that can exist between infant and mother. As I have already argued, acknowledging even a potential for such space is intolerable to the infant. The "illusion of invisible oneness" does not tolerate even the notion of possible twoness, let alone the notion of a space between the two.

Gradually, however, as the neonate becomes observer, smiler, interacter, and eventually crawler and toddler, twoness (myself and mother, myself and other) becomes not just potential, but reality. Winnicott (1971) says that this can happen, however, only as long as the "space" between the two gets filled with something. The infant appears to regard potential space in much the way an adult would view outer space: as a frigid void, intolerant not just of life, but of existence. The only way that the space (void) between mother and infant can be tolerated is if it is filled with something—that is to say, if the space (void) is always kept potential. Winnicott says that the first thing the infant uses to fill potential space is play. As the toddler grows into an adult, play is augmented by other things (culture, creativity, and spirituality), but the space must always remain potential: It must always be filled. Otherwise, the void, the abyss, always looms. The unbearable existential angst, Winnicott is saying, is not death per se, it is separation.

The child first fills potential space with play (play in the sense of creativity, of fantasy). Other things will follow to fill potential space as the child develops, but all, in some sense, retain an element of play. Winnicott (1971) says that therapy happens "in the overlap between two play areas, that of the patient and that of the therapist" (p. 54). He then goes on to add, "If the therapist cannot play, then he is not suited to the work. If the patient cannot play, then something needs to be done to enable the patient to become able to play, after which psychotherapy may begin" (p. 54). The client's ability to play in therapy refers essentially to the ability to have a "what if" experience. The client must be able to play with the ideas "What if you were really my father, my mother? What if I were to try and seduce you, stop paying you, go silent, stop coming?" This must be real play rather than just an intellectual exercise. That is to say, the client must be able to enter deeply enough into the fantasies that the affective component becomes real and palpable.

If the client cannot play, the issues will be expressed not as a fantasy dialogue in the therapy, but as concrete behavior. The client will attempt to seduce, will stop paying, will stop coming. This is one of the differences between working with neurotic clients and working with borderlines and psychotics. Neurotics will wish that you were their mother. Borderlines will become enraged when you "refuse" to become their mother.

The therapist must be able to enter into the play of the client and play with the ideas as well. The intern Joan whom I mentioned earlier in this chapter could not do so, at least where the fantasies had to do with sex and intimacy. Every time her client brought in a sexual fantasy, Joan coldly reminded him of the boundaries of the relationship. She would thus bring any work on sexuality and intimacy to an abrupt halt as soon as he brought it into the room. I am not saying here that an exploration of sexual fantasies should ever be done "playfully" (in the common sense of the term) or flirtatiously. But in prematurely shutting down the client's expressions of sexual desire, Joan was never able to explore them with her client to see what lay beneath them. (Anger? Loneliness? Love? Some combination of these?)

Winnicott says, at various times, that potential space is the space between infant and mother, between fantasy and reality, between symbol and symbolized. We may well ask what all these things have in common that they should be referred to by the same term. I have found it helpful to visualize potential space as the potential space that may or may not exist between the two wings of a hinge. The two wings may be labeled "mother and infant," "fantasy and reality," or "symbol and symbolized." What they have in common is the pivot pin around which they open or close. That pivot pin is the sense of self-as-agent, the experience of "I-ness" that distinguishes the depressive position from the paranoid–schizoid position (see chapter 2). It is I-the-active-observer who distinguishes between self and other. It is I-the-creator who creates a symbol to stand for what is symbolized. It is I-the-thinker who creates and uses a fantasy while at the same time distinguishing it from reality.

When the experience of I-as-agent is lost, potential space collapses into itself like the wings of a hinge slamming shut. This can happen in a number of ways. Fantasy can collapse into reality, or reality can collapse into fantasy. Symbol can collapse into symbolized, or symbolized can collapse into symbol. In any case, the sense of I-as-agent is gone, replaced (at best) by me-as-object. All of these different ways of collapsing potential space can be seen readily among the adolescents at the Center.

Raquel, a seventeen-year-old at the Center, eagerly collapsed reality into fantasy. Nearing the end of her stay, she announced that her plan was to go home and live with her mother and that everything would be "fine" between them. Her mother, a chronic drug abuser, had spent most of Raquel's life in and out of jail. When the two of them were together, they fought sadistically. But Raquel could not be persuaded to consider any potential problems with her plan. Everything would be fine and that was that. Raquel experienced no sense of I-as-agent (I-as-problem-solver), but that was okay with her because she felt no need for agency. Her mother would love and take care of her in a way she never had before, and Raquel would be fine.

Juan, a sixteen-year-old at the Center, characterologically collapsed fantasy into reality. Although he had done well at the Center and had never gotten into any significant trouble there, he announced matter-of-factly that upon release he would go back to hanging out with his homeboys on the street corner and would probably soon be back in jail. Why? Because "that's what you do" when you are outside of an institution. The world is what it is, and the most you can hope to do is adjust to it. Again, no sense of agency, no sense of I-as-the-master-of-my-fate, was even considered.

A therapist I supervise, Dr. C., presented to me a case of a middle-aged client who had emphatically collapsed symbolized into symbol. In their first session he announced determinedly that what he wanted from her (and from therapy) was advice on how to get a woman to have sex with him. "You are a young woman. You know what women want in a man. Tell me what I have to do to get laid." Dr. C. spent some time asking questions trying to find out if there was anything else, any other issue that he might want to work on in therapy. To all of her questions she got the same answer, "No, I just want to get laid. Tell me how I can get laid." Finally, Dr. C. asked the client what sex meant to him. "Oh," he said, "it means everything. It means acceptance of my manhood. It means love. It means escape from my loneliness." Dr. C. heaved a sigh of relief and suggested that they discuss some of these issues. "No," he shouted at her, "that's not what I'm here for. Just tell me how to get laid." Potential space had opened briefly and then slammed shut. Symbolized (love, acceptance, manhood) had collapsed back into symbol (getting laid).

The collapsing of symbol into symbolized leads to a kind of distressing concreteness in which there is no ability to deal with image, sign, or metaphor. Such a client was Mark (discussed in the introduction), who, while at the Center, we thought likely to be brain damaged. When Mark spoke of his thoughts of becoming a bricklayer, the entire group was struck by the aptness of this as a metaphor for the dullness (laying brick after brick after brick) of his life and of his mind. Yet it was not until years later, when Mark returned to the Center, that he himself was capable of using metaphor. It was not until then that he had acquired a sufficient sense of agency to be able to create and use symbols.

The collapsing of potential space, whatever its form, produces what behavioral psychologists now commonly refer to as "cognitive distortions." These include, among others, concreteness, poor reality testing, inability to use metaphor, and inability to fantasize. What Winnicott and object relations theory suggest is that these cognitive distortions are simply symptoms of what might better be called a disorder of self: a regression to an experience of self-as-object (me-ness) from a more mature sense of self-as-subject (I-ness). This regression, furthermore, is caused by anxiety relating to separation and loss (the earliest potential space, after all, is the space between infant and mother).

Object relations therapy would have us look at the underlying issues rather than the cognitive distortion that may be symptoms of those issues. The middle-aged man who just wanted sex did return for more therapy and was able to do some meaningful work. And the issues he ended up working on were those he presented in the initial session when he had allowed for a brief, momentary opening of potential space: acceptance, loneliness, and love, issues essentially having to do with his profound sense of existential isolation.

Winnicott and Kalsched

Writing from a Jungian perspective, but paying considerable homage to Winnicott, Donald Kalsched (1996) offers ideas that may considerably expand traditional object relations theories. Kalsched has worked extensively with the victims of both acute and cumulative trauma. He describes in these survivors the presence of what he calls a "demonic" internal voice or figure who appears primarily in dreams, but also in waking thought and reverie. This demonic figure represents the personification (objectification) of the trauma itself, and of the psyche's response to the trauma.

This figure can be highly sadistic and has the effect of frequently retraumatizing the subject, but its function is not entirely malevolent. Much like Winnicott's (1960, 1986a) False Self, the demonic objectification of trauma has the role of protecting the subject as well. It is a voice that (by making the subject reexperience the trauma) reminds the subject that trauma is always a possibility and that eternal vigilance is necessary. It is like a voice that says, "I (trauma) am always lurking, always ready to devastate you again, without warning. Never let your guard down!" As one would expect, this demonic voice becomes most strident, and most sadistic, at times when the subject is beginning to consider the possibility of feeling hope (as, for example, in a successful psychotherapy). Hope is the one feeling the demonic presence cannot allow the subject to experience since hope may lead to the lowering of one's guard.

Winnicott's False Self, a similarly malevolent process, also serves to protect the subject from further trauma. But there appear to be significant differences between Winnicott's False Self and Kalsched's demonic presence. False Self functioning seems to be a much more passive, quiet process, involving denial and repression. In False Self functioning aspects of the self (needs, desires, feelings, differences from others) that are in danger of being annihilated by being rejected by a critical other are split off, denied, and repressed. If my need for love, for example, places me at risk of devastation in the face of unloving parents, I can protect that need from annihilation and myself from devastation by burying that need in a place so deep that I am no longer aware of its existence. Of course I pay a terrible price for this kind of protection. In denying my need for love I become a kind of unfeeling machine, seeing life in various shades of gray. But I do not experience the devastation of having what I feel to be an essential need go unmet.

Kalsched's demonic presence is a similarly sinister process that has an ultimately protective function. But the mechanism of the demonic presence is in some ways the opposite of that of the False Self. Instead of denial and repression, the demonic presence involves a constant reminder, a constant re-experiencing, a constant *forcing back into consciousness* of material that the subject wishes desperately to forget. It is as if the victim of trauma no longer has the luxury of repression. The demonic voice says, "Oh no, you can't forget about this. This is too important. The danger is too clear and present. You have to be constantly vigilant."

In most of Kalsched's examples the demonic presence manifests itself as a figure in a dream. This may be a part of the explanation for the clinical observation that depressed people frequently report that their depression is worse in the mornings. Free from the counterbalancing influences of a relatively benevolent reality and of the healing power of rational thought, the demon of trauma wreaks havoc during sleep. Victims of trauma essentially wake up in a more regressed state than they were when they went to sleep.

But the demonic presence is not limited to dream states. Sometimes we speak its words in our own voices.

Lucy (presented earlier), after being date-raped, sat in a darkened room for a week hating herself. She must have been verbalizing the mocking words of the demon personification of her earlier traumas. "How can I have been such a fool? How can I have believed for a second that someone would treat me with love, with caring, with respect? How can I have let myself believe that I am anything more than something for men to use and then discard? How can I have allowed myself to hope? How can I have been such an ass?"

But however cruel and sadistic the words of this punishing demon, the protective function they serve is also clear. Lucy did not soon allow herself to again be so vulnerable.

There are other times in which the function of the demonic presence is taken over by an existing internalized object representation. Lucy again provides a good example of this.

Lucy, as the reader will remember, grew up with a hypercritical, verbally abusive mother whose message to Lucy was always, "If you were only perfect, then I could love you." Along with this cumulative trauma, a second trauma occurred, beginning around age three, with the horrific sexual abuse by her adult brother. Lucy dealt with this second trauma by means of classic repression, and the memory of that nightmare was not recovered until years into therapy.

This left Lucy as a latency-aged child to deal with the one ongoing trauma of which she allowed herself to be conscious, the verbal abuse by her mother. She dealt with this in part by the persistent fantasy that her loving but spineless father would finally stand up to his wife and come to her defense. When she was ten or eleven he came to her instead to begin a years-long incestuous sexual relationship. This was the third and most devastating trauma of Lucy's childhood.

The intensity and duration of this third trauma ruled out repression as a coping mechanism. Instead, the internal demon was created, and rather than adopting a separate identity for itself, it simply took over the already existing spot conveniently created for it in the person of the critical mother.

This, then, is one of the great paradoxes of which the human psyche is so wonderfully capable. In the original childhood fantasy, the father was seen as the potential rescuer from the critical mother. Following the father's ultimate betrayal, the critical mother took on the role of the persecutory–protective demon, to guard against further traumas by men like Dad.

Lucy's newly fused critical mother–demonic presence performed its job with remarkable tenacity. As I mention at the beginning of this chapter, I have never known anyone as determinedly self-hating as Lucy. Still, the mother demon did its work well and, with the exception of the date rape in college, Lucy had never been exploited by another man (at the price, of course, of horrible loneliness, early bouts of drinking and drug taking, severe bulimia, and episodic suicidality).

Five years of intensive psychotherapy proved remarkably effective as a "corrective emotional experience." Lucy developed insight, and with it came compassion for herself. And, not incidentally, the quiet, distant (transference) father figure spoke forcefully and lovingly against the verbal abuse by the (internalized) critical mother.

Then, in the fifth year of therapy, another paradox suddenly emerged. Having had its ability to torture greatly reduced, Lucy's internalized critical mother–demon presence simultaneously had its ability to protect her significantly diminished. I (in the transference) had helped Lucy defeat the critical mother, and yet I (in the transference) was the one against whom the critical mother had represented the strongest bastion against retraumatization.

Lucy's new solution to this dilemma was concrete but eloquent. She suddenly announced that she could no longer stand living in the condominium she had owned for years and was putting it on the market. She also announced that she was sure that she could not afford any other place in Los Angeles County, and that she was planning on moving out of state to a city she could afford. Deaf to all my efforts to dissuade her, she did just that.

To my surprise and deep pleasure, Lucy's solution worked amazingly well. She is happier and more successful than I ever would have predicted. She still keeps in touch with me via e-mail, and, at a safe distance of many hundreds of miles, I am able to continue to offer her a modicum of support.

Kalsched's indirect contribution to object relations theory is twofold. First, he provided (as I hope my examples indicate) new insights and understanding of the puzzling phenomenon that I address in chapter 4 as "addiction to the bad object." Klein saw the splitting of an object into good and bad part objects as a way of protecting both the goodness and the badness of the object by separating them from each other and from mutual contamination. Kalsched takes us a step further in demonstrating how a bad part object can become the active guardian and protector of the self.

Second, from a theoretical perspective, Kalsched expands our understanding of the basic concept of the "internalized object." Kalsched's demonic presence is not, strictly speaking, an "internalized object representation." There is simply no real external object that has been split and internalized. The demonic presence is the internal representation of an event (trauma) that has been personified (objectified) rather than of an object. Although the objectified demonic presence is certainly a split object (purely evil, allowing no experience of ambivalence), it is not strictly speaking part of an ORU, since it is the internalization of an event rather than a relationship. The demonic presence exists in relationship not to a corresponding "self-representation," but rather to the whole self, much as Freud's superego existed in relationship to the whole ego.

Kalsched was not the first to suggest that internal objects do not necessarily correspond directly to split versions of external objects. Bion (1956, 1957) argued that projective identification could be an intrapsychic as well as an interpersonal phenomenon. The implication seems to be that what

Kernberg (1976) would later call "object relations units" (ORUs) exist as much as convenient structural or organizational receptacles of internal thoughts, feelings, and impulses as they do as mirrors, however distorted, of real external relationships. But because Bion tended to take his examples primarily from his work with schizophrenics and psychotics, the general applicability of his observations has not, I believe, been properly appreciated.

Kalsched greatly expands our understanding of internal objects in presenting one that is entirely the creation of the psyche (albeit in response to an external event) rather than the "internalization" of an object that in reality is external. And the "traumas" that give rise to such creations of the psyche can range from as severe as those suffered by Lucy to the everyday traumas of neglect and oversight that Winnicott (1960) cites as leading to the development of the False Self.

Notes

1. For a brilliant and audacious interpretation of Freud's need to absolve the mother from any involvement in the psychological matrix of the child read Stolorow and Atwood's *Faces in a Cloud* (1979). These authors argue that reaction formation to Freud's unconscious rage and sense of abandonment by his own mother caused Freud to create a theory absolving the mother of all blame. For Klein it was not her mother whom she needed to exonerate, but herself for the tragic emotional plight of her own children.

2. Ogden (1986) objects that the term "creating the breast" does not do justice to the infant's need to keep this process invisible. The breast cannot be experienced as a breast (that is, as a separate object), nor (for the same reason) can there be the experience of an "I" who "creates." Instead, self, mother, and breast must all blend together in a seamless, homogenized, undifferentiated field.

3. A female student, after hearing this story, volunteered that the mother was probably "leaking." However, even if this were true, the mother's attention to her own body as an indication of what might be happening in her infant's body would tend to support Winnicott's position.

4. Cf. Ogden (1994), chapter 7.

5. Ogden (1994) prefers the term *interpretive action* to *nonverbal interpretation* because the former is more inclusive. He makes it clear, however, that interpretive action includes "facial expression(s)" (p. 108).

6. I use the word *phantasy* in Melanie Klein's sense of representing a deep psychological structure.

CHAPTER EIGHT

~

Group Therapy

In a cottage at the Center two unlikely boys had formed a close friendship. Both were gang bangers, but one, Thomas, was African American, and the other, Carlos, was Latino. Carlos was a gang leader and Thomas was clearly a follower. Thomas was working in group and being confronted by Carlos on his tendency to yield to passing impulses. Thomas, resistant and whiney, made it clear that he didn't want to hear what Carlos had to say. Carlos, at that point, sat up to his full height, leaned forward, and said, "I am your friend, and because I am your friend I will say what you need to hear whether you want to hear it or not." At this point there was a collective gasp from the group and Thomas's jaw dropped open with surprise and with pleasure. He had never experienced that kind of friendship before.

Now consider Carlos's sentence and imagine crossing out the word *friend* and substituting any of a number of other words, including *parent*, *probation officer*, even *therapist*. We can anticipate that Thomas's reaction would be very different. The most likely picture is one of a teenage boy, head down, staring at the floor, sulking and trying his best to tune out the incoming criticism. This is one of the main reasons that group therapy is the "treatment of choice" for adolescents.

One of the long-recognized tasks of adolescence is the separation from family and the replacement of family bonds with peer attachments. Many well-meaning caregivers frequently fail to appreciate this. I heard a judge admonishing a teenager in his courtroom. The judge was taking this part of his job very seriously and did his best to sound like an Old Testament prophet.

"You need to let go of those gangster friends of yours! None of them is here for you now [ignoring the fact that they wouldn't have been allowed in the courtroom if they had shown up]. Your parents are here for you [for the moment, an indisputable fact]. You need to stick with them!" But in saying this, the judge was essentially telling him not to complete his developmental task. The real problem was not that the boy forsook his parents for his friends, but rather that his choice of friends was ill-advised.

I also hear the same thing from many of the adolescents themselves. When many of them face going home from the Center, I hear them reassuring the staff that they will not return to their old gang or drug-using friends. When asked who will replace these friends the kids will say instantly, "my mother" or "my family." My heart sinks when I hear this. First of all I know that it will not work. But more important, if it were to work, it would be a tragic fixation, a failure to move forward into adulthood.

Healthy peer relationships are essential for a healthy passage through adolescence. The bonds formed among teenagers are a necessary part of development, as is the diminution of the bonds between teenager and family. It follows that teens will be able to "hear" things from peers more readily than they might from adults.

Examples of this pattern abound.

Caitlin was not a typical Center girl. Caucasian and middle-class, she was neither gang affiliated nor seriously drug addicted. Although she had experienced significant trauma in her young life, she exhibited much less psychopathology than most of her peers. She was, in plain English, a spoiled brat (a lovable brat, to be sure, but still a brat). She was used to ruling the roost at home by her dramatic temper tantrums.

When these tantrums did not have the same effect at the Center, rather than giving them up, she simply escalated. Staff would then have to be called in to restrain and seclude her. And she, while not successful in achieving her original goals, would nevertheless still triumph through the punishment she inflicted by means of the chaos she created.

This behavior continued unabated until her peers confronted her in group. Every time she created a disturbance, they had to go down to their rooms so that the staff could deal with the situation undistracted. They were sick of it and they let her know. Caitlin, pleased by the displeasure she evoked in adults, was far less pleased that she was creating displeasure in her peers. Her temper tantrums ceased.

Daphne, one of Caitlin's "cottage sisters," was an extremely beautiful, very bright, articulate seventeen-year-old, who ruled her cottage through a combination of the status afforded by her beauty and the intimidation that resulted from her cutting wit. Aware of her power (she called herself, only partially in jest, "Queen Daphne"), she was in denial about its aggressive origins. Daphne began group one day by announcing that her therapist, Ms. C., had confronted her about intimidating her peers. Daphne, brimming with scorn and derision at such a notion, insisted that, in Ms. C.'s presence, the girls one by one certify the absurdity of the allegation. The round robin indeed followed, but instead of giving Daphne what she wanted, all nine of her peers swallowed hard and said that they were indeed intimidated, and said why. It was a transformational moment in Daphne's program at the Center. Accepting the feedback of her peers in a way that she was not able to from her adult therapist, Daphne saw, and was subsequently able to modify, her capacity for cruelty.

This example raises a couple of important issues. The first is that the therapist and group leader, Ms. C., was strong and much loved by her clients. It is unlikely that Daphne's peers would have had the courage to gainsay her if Ms. C. had not been who she was. This is a way in which a well-run group parallels the bridge between family and peer society that adolescents are trying to navigate. For the shift in alliance from family to peer group should never be precipitous and arguably should never quite be complete.

In a functional family, the role of the parents of an adolescent is to gradually become more and more invisible, but never to disappear. The parents of an adolescent maintain their fundamental parental function, which is to ensure the safety of their children. The trick is to do this in a way that is as unobtrusive as possible, and in a way that must enhance rather than diminish the growing power and autonomy of the child.

The same is true for the leader of the therapy group. One of the primary functions of the group leader is to maintain the safety of the group. This is not done by seeking to avoid conflict or expressions of anger or hostility. To the contrary, as Yalom (1995) points out, groups do not achieve a true feeling of security until after the successful resolution of conflict. The job of the group leader is to assure that subtle undercurrents of anger, hostility, or (as with Daphne) intimidation are brought to the table where they can be processed and dealt with.

On rare occasions a face-off occurs between a group leader and a particularly powerful subversive group member. The group leader should use all his or her technical skills to avoid such a confrontation, but if such an event occurs, the group leader (like the parent) must stand ground. In Daphne's group it was the group's knowledge that Ms. C. would stand firm in this way that gave the group members the extra modicum of courage to speak their truths.

Daphne's group also illustrates the issue of identity formation. Identity formation, or character formation, has long been considered one of the primary "tasks" of adolescence. The terms *identity* and *character* probably have as many definitions as writers on the subject, and I see no need to further muddy the water by adding one more here. Fenichel's definition of character as "the habitual mode of reaction of the ego toward the id and the outer world" (1945, p. 149) is as good as any. But I would like to focus briefly on the word *formation*. "Formation" implies an active, synthetic process. Blos describes it as "the outcome of psychic restructuring" (1968, p. 246). It is certainly this, involving at the very least a dramatic shift in the balance of the part-object–whole-object dialectic. But at the same time, Blos writes of "the silent emergence of character." This leads to some confusion: Is character formed (created), or does it emerge (is discovered)?

I believe that the answer is both. Complete character formation depends on a significant shift in balance in the dialectic harmonic between the part-object position and the whole-object position (chapter 3). Until relative stability is reached in the whole-object position, parts of the self remain split off and denied, and there is no experience of self-as-agent. To be sure, there can be a very marked "character traits" in the part-object position, as Joe (chapter 3) illustrates. But Joe, with his unidimensional self-definition and his me-but-not-me split-off selves, epitomizes a "character disorder" rather than a fully developed character structure.

There is also an element of character (or identity) that is as much discovered as formed. In proposing the concept of the "True Self," Winnicott (1960) suggested that a unique aggregate of characteristics defines each individual as distinct from anyone else. Characteristically, Winnicott declined to specify or delineate these characteristics for fear of unnecessarily circumscribing them. Essentially, they range from near-universal needs such as the need for attachment, and near-universal feelings such as fear in the face of danger, to small idiosyncrasies such as a preference for chocolate over vanilla ice cream.

The emergence of True Self functioning often requires an active and arduous process of self-discovery.

A young therapist I supervise presented the following case. The client was in federal prison and was seen by his therapist after requesting individual therapy. When asked why he had requested therapy he responded, "I don't know." The therapist was sensitive enough to recognize this as a simple statement of fact rather than some defensive maneuver. In the course of their work together it emerged that this man had been raised essentially as an animal, forbidden to enter the house except to eat and sleep. It turned out that his mother saw to this, not out of her own sadism, but as a way of protecting him from his father's cruelty. The father seems to have taken considerable delight in his own sadism and found any excuse to indulge it, including the old proscription that "children should speak only when spoken to." The client remembered coming into the house one day and asking for a glass of water. He was then knocked across the room by a blow to the face, with his father sneering, "Did I ask if you were thirsty?"

When this client would sit in the waiting room for his therapy appointment he would sit staring at the floor and refuse to respond in any way to anyone who might say hello when passing by. He was able to explain later that he was terrified that he would say the wrong thing and make a fool of himself. Staff reported to the therapist that they could tell that the client was beginning to get better when he actually began to make eye contact in the waiting room. A high point in therapy came when his therapist brought in an assortment of cookies so that he could learn which kind he liked best. She reported that he had tears in his eyes at the realization that he actually had a favorite kind of cookie (peanut butter).

Many aspects of the True Self (preference for flavors, greater comfort with a stimulating or soothing environment, love or hatred of Wagner) can be discovered alone through reflection and introspection. But ironically, the majority of the True Self must be discovered not by looking inward, but rather by looking outward at "mirrors." As we cannot really know what we look like physically without looking into a silvered glass or a polished piece of metal, so too are there aspects of our selves that we can discover only by observing the reactions others have to us.

The concept of "mirroring," or of "mirroring objects," is most commonly identified with Heinz Kohut (1971, 1977, 1978, 1984) and self psychology. But it is equally central to the work of D. W. Winnicott and object relations theory. In discussing the infant–mother relationship, Winnicott (1967) asks, "What does the baby see when he or she looks at the mother's face? I am suggesting that, ordinarily, what the baby sees is himself or herself. In other words, the mother is looking at the baby and what she looks like is related to what she sees there" (p. 112). If the baby, happily and warmly nursing at the breast, looks into its mother's eyes and sees adoration, it learns something invaluable there: It learns its own self-worth. And, Winnicott asserts, this cannot be learned any other way.

This brings us back (at long last) to the importance of groups for adolescents, because if mirroring objects are necessary for the discovery of the True Self, then groups provide a veritable "house of mirrors." The house of mirrors metaphor brings up an important issue, for all mirrors, no matter how good, distort at least a little. Some distort grotesquely.

> Rebecca was the victim of the "narcissistic love" of her father. Rebecca's father, a severe narcissist, conceived the idea of his only daughter as a perfect little girl who "adored her daddy." He was sufficiently well read that he was aware of Freud's ideas about the Oedipus complex, and his boundaries were sufficiently poor that he was tickled by this idea too. So when he looked down at her, he loved what he saw there, and he was demonstrative in his love.
>
> The problem was that what he saw in his daughter had very little to do with who she really was. What he loved in his daughter was a figment of his own fantasy world. And Rebecca grew up with as little sense of self as any nonpsychotic person I have known. Being in the room with Rebecca was a disconcerting experience: There was no experience of being with a real person. Everything she said, even casual conversation, was like listening to a bad actress reading from a script that she was barely familiar with.

In group therapy, the sheer number of mirrors can compensate for the distortions provided by a single mirror. Both Caitlin and Daphne were affected by the group's unanimity. Nine peers said to Daphne, "You intimidate us." Nine peers said to Caitlin, "You are childish and we are tired of your antics."

But as powerful as unanimity can be for positive change in a group, it can be equally powerful as a destructive force, especially in a leaderless or effectively leaderless group. Without effective leadership, a group can easily turn into a mob. This was beautifully illustrated in a scene from the television miniseries *The Singing Detective*.

> In the scene, the hero recounts that, as a child, he had accused a classmate of a horrible crime. As the hero had been a popular child, one by one his classmates rose and spoke in witness. They too had seen the accused commit this crime. Finally, overwhelmed by the evidence against him, the accused child rose and confessed. He had done the vile deed, and he was deeply mortified. But of course the accused child hadn't committed the crime. It was the hero himself who had done it: In the single act of rebellion of his whole childhood, the hero had deposited his own turd on a hated teacher's desk.

Lest the examples above mislead, the "lessons" learned in group do not have to be negative nor the voice of the group unanimous. Sometimes a single mirror shines back at us with such intensity that we know a profound truth is being reflected in spite of whatever distortions are present.

> Ana, a seventeen-year-old Latina, was working in group on her desire to give up drugs. Of course, she added, it wasn't really *her* desire. She wanted to do it

for her mother because she was tired of causing her mother so much pain. If it were simply up to her, she would gladly return to drugs. Somehow, she acknowledged, she just couldn't bring herself to care about herself. She loved her mother, but couldn't manage to care at all about herself.

Ana went on like this for some time, always with bland affect. The fact that she didn't care about herself was itself something she didn't seem to care about. The group questioned her, challenged her, debated her, all to no effect. Then the group noticed Samantha, who was sitting quietly with her head averted from the group, but with tears streaming down her face. Samantha, a younger girl, adored Ana and looked up to her as a big sister. When Ana saw Samantha's face, her own defensive veneer of indifference broke and tears began to trickle down her cheeks as well. It was impossible not to recognize the love Samantha had for her friend. And, as with Winnicott's infant at its mother's breast, Ana saw herself in a new light, as mirrored in Samantha's face.

Still another "task" of adolescence that is particularly well served by group therapy is that of mastery. In the psychoanalytic literature, mastery is an issue that is primarily associated with the latency period. Retreating from the overt and flamboyant sexuality of the phallic stage, the child in the latency stage is seen as focused more on the concrete learning tasks of gaining competency at being in the world. Erikson refers to this stage as "industry vs. inferiority" (1950, p. 226).

Rather than diminishing, however, issues of mastery rise to even greater intensity in adolescence. There is a kind of simmering terror just below the surface of the adolescents at the Center. They see adulthood awaiting them on the road just ahead, and they *know* that they are not ready. Some of the anxiety has to do with practical issues: inadequate education, poor job skills, limited employment opportunities. And some of the anxiety comes from emotional issues. These are kids who, by-and-large, have never really been cared for. Now, turning eighteen, they must give up even the fantasy of this ever happening.

In a residential treatment program such as the Center's, a certain amount of healthy regression is inevitable. The wards' basic physical needs *are* met. As much as they rail against the rules and close supervision, adolescent clients thrive under the external structure. And, as many will admit before being released, the Center is the only place where many of them have felt cared for, and where people have taken the time to listen to them. Along with other things, this regression provides an opportunity to revisit and progress in the neglected or uncompleted latency-age task of mastery.

There are few things quite as exhilarating as leading a well-functioning group. The group is doing good work, they know it, and, most importantly, *they are doing it by themselves.* I usually follow the "rule of ten," which simply means that if I am tempted to say something in a group I count to ten first, allowing group members a chance to say it first. In a well-functioning group I will frequently say nothing during an entire session. I am always amazed at how insightful teenage group members are with each other. They are frequently much more patient with resistant members than I am. And their timing tends to be flawless.

Inexperienced group leaders tend to seriously underestimate their teenage group members. The most common mistake is insisting that group members raise their hands before speaking. This seriously disrupts the flow of the group, channeling all interactions through a central "traffic cop" figure. Even more problematic is the message this gives the group members. It says, "I will treat you as though you were transitioning from kindergarten to first grade rather than from childhood to adulthood."

Other common mistakes include these:

- Insisting that the group stay "positive." If the group cited above had stayed positive, Caitlin would never have had the important learning experience that her peers were sick of her tantrums and disgusted by her childishness.

- Encouraging the group to "be patient" or to "be understanding" with each other. In a therapy group, the "therapy" is provided by the group members rather than by the group leader. This does not mean, however, that the group members need to function as "junior therapists." One can see this happening sometimes when one hears one member asking another, "So how does that make you feel?" The job of the group members is to be real with each other. When a member, or the group as a whole, is blatantly impatient or unempathic, this is part of the process and needs to be interpreted rather than chastised.

  An example of this is the group in which Patricia worked (noted at the start of chapter 5). Patricia's work started when the group noticed that she was being rude and disrespectful toward a peer. Rather than insisting on "proper behavior," the group offered Patricia a chance to work on what was upsetting her.

- Prohibiting profanity in group. This is another example of misusing the therapy group to teach "social skills" or proper behavior. It is important that we keep our priorities straight about the goals of the group. Therapy and social skills training are both laudable goals, but they are sometimes incompatible in a single situation. When we encourage an adolescent to "get in touch with your feelings," we should not be overly concerned when what comes out is not particularly pretty.

A corollary of this occurs when particularly concrete teens know how to express feelings only in terms of actions. The phrase, "I want to kill the fool," for example, should be taken as an expression of anger rather than a threat. Too much good work has been missed when a group gets distracted by some lecture on "Well, you've got to think about the consequences of. . . ."

What then is the role of the leader of a group of adolescents? I see the role as essentially twofold. It is important to say right away, however, that if the group members themselves can fulfill either or both of these roles, so much the better. The first role is to assure the safety of the group. As indicated above, this is not done by keeping the group positive, polite, patient, nice, or socially appropriate. Keeping anger out of the room certainly does not do it. There can be no healing without a thorough working through of anger. The statement "You make me sick" can be enormously beneficial in a group if it leads to real work, especially if both parties share the work. Conversely, a seemingly innocuous statement such as "I just don't like you" can be destructive to the group process if it is followed by (implicitly or explicitly) "and that's that! There's nothing more to discuss!"

An extremely powerful group session in a girls' cottage began with Sally asking for help from the group around the issue of her having molested her younger brother. "I hope he doesn't hate me," she said. "I hope he knows that I love him and that for me it was just some kind of sexual experimentation." An almost disembodied voice answered her from across the room. Alicia was sitting rigidly, staring straight ahead. "He knows," she said, in a voice icy with rage, "that you used him for your own pleasure. He knows that when you did that you didn't give a fuck about him or what he was feeling." Alicia, obviously, had been molested several times when she was very young. Feeling blindsided, Sally wanted to retreat and stop working, but I encouraged her to continue working with Alicia. "Your worst nightmare is speaking to you," I said. "Keep working with her."

The work that followed was a classic confrontation between survivor and perpetrator. Sally began an elaborate defensive dance of denial and minimization. With each step she took, Alicia was there, pinning her down with uncanny accuracy. It seemed as though Alicia knew Sally's heart and mind better than Sally did.

In the end, the group proved to be an extraordinary experience for Alicia. She confronted her (surrogate) perpetrator as an accuser rather than as a victim, saying things out loud that she had previously only whispered to herself. It is harder to know if the group was helpful to Sally. In spite of my efforts of support, Sally was never able to emerge out of her defensive position and do any real work. When Sally had asked the group for help, she was asking for absolution. She clearly did not get what she wanted. But it was the opening for her of some important work on her narcissism and her diminished capacity for empathy.

When I run a group of adolescents, it can be a wild and wooly experience. Since I personally exert as little control as absolutely necessary, the group is frequently on the cusp of being out of control. When everyone is involved (which I hope they are), people don't always wait for someone to stop speaking before they start. When emotions are being tapped (which I hope they are), the noise level can make the more controlling of our staff uncomfortable. But the groups are exhilarating. And a good part of the excitement comes from observing a bunch of teenagers mastering a way of relating as adults that many adults themselves cannot hope to achieve.

The second important job of the group leader is keeping the group on task. It is the nature of groups to stray off task, especially in a therapy group when the task is as painful and threatening as confronting the characters of one's peers and having one's own character brought up for scrutiny. Bion, one of the pioneers of British object relations theory as well as of group theory, delineated three "basic assumptions" that can distract a group from its task. Bion's three categories represent just one of a myriad ways of classifying dysfunctional groups. But it is a useful way.

The Basic Assumption of Fight or Flight

One of Bion's basic assumptions is the assumption of "fight or flight." The fight or flight group takes the position that work cannot be done, that the task cannot be performed, because a threat exists that must be dealt with first. This threat can be either external (an enemy) or internal to the group (a scapegoat[1]). The group convinces itself that it can deal with the threat only by fighting it or by fleeing from it.

Bion applied his schemata to all sizes of groups, from the small group of half a dozen to the largest groups of nation-states. For a nation-state the designation of an external threat (an Osama bin Laden or a Saddam Hussein) can distract a group from its true task for years at a time. This can also happen in a small therapy group if the group leader fails to address it.

I was once called in to consult on a problematic group in a boys' unit. The problem was immediately evident. One boy would ask to work in group, saying something like, "I want to work on my anger." This would be accepted as a worthy topic, whereupon the boy would proceed, "Well, I'm mad at Mr. X. (or Ms. Y.). They . . ." And a long and pointless diatribe about how awful (or unjust, or unkind) Mr. X. or Ms. Y. was.

Without disputing the awfulness of Mr. X. or Ms. Y., I suggested to the group that they might have more important issues to work on, issues that were more personal and more central to their lives. "Like what?" the group asked suspiciously. Here I was in a quandary. I did not want to spell out exactly what they should be working on. But I was struggling to say what I wanted in general, without getting too abstract or using too many polysyllabic words. Finally, one boy spoke up. "You mean deep shit?" he queried. "Yes," I replied eagerly, "that's it, deep shit!" "Oh, I'd never talk about deep shit in this group." "Why not?" I asked. "Oh it's just not safe enough in this group."

I don't believe the defense was conscious or purposefully manipulative. But the boys in the group knew they were avoiding something, and on some level they knew *what* they were avoiding.

The problem of an internal enemy (a scapegoat) can be equally disruptive to a group task. The scapegoat, like the "identified patient" in family systems theory, is an interesting creature. The scapegoat distracts the group from its task but simultaneously unites the group and holds it together against a common enemy: himself or herself. Thus, as does the identified patient, the scapegoat sacrifices himself for the greater good. As with the larger group-as-nation-state, the identification of an "enemy within" can be more frightening and more disruptive than that of an external enemy. I have seen entire groups shut down and refuse to work when an identified scapegoat is present.

This problem will escalate if not addressed early by the group leader. The scapegoat, feeling the group's hatred, will simply work harder to earn and justify that hatred. Inexperienced group leaders will sometimes yield to impulse and join the group in attacking the scapegoat. Not only is this destructive to the person cast in the scapegoat role, but it also reinforces the group in its fight or flight assumption. Other leaders will make the mistake of trying to side with the scapegoat, urging the group not to be so mean, not to pick on him or her, to be more patient, more understanding. Unfortunately, this not only further enrages the group because it feels unheard, but it reinforces the scapegoat's perception of himself or herself as the innocent victim of the group's wrath—the sacrificial lamb.

My approach is to speak directly to the scapegoat, wonder aloud with ironic (but genuine) admiration both at the power the scapegoat has gained over the group, and at the good the scapegoat has accomplished by unifying the group. Only after paying this homage will I also allow myself to wonder out loud at the price the scapegoat is willing to pay to achieve these ends.

Basic Assumption of Dependency

Bion's second basic assumption group, the dependency group, is particularly pernicious in its tendency to seduce inexperienced group leaders into its basic assumption. The assumption of dependency, simply stated, is that we, the group members, are hopeless inadequates who need the leader to do all the work. "You are the therapist," they will tell the leader. "We are just a bunch of kids. What do we know about how to help each other? You have all the education. You are the one who needs to be telling us what to do." Or (when the group starts getting angry), "How come you never say anything? Why do they pay you all that money just to sit there listening? Are you listening?"

The group leader who is seduced by the idealization, or shamed by the criticism, ends up reinforcing the group's basic assumption of dependency, helplessness, and inadequacy. It is easy to recognize such groups when one comes in as a consultant. The leader will be "working" with one of the group members, doing what I call "one-on-one-therapy-with-an-audience." The rest of the group members will be struggling to stay awake, staring off into space, having side conversations, or (with the better socialized members) pretending to listen. Typically, after a long and unproductive dialogue, the group leader will then ask, "Does the group have any feedback they want to give?" This request for the group's two cents' worth is then met by those members who have managed to stay awake and who, eager to please the leader, will give "advice" to the one who worked (advice is at the very bottom of Yalom's (1995) list of useful things a group can do).

Those therapists who believe that "real" therapy can be done only by a trained professional are best advised to stick to individual therapy. Individual psychotherapy achieves much greater depth without the "audience" and does not bore to death the nonparticipants.

In the adolescent groups I run I go to considerable lengths to avoid inadvertently contributing to the dependency assumption. I avoid starting a group with the question, "Who wants to work?" as it supports the tacit notion that "work" is one person working at a time. With an established group, I will wait for the group to start itself, and say as little as possible for the first ten or fifteen minutes. After that, most of my interventions will be observations on the group process, occasionally calling the group back to task.

As I have said, I am always amazed at how patient, intelligent, and insightful teenagers are with each other if they are allowed enough space. But as Bion observed, it is the nature of all groups to stray from their tasks, and the role of the group leader is important. At the Center, the adolescents seem to have come up with a basic assumption of their own, which reads, "All mothers love their children." One member will be working on feelings of fear, rage, and worthlessness around the abandonment by a neglectful or drug-abusing mother, and someone is sure to observe, with absolute certainty, that "it wasn't because she didn't love you. It was because she didn't know how to show her love." Without intervention by the leader, the group may well solidify around this notion, leaving the abandoned child's nascent feelings to wither on the vine.

The Basic Assumption of Pairing

Many people (myself included) find Bion's third basic assumption group, the basic assumption of pairing, difficult to grasp. Bion cited national institutions as examples of the basic assumptions functioning at the nation–state level. The institution that meets the fight or flight assumption is the military. The one that meets the dependency assumption is the church. And the institution that meets the basic assumption of pairing is the royal family. So there may well be something particularly British about this third basic assumption.

The basic assumption of pairing refers, at the small group level, to a phenomenon in which two members will pair up and "work" together with particular intensity. Both the leader and the other group members are excluded from this work. But, unlike the dependency group, the other group members will listen with rapt attention to their work, almost with a sense of awe. Bion says that it is as if the paired couple were performing a sexual act, and the group was witnessing the conception of a future messiah.

If one avoids getting lost in the mystical metaphor, the basic assumption of the pairing group is really very simple: Two people do some particular important work, out of which will come, in the future, something magical (the messiah) that will save the group (from having to stay on its task). "Why do we have to do any work now, because when the messiah gets here everything will be okay?"

I have occasionally observed the basic assumption of pairing in outpatient groups, but I have never seen a true one at the Center. The closest I have seen was when a girl worked, essentially alone, in a long monolog about her fantasy of reuniting with her mother (the mother being the second person in the pair). This girl had been thrown out of the house at age twelve by a mother who had added insult to abandonment by keeping in the house all the younger siblings. The mother had obviously been abusive even before the abandonment, and the girl's split from reality was twofold: both in the possibility and in the desirability of a reunion. But no one in the group challenged her. To the contrary, they seemed mesmerized by her words, perhaps silently conjuring up similar fantasies of their own.

It was as if they were waiting not for some future messiah, but rather for the gates of a past Garden of Eden to be reopened so that they could reenter a lost paradise of fusion with the mother.

I believe that the reason the basic assumption of pairing is seen so rarely at the Center is very simple. Each basic assumption is fueled by a different emotion. Fight or flight is fueled by fear. Dependency is fueled by helplessness. And the basic assumption of pairing is fueled by the defensive use of hope. And hope, among the delinquent teenagers at the Center, is not noteworthy for its abundance.

Nontraditional Groups

Yalom (1995) and Ormont (1992), two of the modern masters of group theory, both tend to be wary of the wide assortment of current group techniques such as role playing, "empty chair" work, and group exercises. These techniques do run the danger of derailing the group process, and of reinforcing the one-at-a-time style of group. But teenagers are an adventuresome and flexible lot, and I have seen such techniques used very profitably on occasion at the Center. The following vignette illustrates a case in which both silence and physical contact were among the crucial ameliorative factors in a group therapy session.

The session involved the empty chair technique in which a sixteen-year-old girl (Bea) confronted the man who had raped her at age five. This had definitely not been just molestation, but rather a particularly brutal and violent rape, which Bea remembered as though it were yesterday.

Bea was both eager for the confrontation and doubtful about the technique. Her concern was that the empty chair would not be able to answer her questions, and what she most wanted were answers to questions like "why me?" I had tried, unsuccessfully, for some time to convince Bea that these "questions" were not true questions at all but rather were cries of anguish and outrage.

The compromise we agreed to was that Bea would sit in the circle and speak to an empty chair placed in the center of the circle. I would sit in the circle as well, at a slight distance from Bea, and speak for the rapist as much as possible (I chose not to actually sit in the chair and role-play the rapist because I wanted to protect the fragile positive transference Bea had toward me). I tried to respond as I thought a blunt and honest rapist would answer. Her first question was as expected:

B: Why me?

T: Because you were an easy target. You were too small to fight back.

B: I was so innocent!

T: I didn't care.

B: Why couldn't you have picked someone else?

T: You were available.

My (the rapist's) responses to her questions seemed to do nothing but frustrate her. She became increasingly angry, but the anger appeared to come more out of her frustration at not getting an answer than out of her direct experience of the rape. Her questions became repetitious, and rather than add to her frustration, I chose to become silent.

Bea's questions were now met with silence, and the silence proved to have a much more powerful effect on her than had my words. Bea's words never changed, but her affect changed dramatically, giving the words, her questions, an entirely different meaning. Her voice quality changed as well. Her questioning of "Why me?" changed from being an angry, frustrated confrontation to a long, high-pitched, plaintive wail, an expression of profound narcissistic injury. It became clear that they were not really questions, obvious that they were not even directed to the rapist, but rather to the impersonal, uncaring universe. "Why me?" became a cry of rage and despair at the indifference of the universe, and the universe responded as it does: with silence.

After a crescendo of pain, angst, and rage Bea picked up the empty chair and hurled it against the wall. At that point I moved in to stop her. My aim was not to restrain her nor even to calm her, but simply to make sure that neither she nor anyone else was accidentally hurt. At that point Bea collapsed sobbing into a fetal position at my feet. I, at this point, was in a quandary. I wanted to give some comfort but I was reluctant to touch her. In an earlier group Bea had mentioned that because of the rape she always felt uncomfortable at the touch of a man, and during this group one of her angry questions had been "Why do you men always think with your dicks instead of your minds?" Nevertheless, after a few minutes I put my hand gently on her shoulder. She did not flinch. After several more minutes of sitting with Bea while she sobbed, a female intern who had been working with Bea helped her over to a couch, where Bea curled up with her head on the intern's lap and continued to cry.

After the group was over the intern and Bea went walking on the grounds. Bea began to apologize profusely for having gotten tears and "snot" on the intern's pants. The intern reassured her that it was okay, but Bea persisted in apologizing. "No," the intern insisted, "it really is all right." Bea then looked at the intern with an expression that the intern later described as "absolute bliss!"

Bea had discussed in earlier groups the effects of the rape on her. "When I'm in the shower I look at myself and I don't like what I see. I see that I have breasts and I don't want them. I see that I have a vagina and I don't want one. I don't want to be female." The unit staff had reported that Bea always became upset during her menstrual periods. The menstrual blood reminded her of the rape, and it reminded her that she was a woman, and thus vulnerable to rape.

In the group Bea went through two profound, mutative experiences. She was able to confront and rail against not her rapist but rather the silence (indifference) of the universe. She was able to come closer to accepting the lack of caring by the universe because of the strong caring of the group (needless to say, the group was deeply moving for all present). And, in the combined experience with the group and the follow-up with the intern, Bea was able to experience for the first time since age five that her body functions, her body fluids, were not loathsome and disgusting. Her humanness, her aliveness in its most basic form, had been accepted and validated.

Note

1. Or, as the kids say in a wonderful malapropism, an "escapegoat."

CHAPTER NINE

~

Family Therapy

I do some family therapy at the Center, but I do not consider myself a "family therapist," so this chapter does not pretend to be a technical or "how to" treatise on that form of psychotherapy. Rather, I want to offer some thoughts on the implications of object relations theory for family therapy, particularly family therapy with adolescent family members.

Object relations therapists, and psychodynamic therapists in general, have historically been somewhat resistant to the idea of family therapy. They point out, first of all, that the "object relationships" from which the discipline gets its name are *internal* relationships between *internal* object representations. These internal object representations tend to bear little resemblance to the real, external object they purport to represent. Take the case of superego formation in the Oedipal boy as an example. The four-year-old boy because of his internal logical cognitive processes, in response to internal changes in his own libidinal energy, decides that his father represents a threat of castration, and internalizes this image as a way of appeasing, placating, or controlling the threat. Bringing the "real" person of the father into the therapy would be irrelevant to the internal and libidinal issues (phallic love for the mother) and would therefore be a waste of time.

To use another example, this one from Melanie Kline, the "bad breast" is created in the infant's mind not simply because the real breast is sometimes absent. The child takes the image of the absent breast and projects onto it all of his or her own aggression and sadism, and thus creates (internalizes) an image of a breast that withholds maliciously and sadistically in an effort to torture by teasing and tantalizing. It would be as absurd to say that the infant is responding to its mother's malicious sadism as it would be to say that the four-year-old is responding to some kind of real threat of castration from his real father.

While these points reflect important truths about object relations theory, they miss other fundamental tenets of the theory that in fact make family therapy much more germane. I should like to address three of these object relations tenets in particular.

Modern object relations theory, first of all, dating back to the contributions of D. W. Winnicott, envisions the child as never being completely lost in the autistic world of the paranoid–schizoid position (autistic in that real, external objects are unseen and irrelevant). This is because of the partial boundary dissolution that Winnicott (1971) called the "mother–infant unit." I described the mother–infant unit earlier as a strange, "two-headed beast." One head (psyche) is that of the infant, with its radical splitting and denial of reality (of the reality of separateness, of the reality of historical continuity). The other head is the adult psyche of the mother with the wisdom, reality orientation, and emotional complexity of the adult. Thus, according to Winnicott, even in infancy there is always an interpersonal component to the psyche, complementing and modifying the intrapsychic component. And this interpersonal component to the infantile psyche relates essentially to the mother.

The second point (and this is, in a way, a continuation of the first point) is that object relations theory is not simply a theory of the paranoid–schizoid position. Rather, it is a theory (a set of theories) about the complex growth or transition (though never complete) out of the paranoid–schizoid position and into the depressive (interpersonal) position. Winnicott's contribution is again critical here. Winnicott postulated that the success of this transition depends on the functioning of the mother. The mother, as I quoted earlier, must "allow herself to be killed a thousand times and never die." That is to say, she must patiently tolerate the infant's "creative destruction" of its internal objects (including that of the internalized "good mother"), and be waiting to catch it in her (real) arms when it turns to her as a real, external object. This is no easy task for the mother, for the destruction of the internal mother, however little it has to do with the real person of the external mother, is being done on *her* bones!

A therapist I supervised reported that, when he was in his early twenties, his mother had told him about, and apologized for, the following decision. When he had been a toddler his mother had reached down and picked him up one day. He clearly had not felt like being held and, as toddlers will do, had squirmed and struggled in her arms. She had put him down and, narcissistically wounded by this momentary rejection, she had sworn never to pick him up again (and indeed, never did).

The young toddler, in struggling to get out of his mother's arms, was fleeing from (killing off) the (momentarily) bad internalized mother whom he had projected onto the person of the real mother. The real mother, unable to accept the injury, had not allowed herself (the internalized object representation of herself) to be thus killed and had, instead, retaliated. It took many years and much therapeutic work as an adult for this young therapist to eventually rid himself of the internalized bad mother that his real mother did not help him destroy when he was young.

As I form a prognosis of success at the beginning of family therapy, the crucial variable I look for is the mother's ability to tolerate the rage, the hurt, and the accusations (both founded and unfounded) of her troubled child. With mothers who react with denial or counterattacks or, worst of all, with mothers who storm out of the therapy room not to return for several weeks, the prognosis is poor. If, on the other hand, the mother is able to courageously acknowledge her mistakes and show genuine concern for the pain and damage that her mistakes have caused, while also having the composure to disavow the mistakes she did not really commit, then great things can come out of family therapy.

The third facet of object relations theory relevant to family therapy is the concept of transference. The issue of transference as the primary vehicle for therapeutic change is one of the last great commonalities of psychodynamic theories. One may define transference, as did Freud (1910a), as the residue of unresolved feelings from one early relationship transferred onto a current relationship or, in object relations terms, as the projection of an internalized object representation (or self-representation) onto an external object. But in either case, the therapist, the recipient of the transference, is acting as a medium, as a middleman in the resolution of the conflict. How much more powerful it can be to have this conflict resolved in person, with the original object.

The issue of transference brings up one of the problem areas of family therapy. If, in psychodynamically oriented therapy, transference is the vehicle for change, then the transference object has the advantage of being a highly trained, highly skilled, experienced therapist. Family therapy is inherently on more shaky (though potentially more fertile) ground. The parent may simply not have the ego strength, the motivation, the capacity to do a good enough job as a parent. When this is the case (and this happens often at the Center), all is not lost. With the help of the therapist, the adolescent is sometimes able to gain some perspective on the parent's shortcomings: "My parent abandoned me because they are incapable of love, not because I am unlovable."

Goals of Family Therapy

There are a number of different schools of family therapy, which differ from each other as much in their goals as in their techniques. The goal of object relations family therapy is the same as the goal of any other modality of object relations therapy: to move the clients increasingly out of the paranoid–schizoid position and into the depressive position. It is to get family members, as much as possible, to see each other as whole objects rather than as part objects; it is to get them to relate to each other as real, external objects rather than continuing to relate to their autistic internal objects, projected onto the bodies of external objects.

There is frequent discussion in the Center of the concept of forgiveness. Religious services, led by visiting clergy, often stress this as a Christian virtue, and the kids at the Center are frequently pressed by the clergy to forgive those who have injured them. The wards will sometimes come to me in considerable distress, wanting to do what they believe God wants them to while at the same time finding themselves emotionally unable to do anything of the kind. I generally urge patience, validating forgiveness as an ultimate goal, but cautioning that all things must come at their own pace, that it is a mistake to try and force oneself to do what one is not yet ready to do.

But my real agenda is not forgiveness, it is acceptance: It is the acceptance of another person, the parent, as a complex, flawed, mixed bag of a human being. Rather than "My father beat me but I forgive him," I would much rather hear, "I hate my father for having beaten me, but I also recognize that he was beaten as a child and that was the only way he knew how to parent."[1]

I have been present a disconcerting number of times when girls have told their mothers for the first time that they had been raped some time earlier. The girls invariably feel much anxiety before revealing this. They can rarely articulate exactly what they dread in their mothers' reactions, but they clearly do not expect anything positive. Many of them have kept the rape secret for years.

What the girls hope for (if they allow themselves to hope for anything), and what I hope for along with them, is something along the lines of the mother, in tears, rushing over and throwing her arms around her daughter, saying, "Oh my God darling, I am *so* sorry." Sometimes this happens. More often the mother sits in stunned silence before blurting out, with discernable anger, "Why didn't you tell me sooner?" A few will continue in this mode of attack disguised as questions ("Why were you out that late? Why were you in that place? Why were you with that crowd?") before I can redirect them to a place where they are able to express more empathy for what their daughters have suffered. Only a very few remain completely unable to get to this place of love and compassion.

My goal in such therapy is to help each party recognize the other as a whole object. The mother needs to be able to see that her willful, defiant, rebellious child, who shouted profanities and hateful things at the mother before running out of the house, is also a fragile and delicate girl whose body and emotions have been ravaged. The daughter needs to be able to understand that the mother's initial expression of anger is not the tip of an iceberg of hatred and loathing. The daughter needs to see that the mother felt betrayed by her daughter's silence as, most likely, any mother would. The mother's staccato of angry I-told-you-so's is, again, not necessarily an expression of deep-seated hatred so much as of the frustration of someone who for years had been struggling to control and protect an out-of-control and unprotectable child. It is certainly always preferable if the mother could express love and empathy before expressing betrayal, rage, and frustration, but this does not mean that the mother's love and empathy are any less real if expressed second. Forgiveness is not the issue here: Understanding and acceptance are.

I worked for many months with Araceli (see chapter 7) and her mother Rosa. Rosa was rare among the mothers at the Center in that she really was, or at least had become, a good mother. How she had managed to do this I was never able to figure out. She reported having had some good mothering herself in the person of an aunt, but most of her life had been horrendous. Growing up in poverty in Guatemala, she had been molested by a grandfather and at least one uncle. Escaping one hell, she exchanged it for another. Coming illegally into the United States, she sought protection and identification by joining one of the most notorious street gangs of Los Angeles. Pretty and vivacious, she married one of the gang leaders and gave birth to two daughters. Her husband physically and verbally abused her. Her self-esteem fell to such a low point that, when he left the family (to begin an extremely long prison sentence), she believed him when he told her that she was an unfit mother, and she gave up the care of her two daughters to his mother. Rosa then further declined into heavy drug use and petty crime, finally ending up herself spending two years in prison.

What happened to Rosa in prison is the opposite of most of the stereotyped prison stories: She turned her life around. She reports that the first thing she did was decide to give up hating. She gave up the racial hatreds that had been indoctrinated into her by the gang culture and by her life on the streets. She formed close friendships with other women prisoners, some of whom were African American and some Caucasian. In giving up so much of her hatred for others, Rosa was able to shed much of her self-hatred as well. When she left prison she was determined to regain custody of her two children.

Araceli remembers her mother's return to the family as a mixture of joy and terror. She says that she wanted to climb into her mother's lap and never leave. She was terrified that whenever her mother left to go to the store she would never return. Araceli stuck to her mother like glue (her mother's phrase was "like a fly to shit," which speaks to the fact that Rosa still had a ways to go in giving up all of her self-hatred). And when Rosa appropriately urged her young teenage daughter to go out and have age-appropriate fun, Araceli felt rejected and dismissed. Araceli fought bitterly with her mother and returned to the more "predictable" comfort of her gang and drugs and got arrested. Rosa subsequently underwent her own brief drug relapse.

This was where I began working with them in the Center. Araceli assured me in individual sessions that her mother was childlike, irresponsible, "more like a friend than a mother," and had no boundaries. I saw little of this in family sessions. Rosa seemed to have an instinctual sense of how to be a mother. I saw a joy and enthusiasm about her that did at times appear childlike, but she seemed determined to be responsible and always maintained appropriate boundaries. She would not, for example, tolerate her daughter's casual profanity but accepted without comment whatever words came out when Araceli was truly upset. Most impressively, and most critically, Rosa was willing to hear and accept all the pain she had caused her daughters by her own abandonments of them.

Several months into treatment, Araceli reported to me in individual therapy that she and her mother had had a disastrous weekend visit. Rosa had thought that Araceli was "looking down at her" and had left in a huff. Araceli had shouted after her, "Good! So don't come back!"

Rosa did come back that week and in the family session said that the cause of the blowup had been her announcement that she had become an "exotic dancer" to earn extra money. Rosa continued to want to focus on her daughter's contempt rather than her own provocation of it. However, it took very little work on my part to help her acknowledge that most teenage girls would be less than enthusiastic about such a choice of work by their mothers. At this point Rosa broke down and tearfully spoke about how hard it was for her to support, single-handedly, two teenage daughters. This was uncharacteristic of Rosa, who generally worked very hard to shield her children from her financial plight. Rosa, an illegal alien with little formal education, had few marketable job skills, and, she added, Araceli was "high maintenance."

Characteristically, Araceli took this last remark like a knife to the heart. Araceli had always acknowledged that her mother "loved" her but was convinced that the love was a hollow, duty-bound thing. She could not believe that her mother ever took real joy in Araceli's existence, and she was convinced that she was an unwelcome burden in her mother's life. For the rest of the session Araceli retreated into a numb withdrawal, out of which I was not able to coax her and which seemed to produce a similar defeated withdrawal in her mother.

Then, in an emotionless, almost disembodied voice, Araceli spoke: "I wish I had a different mother." I was shocked that Rosa did not even flinch. There was a moment's silence that, at my urging, Rosa broke. "Yes, I wish you had a different mother too." She said it with no element of vindictive retribution. She did not say or imply, "I wish I had a different daughter." She meant, as she went on to explain, that she too wished that Araceli had had a mother who had never used drugs, never gone off to prison, never allowed herself to be beaten into a cowed submission by a brutal husband.

I continued the work with Araceli in our next individual session. Araceli, determined to continue feeling hurt and to vilify her mother, became angry with me when I defended Rosa, claiming that I was "taking her side." I denied this, acknowledging Rosa's past egregious failures and the current issue over exotic dancing. Araceli jumped on this last issue. "Ya! Isn't that scandalous!" I acknowledged that the dancing itself was a "scandalous" thing for a mother to do, but pointed out *why* she was doing it: "because she loves you and wants to take care of you."

I knew that I was pushing Araceli very hard at this time, perhaps too hard. Araceli went in and out of withdrawal as I appeared to be selling the idea of her mother's love too forcefully. But I sensed (or I wanted to sense) a side of Araceli that was intrigued by what I was saying, so I persisted. But at the end of the session that side of Araceli claimed defeat. "It's no use," she said (in an apparent non sequitur, but one that demonstrated her understanding of the relationship between her self-love and her perceived object love). "I just can't do it. I try to like myself when I'm alone in my room, but I just can't do it."

Both Araceli and Rosa had a great deal of work left ahead of them. But I believe that at this point the essential task of the family therapy had been laid out, and the work begun. Araceli fired what could have been a devastating broadside at her mother, but she had not destroyed Rosa. Both would fire a great many more such broadsides, both verbally and physically. Araceli returned to drugs shortly after being released from the Center and had to be sent to another program. It remained uncertain whether Rosa would be able to withstand so seemingly endless a series of blows. At this point Araceli's desire to see and love her real mother and her need to hold on to her rage at the bad internalized mother seemed equally powerful, with the rage having the slight upper hand. But the situation was, of course, more complex. Araceli also had a powerful identification with her abusive father, whom she had seen in her childhood as the only object with any strength. My task was to continue to work with both of them, individually and together, to interpret the process as always, and to give each of them as much support as I could in this excruciating process.

Note

1. I likewise reject the "Hate the action, not the person" advice that children and adolescents are frequently given, which, to my mind, is simply another kind of splitting, and completely contrary to our affective experience. When someone spits in my eye, the rage I feel is directed at the person who has thus defiled me, not at some "action." In fact, what it would actually feel like to hate "the action of being spit upon in one's eye," split off from any negative feelings toward the perpetrator of such an outrage is impossible for me to imagine.

PART III

AFTERTHOUGHTS

~

CHAPTER TEN

Thoughts on Delinquency

Early in my career at the Center I was struck by parallels between the gang cultures I was dealing with and what I knew about primitive warrior societies. Both seem based on a necessary fatalism. A confirmed gang-banger will tell you that he does not expect to live past eighteen. If he does that's fine, but he can't allow himself to want it too much. And if he does live past eighteen he has to expect that much of his life will be spent in and out of prison. Again, "That's just the way it goes." Fatalism is often taken to absurd proportions. The fact that one might be killed driving home on the freeway is cited as evidence that one can die at any time and that therefore one might as well engage in gang warfare. A parent in a multifamily group asked a young gangster if he wanted to live. "I'm not afraid to die," the young man answered defiantly. Hip to the gang mentality the parent persisted: "That's not what I asked. I asked if you wanted to live." Caught, the boy answered sheepishly that he did. But it ran against every ounce of his gang ethic to admit it.

Ruthlessness is another quality common to gangsters and warriors. Enemies exist to be hated, to be killed, to be annihilated. When one points out to a gangster that his enemies are teenagers like himself, with mothers, fathers, girlfriends, boyfriends, sometimes even children, one is greeted with a blank stare. "No," the response is (either explicit or implicit), "they are my enemies. That is all they are. They exist to be hated." Occasionally in the Center we see wards from enemy gangs being placed in the same unit and becoming friends, even best friends. But they also share a tacit understanding that the friendship is situational and temporary. As soon as they are released back to the streets they will try to kill each other again.

155

Contempt for and exploitation of women is a third common theme. The current vogue among ghetto youth to refer to women as "bitches" points to the extent to which this denigration of women has become established as a subcultural norm. Women function as sex objects and as little else. Perhaps as a defense against any impulse to actually *need* women, gangsters go out of their way to develop contempt for women.

> I first began to really understand the horror of rape while working at the Center. A young girl was talking about how awful she felt about herself after having been gang raped. Naively, I challenged her on this. "You didn't do anything wrong," I said. "They did! Why should you feel bad? "You don't understand," she replied. "You're lying there naked on the floor and they are all standing around laughing at you, spitting on you, telling you how ugly you are."

Gang-affiliated girls themselves frequently identify with this contempt for females. One of the worst insults one can call a girl in the gang culture is a "hood rat." A hood rat is a girl who is known to sleep with every boy in her gang. Such girls say that they do this to "be accepted" by the gang, but the contempt heaped upon the hood rat, even from the boys she wants to accept her, belies this explanation. My understanding of these girls is much more basic: They act as sex objects because that's how they see themselves. It is not just their fates in life; it is who they think they are.

There are undoubtedly many more parallels between current gang mentality and the mentalities of earlier warrior societies. Gang societies are, after all, a kind of warrior society. But all of the characteristics are merely exaggerated (culturally reinforced) qualities of the paranoid–schizoid (part-object) position. In the paranoid–schizoid position one does not look forward to a future life, because life is experienced as an endless present. One does not show ruth to one's enemies, or to anyone else for that matter, because ruth can exist only in the depressive position. One exploits women, and everyone else, because part objects exist to be exploited.

D. W. Winnicott, along with his pioneering work on the mother–infant relationship, transitional objects, and the like, wrote more on delinquency than any other object relations theorist. Winnicott made two important contributions to our understanding of delinquency. The first (Winnicott 1958b, 1963, 1966) is that the way out of delinquency is to get out of the paranoid–schizoid position and into the depressive position. On the face of it, this does not seem like a particularly profound observation, and indeed, one senses a certain embarrassment in Winnicott when he posits it. Yet its implications are profound. One does not move from the paranoid–schizoid position into the depressive position easily, nor does one move there piecemeal. Both the paranoid–schizoid position and the depressive position come as packages. Each "position" represents an elaborate set of implications or consequences of a single mental action: the splitting of a whole object into two, unambivalently held internal part objects, versus the recognition and acceptance of ambivalently held whole, external objects. One cannot simply "teach ruth" to someone firmly entrenched in the part-object position, because ruth makes no sense in that position (see chapter 3). Yet this is exactly what some therapists try to do. A standard part of the treatment of sex offenders is something called "empathy training." In this kind of training the perpetrator is taught to put himself in the position of his victim and imagine what she goes through when she is being abused. I have worked with several young sex offenders who have been through such training, and I find that they have learned well. They are able to systematically and sequentially name every emotion that their victims must have experienced. What I find chillingly absent is any sense that they care.

Psychodynamic psychotherapy (sometimes referred to as "talking therapy" even in the research literature) is not currently in vogue in the treatment of delinquents, and certainly not in the treatment of sex offenders. I do not wish here to dispute the "evidence" upon which "evidence-based treatment" is based, nor do I want to denigrate the cognitive–behavioral therapies that the "evidence" purports to support. The "skills" that these approaches teach are invaluable. It is essential for any client to be able to tolerate his or her anger without immediately lapsing into violent aggression. It is equally crucial for a client to be able to feel sadness without being swallowed by depressive rumination.

But I do not believe that teenagers, delinquent or otherwise, can be treated by shortcuts. Teaching someone a set of skills cannot replace psychotherapy. One cannot "modify a person's behavior" without somehow changing who that person is. The addiction to the bad objects (chapter 3) is too tenacious. The painstaking processes of individual, group, and family therapies simply cannot be gotten around. Our clients deserve no less.

Delinquency as a Sign of Hope

Winnicott's (1956a, 1986b) other contribution to our understanding of delinquency is his somewhat startling assertion the delinquency is "a sign of hope." By this he certainly did *not* mean that we, the outside observers, should in any way feel hopeful when a teenager lapses into delinquency. Rather, Winnicott was suggesting that an adolescent's choice of engaging in delinquent behavior represents that adolescent's continued *hope* that object relatedness (care, nurturance, love) can somehow be regained. The alternate would be despair and depression (hopelessness).

In saying this, Winnicott connects delinquency directly and explicitly to abandonment and loss. Delinquent children are in some way, physically or emotionally, abandoned, and their choice of delinquent behavior is a way of assuring that some external object will intervene, to protect them from their own impulses, and provide the containment that they feel they have lost.

The term *containment* is another of those difficult to define but essential concepts that permeate object relations theory. In its most basic form containment speaks to the human need for physical limits. Throughout history and across cultures, those dealing with neonates have recognized the newborn's need to be swaddled. Suddenly released from the natural swaddling of the womb, the neonate, lacking the physical ability to control its own muscles, flails about uncomfortably without the artificial constraints imposed by swaddling.

> The image of swaddling becomes a metaphor for all sorts of pleas for external controls. Margaret Mahler's (1968) case of "Jay, the Painless Wonder" is illustrative. Jay, a toddler participating, with his mother, in Mahler's laboratory nursery school, was noteworthy for persistently climbing to the very top of any available climbing apparatus and performing some toddler daredevil feat up there, until he fell. Having fallen, he would never cry (hence his sobriquet given to him by the other mothers) but simply start climbing all over again. Jay's mother was not completely uninvolved. Rather, she would watch Jay "like a hawk," but she would never do what Jay was so clearly begging her to do: shout out, "Wait sweetheart, that's high enough! It's dangerous up there." (Jay did not perform this ritual unless his mother was present.)
>
> In the terms of modern object relations theory Jay and his mother represent a classic case of the failure of maternal "containment." Jay appears to have been desperate to project his fear onto his mother and, by his manipulative behavior, to have turned simple projection into projective identification,[1] to get his mother to "contain" his fear.
>
> For whatever reasons of her own, Jay's mother refused to do so. And in this refusal she failed Jay and she failed herself terribly, for she essentially refused to allow herself to become a "mother." On the most superficial level she refused to become a mother in that she refused to perform the motherly function of protecting her son from harm. On a deeper level she refused to participate equally in what Winnicott (1956b) called the "mother–infant unit." She would not let herself feel (contain) the feelings her son was projecting onto her, and thus could not function as the adult surrogate ego that makes up an essential half of the mother–infant unit. Jay was clearly willing to do his part.

He projected his fear onto someone who should have been able to contain it and should have been much better able to make sound decisions on what to do with it, and he did his best to manipulate her into doing her job. He was also quite willing, on his part, to contain *her* projections: For whatever reasons, she seems to have needed her son to be oblivious to pain.

Mahler reports that she and her colleagues were extremely concerned about Jay, and that the case sorely challenged their collective decision to remain scientifically detached throughout their study and not to intervene in cases of perceived bad mothering. She predicted that Jay would achieve "a borderline adjustment with schizoid features." (p. 756)

Winnicott might have predicted that Jay would likely decline into delinquency. The kind of failure of containment just described is precisely what Winnicott (1986a) was referring to when he spoke of delinquency as resulting from "abandonment." Of course the more obvious physical kind of abandonment can also lead to delinquency. But I am frequently amazed to find apparently healthy, high-functioning people emerging out of horrific childhoods. Almost invariably, such people are able to identify one person—neighbor, teacher, aunt, uncle—to whom they were able to turn, and use, for mothering. Jay continually turned to his biological mother, and her failures were continuous.

The kind of abandonment that the failure of maternal containment constitutes leaves the child emotionally alone in the world: with no stronger ego extension to contain unbearable feelings, and no adult ego component to make decisions essential to safety and survival. When children such as Jay eventually tire of the endless failures of the biological parent, they have two choices. If they give up hope, they fall into despair and depression. If they maintain hope, they turn to delinquency.

Delinquency, according to Winnicott, represents the child's continuing hope of finding some kind of containment. Often the containment found is crude and physical: jail or a facility such as I have described as "the Center." Sometimes it is an even more basic form of containment. Boys at the Center will sometimes describe purposefully "going off" when they are upset, forcing the staff to physically restrain them. The experience of thrashing about, and being held by a number of strong, adult staff, is fundamentally satisfying (in some ways it is reminiscent being swaddled as a newborn).

The extraordinary recidivism rates for our nation's prisons have a number of contributing factors (the failure of prisons to teach productive alternatives to crime, the dehumanizing effects of prison life, the lifelong stigma placed on ex-convicts). But one factor may also be the containing function provided by jails and prisons.

A therapist I supervise worked with Ed, an unusual ex-con in that he had a college degree and even a graduate degree. He had served some prison time in his twenties for an impulsive but violent assault. When he was released from prison, he was depressed and despondent and unable to pursue his original career. After a few years of barely getting by, going from one unsatisfying job to another, Ed held up a liquor store and then waited across the street for the police to arrive.

After his second release from prison, Ed was court-ordered into therapy. In therapy he repeated the same dynamics. Instead of talking to his therapist about his anger at various people, he would rant floridly about what he would like to do to them. His therapist would sit through their sessions frequently wondering if she would have to make a Tarasoff report or call his parole officer. Ed's provocative ranting diminished considerably (for a while) when the therapist interpreted to him his need to use her as he had used the police and the judicial system, to contain him.

The term *containment* refers to much more than just a need for external restraints on one's impulses. *Containment* refers to a feeling of being held, appreciated, and understood (see chapter 7 for a discussion on the importance of being understood). And containment involves even more than these. It refers to a situation in which one's projections can be contained by a willing recipient. This is essential for a complete experience of containment. Physical containment, even with love and appreciation, is not enough.

When Shannon (see chapter 7) was due to be discharged from the Center, the staff had a lot of concern for her well-being. The level of concern spoke both to the fact that Shannon had become a favorite at the Center, and to the reality of the poor prognosis she faced. At age fifteen, before coming to the Center, Shannon had been a heroin addict, and throughout her stay at the Center she had spoken of drugs with a kind of palpable love and nostalgia. She was being discharged to a family situation that was far from ideal.

Two days after she was discharged I spoke to her primary therapist about my worries. The therapist responded that she had just been having a similar conversation with another staff. "Yes [she said], Shannon was so contained here." I was struck by this word for two reasons. First, it was so appropriate. Second, it was unusual coming from a therapist who was "cognitive–behaviorally" oriented. There are many overlaps between cognitive–behavioral therapy and object relations therapy, but the concept of containment is not one of them. There is no behavioral manifestation of containment. Nor is there any set of learned skills that is associated with it. Shannon was "contained" in that the staff and the institution were willing to identify with, and contain, her projections.

I had worked with Shannon every week for the almost one year she stayed in the Center. She would begin every session in my office with an almost ritualistic rant about how much she hated the Center and how much she needed to leave. About halfway through her stay I suggested to her that when she actually did leave she might even miss the place. "Yes," she whispered, sotto voce, "sometimes I think so too, but I'm afraid to say it out loud." For the last week of her stay at the Center, Shannon beamed rapturous joy. "I'm so happy," she would say, adding occasionally, "I'm also scared to death." But her face never betrayed any of the fear, maintaining a constant expression of ecstasy.

It was the staff and I who contained her fear, accepting as our jobs what Jay's mother was unable to accept. We pointed out the dangers to her, tried to boost her coping skills, and made sure she had resources to fall back on. We begged her to consider not returning to her mother, but rather to live in a small group home for girls. She refused. Mostly, however, we allowed ourselves to feel what she could not yet let herself feel (at least not for very long): the nagging dread that corresponded to the reality she was returning to. And in this case our containment seems to have been successful. One week after returning to her dysfunctional mother, she called her caseworker and asked to be moved to a small group home.

Shannon had sat as a child with her psychotic mother repeating to herself over and over again, "I have to be responsible. I have to be responsible." So for the Center to be willing to act as an adult container for her fears (and for her to allow us to do so) was crucial. But even more important, the Center contained for Shannon her self-love. Shannon's bipolar mother had alternated between an anxious, smothering love; abandonment into her own depression; and hate-filled verbal abuse. While there had been some loving mirrors in her life (her grandparents doted on her), Shannon had dutifully internalized the venomous view of herself that she had heard so often from her mother.

At the Center, Shannon's wonderfully expressive face charted the work she did. Most of the time her face was hard and cold, avoiding eye contact, congruent with the rage she would express through streams of profanity. But increasingly over the course of her stay, she allowed herself timid glances into the eyes of those she was with, her shy smile saying, "So you really do like me?"

One last element of containment needs to be mentioned: The Center contained Shannon's hope. Near the end of her stay, cognizant of how much I cared for Shannon, staff would approach me with a cautionary note: "You know she's not going to make it, don't you?" And I would grudgingly acknowledge that I knew that the odds were heavily against her. But the important thing was that even the doubters had more hope for Shannon than she had for herself. Shannon paid lip service to hope but could not allow herself actually to feel or experience any such thing. We at the Center saw her potential. Our doubts came from knowing how much the deck was stacked against her, not from any failure to believe that Shannon had the potential to make it. This was what we all carried for her, and this was why it was crucial that, upon discharge, she not lose contact with us, or with people like us, with whom she could bond.

Note

1. Interestingly, Mahler herself does not use the term projective identification in the article.

~

CHAPTER ELEVEN

Object Relations Theory in Clinical Supervision

The degree to which we are locked in to the particular constellations of object relations units that inform the paranoid–schizoid position, and the degree of willingness we have to seek, meaning externally through intersubjectivity—both of these fundamentally determine our ability to take in new information in a way that *changes* the way we see our worlds. As such, considerations of object relatedness functioning are critical to the supervisory process.

I include a chapter on clinical supervision in this book because I believe that the supervisee, whether intern or neophyte therapist, is in a kind of professional adolescence, dealing with developmental issues, regardless of his or her chronological age, that parallel those of biological adolescence. The intern or young supervisee is in a "transitional period" between student and professional, a period that raises the same questions and concerns that preoccupy the mind of an adolescent in transition between childhood and adulthood. In both, issues of identity are critical: "Should I model myself as a therapist on supervisor Dr. A or supervisor Dr. B or on my own therapist, Dr. C? How can I incorporate the modeling of these mentors and still be myself as a therapist?" Doubts about competency are at least as agonizing as they were in chronological adolescence: "When I go out there and market myself as a licensed professional, will people recognize how ignorant and incompetent I truly am? Do my peers feel as utterly fraudulent as I do?" Dependency issues abound: "Can I actually support myself as a professional? Who will refer clients to me knowing how many better, more experienced therapists there are out there?" Separation anxiety diminishes the joy of independence and autonomy: "How will I know what to do with my clients without my weekly supervision? What if I make a terrible mistake?" Even sexual identity is an issue for the young therapist transitioning from student to professional: "How, without entirely splitting off and denying my sexuality, can I learn to have a deeply intimate relationship that is not sexual with another person, that is emotionally intimate without being physically intimate?" In short, the whole host of issues, doubts, anxieties, questions, and dilemmas that form the "task" of chronological adolescents are revisited with equal power in our professional adolescence.

The introduction of theories such as object relations theory into the supervision process is, however, controversial. This is not to say that a solid grounding in a theory of psychotherapy is not considered essential for any young therapist. The ability to articulate and apply the tenets of a recognized and accepted psychotherapeutic orientation is now considered mandatory for entry into the professions ("eclectics" need no longer apply!). But for a supervisor to utilize in the supervision session techniques developed for therapy sessions is far from universally accepted.

The long-lived issue at stake is what is sometimes called the "teach–treat controversy." Having named this controversy, however, I immediately find myself having trouble defining it. This is because (as with the primary controversy in adolescence over the "inevitability of turmoil") it is a controversy in which each side so distorts and exaggerates the position of the other side that the defining poles of the disagreement bear little resemblance to anything professional psychotherapists actually do. I am aware of no supervisors, however entrenched they might be on the "teach" side, who define their roles primarily as pedagogues. This kind of dry teaching is what is supposed to happen in the classroom, and, while it is a critical adjunct to what happens in the supervision, it does not address the kind of experiential learning that the intern or supervisee is engaged in with his or her clients. Similarly, I have never heard anyone advocate doing psychotherapy with one's supervisees. To do so would not only be grossly inappropriate, it would be unethical. Rudolf Ekstein (Ekstein, Busch, Liebowitz, Perna, and Tuma, 1976), one of the earlier proselytizers of the "treat" side of the controversy, was very far from advocating doing therapy with one's supervisees. What Ekstein said was, "The professional teacher of psychoanalysis is certainly aware that students cannot make use of new ideas that are suggested to them until they are good and ready for them. The challenge of our training work . . . consists of creating situations which help prepare students for new ideas that they can use" (p. 32). Ekstein emphasized primarily the need to reduce the anxiety of the neophyte therapist, an approach that seems more an act of kindness than a process of psychotherapy.

To a certain extent, at its essence, the teach or treat controversy is not so much a true debate over how clinical supervision should be done, but rather a displaced conflict over how therapy should be done. Liddle (1979) suggested a "parallel" between the supervision orientation of a supervisor and his or her clinical orientation. This hypothesis received strong empirical support from the research of Davenport (1985). Davenport found that clinicians who espoused a behaviorist clinical orientation favored a "skills development" model of supervision, while those clinicians who claimed a humanistic or existential orientation preferred a "personal growth model" or "collaborative model."

Thus the entire teach or treat debate should be reframed from what is the "better" form of supervision to what form of supervision is most appropriate to the kind of therapy being taught. Behavioral therapies, which emphasize skills acquisition by the client, are obviously more suited to a skills acquisition philosophy of supervision. Humanistic, existential, and the more intersubjective forms of psychoanalytic psychotherapy all focus on the human interaction (Ogden's "analytic third") as the agent of change. It follows that in supervising this type of therapy the interaction between supervisor and supervisee should be the object of scrutiny.

There turns out to be, therefore, much more unanimity of thought in the supervisory dialogue than there is divergence. It is generally agreed, for example, that the person of the therapist is a crucial factor in the therapeutic process. Even Freud, advocate of the "blank screen" role for the analyst, insisted that the essential feature in the training of an analyst was his or her own thorough psychoanalysis. In order to approach the analysand with "scientific objectivity" the analyst must be as free from unconscious and neurotic functioning as possible. With the shift to a more interactive and intersubjective analytic technique, the person of the therapist became even more important. Winnicott (1971) implies that there cannot be the same analysis with two different analysts, a remarkably intersubjective statement. Surely, as the person of the therapist becomes more and more salient in the therapeutic process, issues such as the therapist's ability to tolerate anger and hatred, to recognize and be inured to flattery and sexual seduction, to be cognizant and careful of his or her capacity for sadism, to allow the client enough space and place the client's needs above his or her own, become all the more important.

The question, then, is not whether or not the issue of the character structure of the supervisee therapist is important. It is universally acknowledged to be so. The question is in which arena issues of the supervisee's character should be addressed. Should the supervisor do it, or should the supervisee be referred back to his or her own therapy for such work?

We may be better off if we reformulate the hoary teach or treat controversy altogether and instead pose a single complex question: At what points does a supervisor's attempts to be kind, empathic, empowering, and modeling of a therapeutic stance with our supervisees run the danger of crossing some crucial but difficult to define "boundary" to become "therapy?"

Resnick and Estrup (2006) suggest that such a boundary lies at the point at which inquiry into the supervisee's behavior in the therapy session turns to questions of the supervisee's personal history (i.e., when a genetic understanding is sought). There is much to be said for this formulation. The seeking of a genetic understanding of the supervisee's behavior, the probing of the supervisee's past, does run the danger of lapsing over into the supervisee's own therapeutic work.

But I find this formulation unsatisfactory. For one, history taking is not the same as psychotherapy. Indeed, one rather formulaic school of psychotherapy instructed its students to spend many initial hours "taking a history" before beginning to "do therapy." Thus Resnick and Estrup's suggestion seems to be an arbitrary and misleading place to draw the distinction between supervision and psychotherapy. More importantly, I have frequently found it essential to know as much as possible about my supervisees in order to provide adequate supervision.

> I was extremely disturbed, for example, (and more than a little angry) when an intern at the Center volunteered near the end of her year there that she had an older brother who was gang affiliated and incarcerated for delinquent activities. A piece of information crucial to my ability to help this young therapist with her countertransference issues had been withheld from me.
>
> Another intern presented an even more striking example. Carol, a particularly bright and talented young therapist, was also enormously dedicated to her clients and unusually willing to be touched by their pain, to actually feel much of what they were feeling. I realized, during the course of the year, that Carol was also clinically depressed.
>
> Because I was so impressed by her talents, and touched by her dedication, I set out to be particularly supportive with Carol. I encouraged her to trust herself, to trust her intuitions, to value her feelings (countertransference), to take risks with her clients. I encouraged her to listen to her clients and observe their responses rather than coming to me to ask if her interventions had been "right or wrong." I told her that her clients could be much more powerful teachers than could I.

I was certainly not trying to be a "therapist" to Carol, merely supportive. Nevertheless I was distressed to see that through the course of the internship year her depression seemed to worsen rather than diminish.

About three weeks before the end of the year Carol ended a supervision session with the words, "Well, at least you were there for me today." As I had bent over backward to "be there" for her the entire year, I was flabbergasted. The next week we talked about her words. Carol's immigrant parents had put her to work in the struggling family business when she was ten or eleven. In response to Carol's protests that she was still a little girl being asked to do an adult's job, her parents tried to reassure her. "No," they said, "you are smarter than other children your age. You are more mature. You can do this (adult) job. You are special."

In our second-to-last session it became immediately and horrifyingly clear to both of us what had happened. In my zeal to be "supportive" of Carol, I had inadvertently reenacted her experience of parental abuse and abandonment.

It seems to me that the problem lies in attempting to single out a specific feature of psychotherapeutic technique and then proscribing that feature to anyone doing supervision. The result is an awkward "Thou shalt not . . ." conundrum that appears arbitrary and confining: Thou shalt not take history of your supervisees, look for genetic understanding, or work in the transference. Thou shalt not do whatever is deemed exclusive to the process of "therapy." Rather than singling out *aspects* of our professional repertoire to distinguish between therapy and supervision, I suggest that we look instead at the *focus* of our work. If the focus of our work aims to enhance a person's happiness, self-awareness, sense of empowerment, experience of wholeness, then we are doing psychotherapy. If we focus on helping someone become a better therapist, understand a certain client better, or understand his or her own role in a therapeutic relationship, then we are doing supervision. When we look back at Ekstein's original formulation, we can see that not only was Ekstein broadening the scope of our work as supervisors, he was focusing it and circumscribing it. The work of the supervisor is to facilitate the experience of the supervisee in becoming a therapist.

Dr. K., a young psychologist I supervised, was presenting her difficulties in working with a resistant young woman (Ms. C.) who wanted to cut her sessions back to every other week. Dr. K. was clear about Ms. C.'s dynamics. As a child Ms. C. had been passed from caretaker to caretaker and in every situation had ended up taking care of the caretaker. This had included at least one previous therapist. Ms. C. was terrified of closeness and intimacy because she had always been lost in and subjugated by close relationships.

In enumerating the reasons she had presented to Ms. C. for opposing her desire to cut back to every other week, Dr. K. listed that she "didn't work that way," that "it wasn't effective," and that it would leave her with an empty, unprofitable hour on the odd weeks and that she "needed to take care of herself financially." I indicated that I thought all of the stated reasons were valid and that there were times in which it would be appropriate for clients to be reminded of all of them, but that I was struck by the one-sidedness of her arguments. What had she said about Ms. C.'s resistance to closeness?

Dr. K. immediately said that they had discussed this, that she had interpreted to Ms. C. her anxiety about closeness and gone into the history behind the anxiety. "And how did Ms. C. respond?" I asked. "She said, 'Yes, you're absolutely right.'" "And then?" And then the subject had apparently been allowed to drop.

At that point I suggested to Dr. K. the following intervention: "I know, Ms. C., that you have good reason to fear closeness and intimacy. Historically you have always lost yourself in any relationship you have gotten in. So you learned to protect yourself by putting up barriers and keeping distance in all your relationships. You do that in here with me, and I suspect you do that in all your relationships. If you are satisfied with this way of being then you are correct in wanting to reduce the frequency of our meetings and perhaps even work towards termination. But I suspect from our work together that you are not satisfied with this, that there is a huge loneliness in you of which you are very tired. If this is true then increasing the distance in our relationship is not going to help you get what you want."

Dr. K. smiled at my suggestion. "That's just what I wanted to say," she responded, "but I couldn't come up with the right words." Had I been a supervisor more in the "teach" school I might have stopped here. I had offered a suggestion on how she could be more effective with her client and my suggestion had been accepted. But I chose to go on.

"I don't quite believe that," I said. "You are every bit as articulate as I am, and everything I know about your client I learned from you. I suspect that the problem lies elsewhere. In my intervention I was willing to suggest to your client that she might not be willing to do the work I was proposing and, if that were true, that it would be understandable for her to consider cutting back on or even dropping out of therapy. I'm not sure you would be willing to suggest that to her."

Dr. K. agreed with this. She had been losing a lot of clients recently. She "needed" to have this client remain in therapy. We spoke about the narcissistic injury that comes with losing a client. We spoke of her financial anxieties. We spoke about her fears about her competency.

I validated all of these concerns but ended on a cautionary note. "I understand your feelings, but you cannot 'need' your client to stay in therapy. She has to choose to stay in therapy because of *her* needs, not because of *yours*. Otherwise you will be abusing her, as did all the other caretakers in her life.

I believe that taking the extra step with Dr. K. was necessary, even if it ran the risk of bumping into a boundary of something called "doing therapy." To have rested at the "suggestion offered–suggestion accepted" point would have turned the supervision into a charade. I would have had to give tacit acceptance of Dr. K.'s premise that the problem was her inability to "find the right words." The real problem interfering with Dr. K.'s ability to work effectively with her client stemmed from her unspoken and unresolved fears and anxieties, from the sense of "neediness" that those fears provoked in her, and that she then acted out on her client.

As the style of psychodynamic psychotherapy evolves increasingly in an intersubjective direction, the style of supervision must shift in a comparable way away from an exclusive focus on what is happening with the *client* in therapy, and more toward a focus on *what is happening in the room between the client and the therapist*. This will necessarily involve a similar shift in focus toward an increased willingness to look at *what is happening in the room between the supervisee and the supervisor*. For some time this has been happening in the name of "working in the parallel process."

Working in the parallel process is based on the observation that, if an issue interferes with the therapeutic work between client and therapist/supervisee, that same issue frequently will be brought unconsciously into the room with the supervisor and supervisee and interfere, in the same way, with the supervision process. In object relations theory, the "parallel process" can be understood in terms of mutual projective identification. If a client and therapist/supervisee are locked in an unyielding process of mutual projective identification—what Ogden (1994) called a "subjugating third'—then the therapist/supervisee is likely to bring those same projections into the supervision room and attempt to manipulate the supervisor into identifying with them. As with all projective identification, either half of the object relations unit (the self-representation or the internalized object representation) can be projected out, and either half retained and identified with (see Racker 1972).

A young therapist, Dr. M., asked for some time in a supervision group I led. She made it clear in the beginning that she was not asking for any feedback from the group. She merely wanted a chance to "ventilate" and "get the group's support" concerning a "horrible" experience she had just gone through with a client.

The client in question was a woman in her mid-fifties, Ms. P., who was being seen in couple's therapy with her husband. What made the experience so horrible for Dr. M. was that Ms. P. had spent the entire session verbally attacking, belittling, and humiliating her husband. She would not, in this process, allow Dr. M. to get a word in edgewise. She seemed to want nothing from Dr. M. beyond her bearing witness to the worthlessness and loathsomeness of her husband. Mr. P., on his part, sat in mute acceptance of the abuse.

Dr. M. went on in great detail for about twenty minutes, raging about how abusive Ms. P. had been, how rejected all of her attempts at intervention had been, how unproductive the session had been, when she finally said, "I felt like saying to her, 'Shut the hell up!'"

I intervened at this point saying that I suspected that some parallel process was going on because I, at that exact moment, had found myself suppressing the urge to shout out to Dr. M. those exact same words. Dr. M., I suggested, had become, vis-à-vis the supervision group, what her hated client had been to her.

One can only speculate on the dynamics of this complex situation. It seems very likely that Ms. P. had taken a powerful object relations unit, probably critical and abusive parent and loathsome and unworthy child, identified with the critical parent (identification with the aggressor) and projected the unworthy child representation onto her husband (who, for his own reasons, seemed willing to identify with the projection).

This explanation, however, is insufficient because Ms. P. also seems to have needed a *witness*. The function of this witness is interesting. Ostensibly, the witness was called on to observe the loathsomeness of the husband. But the effect was so powerfully in the opposite direction that Ms. P.'s own loathsomeness was flaunted; this may have been the unconscious intent.

In chapter 4 I suggest that one motivation for the addiction to the bad object might be to punish it by publicly demonstrating its evilness. What Ms. P. *may* have been enacting was a drama that said something like, "Look how evil my critical parents were. They were so evil that they have turned me into one of them."

Unfortunately, Dr. M. herself grew up with critical, verbally abusive parents. She was not in a position, therefore, to have empathy for the abusive parents or the abusive wife they had created, at least not when she herself was feeling re-abused. What seems to have happened is that in the couple's therapy session Dr. M. identified with the worthless, loathsome child. Her contributions were devalued, she was not allowed to speak, and she was coerced into bearing impotent witness to the abuse of another human being.

In the group, however, she turned the tables. She asked others to remain silent, she had no use for their input, and she forced them to experience what she had gone through. Rather than identifying with the victim, she now identified with the aggressor.

The difference was that I and the group members represented different subjectivities from those of her clients or parents. When I told Dr. M. that I had the urge to shout "Shut the hell up" at her too, I was telling her that I did not like what she was doing to me or to the group. But I was not telling her that I wanted to annihilate her, degrade her, humiliate her, devalue her, or disrespect her. Just the contrary! I had enormous empathy for Dr. M. and, once removed, for Ms. P., with whom she was momentarily identified. I felt certain the Dr. M. did not like herself when she was like this, any more than I believed that Ms. P. truly liked herself when she identified with her own hated parents. I felt and expressed empathy for Dr. M., who, I hoped, would then be able herself to feel and express more empathy for the unhappy Ms. P.

There is another situation in which the supervisor is sometimes required to step "out of role" and, while not becoming a therapist, again push the boundaries. This is when the transference–countertransference relationship between supervisee and supervisor becomes so problematic that the work of supervision cannot proceed, and the supervisee cannot learn what it is necessary to learn. The transference and countertransference that develops between a supervisee and supervisor is frequently as powerful, or almost as powerful, as that which develops between client and therapist. In most cases it is not problematic, and in some cases, as in therapy, it empowers the learning experience. In other cases the transference presents a clear impediment to learning and must be addressed directly. The goal in such cases is not to "work through" the transference or to "resolve" it, as would be the goal of psychotherapy. Instead, the goal is to depotentiate or detoxify the transference as efficiently as possible, so that the real work of supervision can resume.

An intern I supervised at the Center, Annie, immediately formed a powerful father transference toward me. Annie's father was a narcissistic and demanding figure, and Annie had spent much of her life trying to please him. She immediately repeated this with me. I frequently pointed out to Annie that learning to be an effective psychotherapist and pleasing me were two different things, and that to the extent that she focused on the latter, she would be missing out on the former. These reminders had the effect of temporarily refocusing Annie on the task at hand, but had little impact on the transference itself.

Annie's narcissistic, demanding father had held a specific picture of what he wanted Annie to be and had been uninterested and intolerant of who she really was. This had produced a powerful level of False Self functioning in Annie that seriously interfered with her functioning as a therapist. She was not able to use her countertransference to inform her therapeutic work because she was not sufficiently aware of how she really felt. In supervision, when I asked her what it felt like to be in the room with a client, she would respond with how she thought she *should* have felt, or with how she thought I *would like* her to have felt. Again, I would frequently point this out, help her identify some true feelings, and refer her back to her own therapy to do the real work.

About eight months into her year at the Center she came into a supervision session clearly too agitated to do any real supervision work. She was upset, she said, because I seemed to be impatient with her. She demanded to know whether or not I really was impatient with her and if so, why.

I had three choices. I could have lied and said that I was not. This would have accomplished nothing. I could have told the truth, and tried to explain why I was, but I sensed that this would accomplish worse than nothing. Annie had a tendency to feel sorry for herself and to want others to feel sorry for her, and to take pleasure in the role of the victim. I felt sure that to acknowledge my impatience would have sent her back to that unproductive place. Instead, I determined not to answer her question.

"Maybe I am, maybe I am not," I said with studied indifference. "In either case it is my business and not yours." "Oh come on," she protested. "An intern feels her supervisor might be impatient with her and you say it's none of her business?" "Look," I explained, with impatience creeping into my voice, "you have your learning to do. And you have to do your learning at your own pace. If the pace at which you need to learn and the pace at which I would want you to learn are different, that is my problem. It is not your problem, nor even your business."

Annie reacted with amazement. This was a sentiment she had never heard or expected to hear from a father figure. The sense of rejection she had expected from me was replaced by a kind of caring that she was totally unused to. We were able to return to our primary focus on supervision. A bit of personal growth had taken place, and a shift had occurred in our transference-based relationship.

Let me end this chapter with one last comment on object relations theory. Cognitive behavioral therapists might want to describe my interventions with Annie and with Dr. M. as "modeling." This is certainly true. With Dr. M. I was modeling a kind of empathic responding in a case in which she felt no empathy toward the client. With Annie I modeled a kind of selfless caring, a willingness to place her needs above mine, that would serve her well with her clients. But the intersubjective relationship in which projective identification is altered goes much deeper than that. "Modeling" implies the teaching of a behavior through the acting of that behavior. But when one projects in projective identification, one projects much more than just a behavior, a feeling, or an idea. One projects part of one's ego, part of one's psyche, part of who one is. When that projection is altered or modified through contact with another human subjectivity, who one is changes. When Dr. M. encountered a group of people who responded with empathy and more than a little sadness at her having chosen to identify with the aggressor rather than with the victim, she was able to modify the loathing with which she viewed herself. When Annie encountered a subjectivity willing to place her needs above his own, the rage with which she viewed the world was dampened somewhat.

References

Adorno, T. W., Else Frenkel-Brunswik, Daniel J. Levinson, and R. Nevitt Sanford (1950). *The Authoritarian Personality*. New York: Harper & Row.

Atwood, George E., and Robert D. Stolorow (1984). *Structures of Subjectivity: Explorations in Psychoanalytic Phenomenology*. Hillsdale, NJ: Analytic Press.

Atwood, Margaret (1988). *Cat's Eye*. New York: Bantam Books.

Bion, W. R. (1956). "Development of Schizophrenic Thought." In *Second Thoughts*, pp. 36–42. New York: Jason Aronson, 1967.

——— (1957). "Differentiation of the Psychotic from the Non-psychotic Personalities." In *Second Thoughts*, pp. 43–64. New York: Jason Aronson, 1967.

——— (1959). "Attacks on Linking." *International Journal of Psycho-Analysis* 40: 308–15.

——— (1961). *Experience in Groups and Other Papers*. New York: Basic Books.

——— (1963). *Elements of Psycho-Analysis*. London: Heinemann.

——— (1967). *Second Thoughts*. New York: Jason Aronson, 1967.

Bird, Brian (1972). "Notes on Transference: Universal Phenomenon and Hardest Part of Analysis." *Journal of the American Psychoanalytic Association* 20: 267–301.

Blos, Peter (1967). "The Second Individuation Process of Adolescence." *Psychoanalytic Study of the Child* 22: 162–86.

——— (1968). "Character Formation in Adolescence." *Psychoanalytic Study of the Child* 23: 245–63.

Braun, B. G. (1988). "The BASK Model of Dissociation." *Dissociation* 1: 16–23.

Briggs, Stephen (2002). *Working with Adolescents: A Contemporary Psychoanalytic Approach*. New York: Palgrave Macmillan.

Brodie, Bruce R. (1998). "Hate in the Countertransference with Criminal Clients: Winnicott Revisited, Implications for Treatment and Therapist Burnout" (paper presented at the annual conference of the Forensic Mental Health Association of California, Asilomar, California, March 1998).

Davenport, Judith J. (1985). "An Investigation of the Relationship between a Clinical Supervisor's Theoretical Orientation and Preference for a Model of Supervision." Doctoral dissertation, the California Institute of Clinical Social Work.

Demos, John, and Virginia Demos (1969). "History of the Family: Adolescence in Historical Perspective." *Journal of Marriage and the Family* 31, no. 4: 632–38.

Diagnostic and Statistical Manual of Mental Disorders, 4th ed., text revision (2000). Washington, DC: American Psychiatric Association.

Ekstein, Rudolf, Fred Busch, Joel Liebowitz, Doris Perna, and June Tuma (1976). "Notes on the Teaching and Learning of Child Psychotherapy within a Child Guidance Setting." In *In Search of Love and Competence: Twenty-Five Years of Service, Training, and Research at the Reiss-Davis Child Study Center*, ed. Rudolf Ekstein, pp. 31–61. Los Angeles: Reiss-Davis Child Study Center.

Ekstein, Rudolf, Judith Wallerstein, and Arthur Mandelbaum (1992). "Countertransference in the Residential Treatment of Children." In *Countertransference in Psychotherapy with Children and Adolescents*, ed. Jerrold R. Brandell, pp. 59–87. Northvale, NJ: Jason Aronson.

Erikson, Erik H. (1950). *Childhood and Society*. New York: W. W. Norton.

——— (1959). "Identity and the Life Cycle: Selected Papers by Erik H. Erikson." *Psychological Issues* 1, no. 1.

——— (1968). *Identity, Youth, and Crisis*. New York: W. W. Norton.

Fairbairn, W. R. D. (1952). *An Object Relations Theory of Personality*. New York: Basic Books.

Fenichel, Otto (1945). *The Psychoanalytic Theory of Neurosis*. New York: W. W. Norton.

Fishman, H. Charles (1988). *Treating Troubled Adolescents: A Family Therapy Approach*. New York: Basic Books.

Freud, Anna (1936). "The Ego and the Mechanisms of Defense." In *The Writings of Anna Freud*, vol. 2. New York: International Universities Press.

——— (1958). "Adolescence." *Psychoanalytic Study of the Child* 13: 255–78.

——— (1969). "Adolescence as a Developmental Disturbance." In *The Writings of Anna Freud*, vol. 7. New York: International Universities Press.

Freud, Sigmund (1900). "Interpretation of Dreams." *Standard Edition*, 4 & 5.

——— (1910a). "Five Lectures on Psychoanalysis. Fifth Lecture: Transference and Resistance." *Standard Edition*, 11: 49–58.

——— (1910b). "The Future Prospects of Psychoanalytic Therapy." *Standard Edition*, 11: 139–52.

——— (1912). "The Dynamics of Transference." *Standard Edition*, 12: 97–108.

——— (1913). "Further Recommendations on the Technique of Psychoanalysis I: On Beginning the Treatment." *Standard Edition*, 12: 121–44.

——— (1914). "Further Recommendations on the Technique of Psychoanalysis II: Remembering, Repeating, and Working Through." *Standard Edition*, 12: 145–56.

—— (1920). "Beyond the Pleasure Principle." *Standard Edition*, 18.

—— (1923). "The Ego and the Id." *Standard Edition*, 19: 3–66.

—— (1938). "Splitting of the Ego in the Process of Defense." *Standard Edition*, 23: 271–78.

Gates, Henry Louis Jr., "The End of Loyalty." *The New Yorker*, March 1998, 34–44.

Gill, Merton M. (1979). "The Analysis of the Transference." *Journal of the American Psychoanalytic Association* 27: 263–88.

Goffman, Erving (1959). *The Presentation of Self in Everyday Life*. New York: Anchor.

Greenacre, Phyllis (1957). "The Childhood of the Artist: Libidinal Phase Development and Giftedness." *Psychoanalytic Study of the Child* 12.

Greenson, Ralph (1971). "The 'Real' Relationship between the Patient and the Psychoanalyst." In *Explorations in Psychoanalysis*, pp. 425–40. New York: International Universities Press.

Hall, G. Stanley (1904). *Adolescence: Its Psychology and Its Relationship to Physiology, Anthropology, Sociology, Sex, Crime, Religion, and Education*. 2 vols. New York: Appleton.

Kalsched, Donald (1996). *The Inner World of Trauma: Archetypal Defenses of the Personal Spirit*. New York: Brunner-Routledge.

Kernberg, Otto (1976). *Object Relations Theory and Clinical Psychoanalysis*. New York: Jason Aronson.

—— (1980). *Internal World and External Reality*. Northvale, NJ: Jason Aronson.

Klein, Melanie (1952). "On Observing the Behavior of Young Infants." In *Envy and Gratitude and Other Works, 1946–1963*, pp. 94–121. New York: Delacorte, 1975.

Kohut, Heinz (1971). *The Analysis of the Self*. New York: International Universities Press.

—— (1977). *The Restoration of the Self*. New York: International Universities Press.

—— (1978). *The Search for the Self*, vols. 1 and 2. ed. P. Ornstein. New York: International Universities Press.

—— (1984). *How Does Analysis Cure?* Chicago: University of Chicago Press.

Kushner, Harold S. (1981). *When Bad Things Happen to Good People*. New York: Avon Books.

Lewis, C. S. (1989). *A Grief Observe*, reprint edition. San Francisco: Harper.

Liddle, H. A. (1979). "Training of Contextual Therapists: Steps toward an Integrative Model of Training and Supervision." In *Marriage, Marital, and Divorce Therapy*, ed. P. Sholevar. New York: Springer.

Linehan, Marsha M. (1993). *Cognitive Behavioral Treatment of the Borderline Personality Disorder*. New York: Guilford Press.

Mahler, Margaret S. (1968). "On Human Symbiosis and the Vicissitudes of Individuation." *Journal of the American Psychoanalytic Association* 15: 740–63.

—— (1972). "On the First Three Subphases of the Separation-Individuation Process." *International Journal of Psycho-Analysis* 53: 333–38.

Masterson, James F. Jr. (1967). "The Symptomatic Adolescent Five Years Later: He Didn't Grow Out of It." *American Journal of Psychiatry* 123: 1338–44.

Miller, Alice (1981). *The Drama of the Gifted Child*. New York: Basic Books.

Mitchell, Stephen A. (1993). *Hope and Dread in Psychoanalysis*. New York: Basic Books.

Natterson, Joseph (1991). *Beyond Countertransference: The Therapist's Subjectivity in the Therapeutic Process*. Northvale, NJ: Jason Aronson.

Offer, D., M. Sabshin, and D. Marcus (1965). "Clinical Evaluation of Normal Adolescents." *American Journal of Psychiatry* 121: 864–72.

Ogden, Thomas H. (1986). *The Matrix of the Mind*. Northvale, NJ: Jason Aronson.

—— (1994). *Subjects of Analysis*. Northvale, NJ: Jason Aronson.

—— (1997). *Reverie and Interpretation: Sensing Something Human*. Northvale, NJ: Jason Aronson.

Ormont, Louis R. (1992). *The Group Therapy Experience: From Theory to Practice*. New York: St. Martin's Press.

—— (2006). "The Ormont Method: The Observing Ego." At www.ormont.org/methods2.cfm (accessed July 25, 2006).

Phillips, Adam (1993). *On Kissing, Tickling, and Being Bored: Psychoanalytic Essays on the Unexamined Life*. Cambridge, MA: Harvard University Press.

Racker, Heinrich (1972). "The Meanings and Uses of Countertransference." *Psychoanalytic Quarterly* 41: 487–506.

Resnick, Rita, and Liv Estrup (2006). "Supervision: A Collaborative Endeavor" (workshop presented at the Los Angeles County Department of Mental Health, April 26, 2006).

Stolorow, Robert D., and George E. Atwood (1979). *Faces in a Cloud: Subjectivity in Personality Theory*. Northvale, NJ: Jason Aronson.

Stolorow, Robert D., B. Brandshaft, and G. Atwood (1987). *Psychoanalytic Treatment: An Intersubjective Approach*. Hillsdale, NJ: Analytic Press.

Stolorow, Robert D., George E. Atwood, and Bernard Brandshaft, eds. (1994). *The Intersubjective Perspective*. Northvale NJ: Jason Aronson.

Winnicott, Donald W. (1947). "Hate in the Countertransference." In *Through Pediatrics to Psycho-Analysis*, pp. 194–203. New York, Basic Books.

—— (1951). "Transitional Objects and Transitional Phenomena." In *Playing and Reality*, pp. 1–25. New York: Brunner-Routledge, 2002.

—— (1954–1955). "The Depressive Position in Normal Development." In *Through Pediatrics to Psycho-Analysis*, pp. 262–77. New York: Basic Books, 1975.

—— (1956a). "The Antisocial Tendency." In *Deprivation and Delinquency*, pp. 120–31. New York: Brunner-Routledge.

—— (1956b). "Primary Maternal Preoccupation." In *Through Pediatrics to Psychoanalysis*, pp. 262–77. New York: Basic Books, 1975.

—— (1958a). "The Capacity to Be Alone." In *The Maturational Process and the Facilitating Environment*, pp. 29–36. New York: International Universities Press, 1965.

—— (1958b). "Psychoanalysis and the Sense of Guilt." In *The Maturational Process and the Facilitating Environment*, pp. 15–28. New York: International Universities Press, 1965.

———— (1960). "Ego Distortion in Terms of True and False Self." In *The Maturational Process and the Facilitating Environment*, pp. 37–55. New York: International Universities Press, 1965.

———— (1963). "The Development of the Capacity for Concern." In *Deprivation and Delinquency*, pp. 100–105. New York: Brunner-Routledge.

———— (1966). "The Absence of a Sense of Guilt." In *Deprivation and Delinquency*, pp. 106–12. New York: Brunner-Routledge.

———— (1967). "Mirror Role of Mother and Family in Child Development." In *Playing and Reality*, pp. 111–18. New York: Brunner-Routledge, 2002.

———— (1968). "The Use of an Object and Relating through Identifications." In *Playing and Reality*, pp. 86–94. New York: Brunner-Routledge, 2002.

———— (1971). "Playing: Creative Activity and the Search for the Self." In *Playing and Reality*, pp. 53–64. New York: Brunner-Routledge, 2002.

———— (1986a). "The Concept of the False Self." In *Home Is Where We Start From: Essays by a Psychoanalyst*. New York: W. W. Norton, 1986.

———— (1986b). "Delinquency as a Sign of Hope." In *Home Is Where We Start From: Essays by a Psychoanalyst*. New York: W. W. Norton, 1986.

Yalom, Irvin D. (1995). *The Theory and Practice of Group Psychotherapy*, 4th ed. New York: Basic Books.

Index

Adorno, Frenkel-Brunswick, Levinson, and Sanford, 51
alterity, 72, 74, 75, 103, 111
anger, 11, 16, 17
anxiety, 17, 18
attribution of meaning, xix, 23, 33, 34, 46, 47, 51, 54, 72, 106, 163
Atwood, George E., xx, 84, 85
Atwood, Margaret, 3

basic assumptions groups, xxi, 138; dependency, 139; fight or flight, 138; pairing, 141, 142
Beck, A., 82
Bion, Wilfred, xxi, 20, 22, 44, 54, 85, 91, 114, 127, 128, 138, 140, 141
Bird, Brian, 105
Blos, Peter, 10, 81, 87, 132
boredom, 11–13
Braun, B. G., 22
Briggs, Stephen, 13

capacity to be alone 10, 178
cases, clinical: Alice (and intersubjectivity), 89–91; Ana (wanting to give up drugs) and Samantha (in group), 134, 135; Annie (intern with father transference to me), 171, 172; Araceli (with mother Rosa), 110–112, 149–152; Bea ("Why me?"), 142–144; Caitlin (temper tantrums), 129, 136; Carol (intern with abandonment issues), 166, 167; Clara (storytelling of lost virginity), 112,113; client (and projective identification),108; client ("deep shit?"), 138, 139; client (favorite cookies), 132, 133; client ("How can I get laid?"), 123; client (mythical reunion with mother), 141, 142; client (oral sex with father fantasy), 86, 87; client (refusal to work "in the transference"), 112; Daphne (queen Daphne), 9, 10, 130, 131, 134; Dr. M. (enraged at client Mrs. P.), 169–171, 172; Dr. K. (needing to keep her clients), 167–169; Ed (contained by prison), 160; Emma (felt abandoned by me; my "Mexican

daughter), 74, 119, 120; Frank (from F13), 8; Helen (my momentary hatred of), 114, 115; "Jay the Painless Wonder" (Mahler's case), 158, 159; Joan (therapist) and Sam (client), 116,117, 122; Joe (the bad kid), 27, 47–54, 60, 64, 102–104, 132; Juan ("that's what you do"), 123; K., 15; Krystal (wanting to love herself), 57, 65–67; Lucy, 24, 25, 31, 45, 46, 58–60, 66, 96–98, 125–128; Maria (abandoning mother), 40, 65, 66; Marissa, 16; Mark, xvii, xviii, 123; Max (death of mother, birth of child, intimidated by Elizabeth), 22, 23, 62, 71–72; Niki, 8; Patricia (moving into adulthood), 69, 70, 136; rape victim, 156; Raquel ("everything will be fine"), 122, 123; Rebecca (victim of father's narcissistic love), 134; Rosa (mother to Araceli), 149–152; Sally (molested younger brother) and Alecia (was molested), 137, 138; Shannon (time-warped flower child), xi–xiii, 13, 14, 21, 22, 111, 160–162; "Singing Detective" case, 134; Tanya ("nasty little girl"), 79, 118–120; therapist (never picked up by mother again), 146, 147; Thomas and Carlos (unlikely friends in group), 129; Tom (shot grocery store clerk), 115,116; Tommy ("I'll show you failure!"), 61; Veronica (burned by mother), 79, 80
character formation, 132
container, xii, 72, 107, 113, 119, 161
containment, 109–113, 159–160
countertransference. See transference–countertransference matrix
creative destruction of the mother, 71, 117, 118, 120, 146

Davenport, Judith J., 165
demonic internal object, 25, 124–127
Demos, John, and Virginia Demos, 4
dependency (basic assumption group), 140
depression, 11, 13, 18, 158, 159
depressive position, xvii, xix–xxi, 19, 22, 38, 39, 65, 66, 72, 82, 95, 96, 98, 102–106, 122, 148, 156, 157
dialectics, 85, 86, 92, 93, 115, 120
disrespect, 90–92

Ekstein, Rudolf, 164, 167
Ellis, A., 82
Erikson, Erik H., 7, 8, 135

Fairbairn, W. Ronald D., 44, 50, 54, 60, 63, 176
false self, 25, 72–76, 124, 125, 128, 171
fatalism, 155
feelings, limited (a world of), 37–40
Fenichel, Otto, 84, 132
fight or flight (basic assumption group),138
Fishman, H.Charles, 3
forgiveness (in family therapy), 148–152
Freud, Anna, 6, 10, 81, 106
Freud, Sigmund, xvi, xvii, 6, 7, 19, 20, 43, 44, 58, 71, 73, 82, 85, 98, 102, 104–106, 117, 118, 127, 128, 134, 147, 165

gangs, 7, 9, 81, 82, 87, 88, 149, 155
Gates, Henry Louis Jr., 87
Goffman, Erving, 7
good enough mother, xxi, 71,119
Greenacre, Phyllis, 14, 75
Greenson, Ralph, 120

Hall, G. Stanley, 4
history (sense of), 28–30, 95–98
hope (delinquency as a sign of), 157–162

identification with the aggressor, 51
identity formation, 132
illusion of creating the breast, 111
inevitability of turmoil debate, 6, 164
injustice (a world without), 30–32
interpretation, 101–104
interpretations, non-verbal, 109–113
interpretative action, 109,110
intersubjective third, 87
intersubjectivity, vii, xii, xix–xxii,
    75–89, 93, 113, 163, 165, 169, 172,
    178

Kalsched, Donald, 25, 124, 127, 128
Kernberg, Otto, 45, 106, 128
Klein, Melanie, xvii, xx, 19–22, 39, 42,
    44, 45, 54, 59, 60, 65, 66, 76, 82, 85,
    98, 99, 127, 128
Kohut, Heinz, 59, 133
Kushner, Harold, 30

Liddle, H. A., 165
Linehan, Marsha M., 26

magic, 20, 34, 36, 70
Mahler, Margaret S., 10, 14, 118, 159,
    162
Masterson, James F. Jr., 5
Miller, Alice, 113, 114
mirroring, 133
mother–infant unit, 98–101, 146
mutuality in therapy, 89, 92

Natterson, Joseph, 84, 92, 93

object relations unit (ORU), 45, 46, 50,
    51, 63, 72, 119, 127
Offer, D., M. Sabshin, and D. Marcus, 4
Ogden, Thomas H., ix, xvii, xx, 24, 32,
    42, 48, 49, 68, 75, 84, 85, 87, 89, 92,
    93, 95, 99, 106, 109, 112–114, 120,
    121, 128, 165, 169
omnipotence, 14, 34, 36, 37

Ormont, Louis R., 26, 142

pairing (basic assumption group), 141,
    142
parallel process, 169, 170
paranoid–schizoid position, xvii–xx, 19,
    21, 22, 29, 72, 82, 95, 96, 98,
    102–104, 107, 122, 146, 148, 156,
    157, 163
part–object position (see also
    paranoid–schizoid position), xix, 19,
    20, 24, 26–40, 42–47, 54, 64–67, 70,
    72, 74, 75, 103, 132, 156, 157
part objects, 27, 28
Phillips, Adam, 11, 12
positions, 19, 20
potential space, 120–124
primary maternal preoccupation, 113–117
projective identification, 104–109
puberty, 7

resistance, vii, xxi, 57–59, 61, 63, 65,
    67, 84, 90, 105, 114, 168
Resnick, Rita and Liv Estrup, 166
respect, 80–82, 83, 89, 91
Rogers, Carl (and Rogerians), 82, 84
ruth (and ruthlessness), 40, 41, 103,
    155–157

sadness, 15, 16, 18, 37, 39, 40, 102
self as object, xvii, 32–34, 124
self as subject, xvii, 32–34, 124
space, play, xx
splitting, xii, xiii, xx, 20–26, 40, 47–54,
    59, 63–67, 72, 83, 84, 95, 102, 103,
    108, 119, 120, 125, 127, 132, 141,
    146, 152, 157, 164, 177
Stolorow, Robert D., xx, 84, 85, 128

teach or treat controversy (in clinical
    supervision), 164–169
transference (in family therapy), 147,
    148

transference–countertransference
matrix, 104–109
true self, xxi, 72–76, 132, 133

Winnicott, Donald W., xx–xxii, 10, 12,
25, 33, 40, 63, 64, 71, 72, 76, 85,
98–101, 104–106, 111–114,
117–125, 128, 132, 133, 146,
156–159, 165
women (gang's contempt for and
exploitation of), 156

Yalom, Irvin D., 131, 142